38 HOURS

TO

MONTREAL

38 HOURS

TO

MONTREAL

**William Weller and the
Governor General's Race of 1840**

DAN BUCHANAN

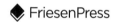 FriesenPress

Suite 300 - 990 Fort St
Victoria, BC, V8V 3K2
Canada

www.friesenpress.com

ISBN
978-1-5255-1988-8 (Hardcover)
978-1-5255-1989-5 (Paperback)
978-1-5255-1990-1 (eBook)

1. HISTORY

Distributed to the trade by The Ingram Book Company

DEDICATION

THIS BOOK OWES ITS LIFE TO DOT CONNOLLY, MY FRIEND AND ASSOCIATE FOR several years in the heritage community of Brighton, Ontario. It was her good advice, persistent support, and dynamic energy that helped make my first book so much fun and left a slam-dunk for taking a second run at publishing another history story.

The folks around Brighton know very well what Dot (NOT Dorothy, thank you very much!) did to create the Brighton History Week events, which are entering their sixth year. She was also instrumental in creating Hilton Hall Heritage Centre and making it a friendly, welcoming place. We often marvelled to each other about the things that Dot could get volunteers to do. Her enthusiasm, love of history, and appreciation for people met up with her organizing and communications skills to make her a formidable administrator and organizer. And we just had so much fun!

Dot had to move along, and we all miss her terribly. This book is dedicated to Dot. Hope you enjoy it.

TABLE OF CONTENTS

PREFACE

CANADIAN HISTORY IS FULL OF FASCINATING CHARACTERS AND AMAZING FEATS, but I have always been interested in that second tier of individuals who toiled in the trenches of society but reached the pages of history books only for a line or two in the context of some other honoured personage. As a technician and self-professed history geek, I love to delve into the lives of characters who made a practical difference in the lives of people and contributed to the development of the country. William Weller was such a person.

38 Hours To Montreal tells the story of a dangerous and remarkable sleigh ride from Toronto to Montreal in February of 1840. It made the papers at the time because the passenger was the governor general of the British North American colonies. Many folks were following the governor general's every move, concerned that he was up to no good. At least that was the view of the elite ruling class, the Family Compact. In today's world, it would equate to the media reporting on the prime minister of Canada. Many folks were interested in where he was going and what he was doing. It was news.

But there was another very popular fellow on the sleigh. William Weller had become famous in a bit more than a decade of operating stagecoach lines along the main routes of Upper Canada, primarily between Toronto and Montreal. He was already known as "The Stagecoach King" and was thought of in glowing terms by all parts of society, from the stable boys he tipped to the lawyers and doctors who rode in his more comfortable coaches. He was a successful businessman, but in reality he had become a celebrity because of the dramatic improvements he had made in the operation of stage lines. These improvements were demonstrated in very practical terms to many people, some of them very well placed in the power structure. Besides all that, he was such a nice fellow that people wanted to speak well of him, no matter how little they actually knew of the man.

But my question about this trip was "Why in such a hurry?" The governor general deliberately sought out William Weller and offered a contract stipulating that he must drive him to Montreal in under thirty-eight hours. Why? Several stories have been floated, such as the need to pardon a prisoner who was to be hanged or the need to catch a ship to London, but none rang true.

I felt that the political situation at the time must provide the answer. Governor General Thomson had been sent to Canada to pass legislation, and he had done that very successfully during the past three months in Toronto. Now, with the volatile politics of the French-English divide threatening his ability to accomplish the same job in Lower Canada, he felt the need to be on the scene right away. He had no interest in waiting for navigation to open in a month. No, he wanted to be in Montreal, **now**!

That being said, it became clear to me that I might use this amazing trip to provide readers with a window into Upper Canada in 1840. This period in Canadian history seems almost forgotten, sandwiched in between the popular and well-reported War of 1812-1814 and the big turning point of Confederation in 1867. Sure, we had our Mackenzie Rebellion in 1837 and 1838, but the boom of guns in a full-fledged war or fireworks at a time of national celebration seems to dwarf the less spectacular but nonetheless serious and fascinating developments in between.

What were the difficulties travelling long distances in Upper Canada in 1840? Where was the road located in those days? Who ran the taverns and inns along the Kingston Road and the King's Highway, places William Weller would rely on to change horses every fifteen miles? And how was the country changing as the sleigh made its way from Toronto to Montreal?

The answers are buried in the many small but fascinating chronicles of local history for each town, township, and county along the way. Both physical and online archives of all sorts provide glimpses of our history, even back into that period before most of our institutions took shape. Many biographies and family histories shed light on certain people, times, and places if we take time to look. There is no shortage of information to tell a story like this.

A lot of discipline was in order to keep my focus on 1840. I love to explore the histories of the communities of Upper Canada and tended to keep turning the pages. The question always came back to "What was it like in 1840?" It was apparent that much had changed after 1840 all along the route. Roads were improved, canals were built, and most of our built heritage was constructed in the decades following the trip. Oh, but not entirely. There are an amazing number of buildings along the road that William Weller might well have seen as he raced by in February of 1840. Who built them and why? How are these old buildings used today?

And as if all that were not enough, did William Weller succeed in his efforts to meet the terms of the contract he had signed with Governor General Thomson?

Come sit on the bench of the sleigh with William Weller and find out.

ACKNOWLEDGEMENTS

A LARGE PART OF THE RESEARCH MATERIAL I COLLECTED REGARDING THE LIFE OF William Weller came from the archives of the *Cobourg Star* newspaper, which is on microfilm at the Cobourg Public Library. In the early summer of 2016, I spent many hours over two months, occupying one of their microfilm readers. My collection of articles from the *Cobourg Star*, which began in 1831 and is amazingly complete for the period of William Weller's life, forms a strong foundation for the story of his trip in 1840 as well as for any further stories that may take shape in the future. I thank the staff at the Cobourg Public Library for their assistance and patience.

The Archives of Ontario are housed in a wonderful new facility at York University, and the staff there were very helpful in providing me with specific items regarding William Weller, John Beverly Robinson, and Charles Poulett Thomson. I now know what "off-site" means.

On my travels to eastern Ontario, I received warm support from various individuals and organizations along the way. Robert Prowse was a gracious host at Chesley's Inn, Cornwall. I stayed two nights in that delightful establishment, and I am sure that John Chesley would be proud of the most current iteration of his popular inn.

Jim Brownell of the Lost Villages Museum was very helpful in providing information about the King's Road, which was certainly one option for Mr. Weller in 1840. However, it turned out to be his second choice. Newspaper reports at the time suggest he took the river route to Montreal instead.

One of my most enjoyable research trips took me to Williamstown and the Bethune-Thompson Historical House where David Anderson was generous with his time and knowledge. I learned a lot and found a kindred spirit as far as early Canadian history is concerned.

The reader who might be interested in the Sources section will see that many of my sources are web pages or documents that have been downloaded from web sites. So much of our history is represented in documents from the 1800s that have been digitized and made available for researchers just like me. As an old IT guy, I find that perfectly delightful.

Online sources were particularly important because my story moves across the landscape of Upper and Lower Canada in 1840 and includes bits of history from all those towns and townships along the Kingston Road and then the King's Highway to Montreal. History purists may scoff at this, but most of the work was done sitting at my computer, making maximum use of the tools in front of me. What a great time it is to be researching our history!

A very important source for my research on individual people was the *Dictionary of Canadian Biography*. It is amazing what connections you can make between disparate things when you have several biographies in front of you, showing details of folks who were active around the same time and place.

The history of Toronto is fascinating and the collection of *Robertson's Landmarks of Toronto* provides so many details about that early period in York and then Toronto. For the story I was telling, it was a wonderful resource.

One of the most useful web sites was *Digital Kingston,* where I found news items from well back into the early decades of the 1800s. The trip in 1840 was well represented here. The big problem was to stop browsing and get back to work.

Some of my research sessions went off track and were extended in time due to a serious weakness for the work of Edwin C. Guillet. I simply can't put his books down. It's not because he grew up in Cobourg or had family ties in Brighton. No, it has to do with his focus on Upper Canada in the first half of the 1800s and the detailed, on-the-ground approach he takes to telling the stories of the people and the times. I'm a fan.

Of all the images that appear in the book, my favourite, without a doubt, is the sketch of the Exchange Coffee House, which originally appeared in one of A.E. Collard's columns in the *Montreal Daily Witness*. I could hardly believe it when I saw this sketch in the book *Steamboat Connections, Montreal to Upper Canada 1816-1843* by Frank Mackey. This book is a fascinating source regarding those early years of steamboat development, as well as stagecoach lines, in eastern Upper Canada and in Lower Canada. The folks at McGill Press were gracious in confirming, through Mr. Mackey, that I could use the image, and I am grateful.

As for my *mea culpa*, let's identify, off the top, that I have stuck my neck out with this story. I have touched on the local history territories of many folks across the country. Every town and municipality along the road from Toronto to Montreal has active local historians who know their own local history and take pride in the work they do. I am one of those for Brighton. I don't doubt that somewhere in the book, the couple of paragraphs I have included for a certain place will pique the history sensibilities of someone. Don't hesitate to let me know.

1

Beverly House

CAPTAIN THOMAS LE MARCHANT SAT BOLT UPRIGHT AND STARED AT THE BLACK-ness around him. He rubbed his eyes and thought out loud to himself, "What time is it?" The clock on the mantle ticked contentedly, but its face was lost in the darkness. Le Marchant reached for a match on his bedside table and lit the whale-oil lamp, which soon cast a yellow glow over the small room.

According to the clock, it was just after 5:00 am. *Very well,* thought Le Marchant, with a sigh of relief. He had not slept in. He strained to hear any sound from the room next door, but there was total silence. On this chilly Monday morning, February 17th, 1840, Beverly House and its grounds were quiet. However, in the next hour and a half, excitement would fill the air as the servants and staff hustled to assist Captain Le Marchant in preparing for the timely departure of a very important person.

Captain Le Marchant was aide-de-camp to the governor general of the British North American colonies, the Right Honourable Charles Poulett Thomson. His Excellency was, at this moment, still sleeping soundly in the next room. They had been living at Beverly House for the last three months, while the governor general worked tirelessly to pass an ambitious package of legislation in the Parliament of Upper Canada.[1] Just a few days ago, he had finally completed this part of the work. His instructions from London had been very clear, and he knew that he was working within a timetable that had more to do with London politics than winter weather in Canada.

At this point, Thomson was a man in a hurry. Now that he had been successful in Upper Canada, he was intent on moving on to Lower Canada to accomplish the same thing. Word came that his enemies in Montreal were working to undermine his plans, and he felt compelled to be on the scene as soon as possible. Unfortunately, in February, navigation was closed and steamboats would not ply Lake Ontario until well into April. The obvious alternative was land travel. To put it plainly, he would take a sleigh ride.

Luckily, the governor general was familiar with William Weller, the Stagecoach King, the only man who might be able to meet the challenge. Weller came highly recommended due to his success in improving stagecoach travel in Upper Canada in the previous decade. Captain Le Marchant had arranged for a meeting, the governor general made his proposal, and Mr. Weller accepted immediately.

Captain Le Marchant grinned in amazement at the audaciousness of his boss, insisting that the trip take no longer than thirty-eight hours or the fees would not be paid. But Mr. Weller did not bat an eye. He signed the contract with a flourish and set about making it happen. If anyone could do it, he could.

The planned departure time was seven o'clock this morning, and the hope was that they would arrive in Montreal on Tuesday evening. It was an ambitious plan, considering the condition of the roads between Toronto and Montreal, but all three men were persistently optimistic that it could be done.

The captain quickly dressed in the plain but warm clothing that had been placed neatly on the chair beside his bed. He then pulled on the fur-lined boots and tied them tightly. As he stood and tried to get comfortable in this unfamiliar footwear, he glanced longingly at his sparkling military boots and told himself it was only for a day or two.

A glint of light drew his eyes to his sword and scabbard, which stood patiently leaning against the wall beside his boots. *Oh, yes,* he thought, *mustn't forget to take the sword out to the stable.* During the planning of the trip, the issue of security had been raised. The governor general was dismissive, feeling that he must defer to the practice of Mr. Weller, who normally did not wish to have weapons on his coaches.

A compromise had been reached, at the insistence of Captain Le Marchant. He would stow his sword, well out of sight in the sleigh, with the intent that it never be used, but with the possibility that it be available to him if a threat presented itself. The whole trip was risky in many ways, but the possibility of bandits or insurgents attacking this fast-moving sleigh, in February, was thought to be minimal. The sword would provide the only soldier on the trip with at least a modicum of confidence that he could do his job if called upon.

A sound from the kitchen interrupted his thoughts. He quickly opened his door and walked down the hall, toward the lamplight that came from the kitchen. The cook had risen early this morning, according to plan. She was stirring the fireplace with a poker and would soon have a fire going to make tea and prepare breakfast. Captain Le Marchant said a pleasant but brief "Good Morning" to the cook as he reached to snatch a carrot from the bundle on the table. He slipped the carrot into his pocket and strode back up the hall, intent on visiting the stables to check on the horses.

At his bedroom door, he entered quickly and grabbed the sword, tucking it under one arm, so as not to be too obvious. He walked up the hall to the front door. As he opened the front door, the cool winter air rushed in, so he quickly stepped outside and shut the door. Two young soldiers were standing on either side of the door, performing the duty of sentry[2] for Government House. It was standard security procedure that any building where the governor general stayed would be designated as Government House.[3] A platoon of soldiers would draw the prestigious, but boring, duty of acting as guards. These two young fellows were cold and hungry, but on this morning they were also anticipating the end of this tedious duty.

Captain Le Marchant strode across the porch and stepped down onto the large circular driveway. He glanced back at the handsome house that had been his home since the governor general had arranged to use Beverly House as his residence while he was in Toronto, back in November of 1839.

The master of Beverly House was the Honourable John Beverly Robinson,[4] who besides holding the post of chief justice of The Court of King's Bench, was the de-facto leader of the Family Compact, that ephemeral yet powerful group of elites that ran the colony. He had been chief justice since 1829 and had acquired this property on the western outskirts of the grimy but growing town of York in 1817. Many of his friends owned country estates to the west of Yonge Street, which were within a quick carriage ride of Osgoode Hall to the east and the Parliament Buildings and other government offices along Front Street near the lakeshore.

In 1840, the Robinson property was bounded on the north side by Lot

1.1 Hon. Sir John Beverly Robinson,
Chief Justice of Upper Canada.

Street, so called because it was the northern boundary of the city with large park lots to the north. This street was soon to be renamed Queen Street in honour of the recently crowned Queen Victoria. The southern boundary was then called Hospital Street, called by this name only west of Bay Street and soon to be called Richmond Street along its whole length. The eastern boundary was then called Graves Street, later to be known as Simcoe. On the west side of the lot was John Street. The large home and stable buildings were in the western section of the lot, up against John Street, surrounded by lovely gardens and forest. The east end contained orchards, fields, and gardens. There were still very few commercial buildings along the streets in this area, although the growth of the town would intrude in the coming years.

The first dwelling constructed on the Robinson property had been built around 1812 by D'Arcy Boulton, Jr., the eldest son of Judge D'Arcy Boulton.[5] The senior Boulton had been a young lawyer who happened to be in the right place at the right time in late 1804 when H.M.S. *Speedy* was lost in a storm near Presqu'ile Point. The solicitor general of Upper Canada, Robert Isaac Dey Gray, was on the *Speedy* and his loss punctuated the disastrous nature of the event. Shortly after, D'Arcy Boulton was appointed to replace Gray as solicitor general.

Considerable grants of land in the western outskirts of York resulted from his elevated position, including land north of Queen Street that would later be donated for St. Patrick's Market. In 1808, his son and namesake, D'Arcy Boulton, Jr., married Sarah, a sister of John Robinson, another promising young lawyer in York. Robinson would purchase part of D'Arcy Boulton's property in 1817 and over the years would improve the house to the point that some would call it a mansion, although it was not extravagant in comparison with other notable homes of the time.

Conveniently, the Robinsons were not living at Beverly House at this time. Chief Justice Robinson had gone to England with his family for health reasons late in 1838 and would remain there until May of 1840. He had applied for and received a leave of absence from his duties as chief justice with the expectation that he would recover his health at Cheltenham Spa and return to Canada when his leave expired. Of course, the chatter of his critics suggested that the chief justice was in England to counter the reforming tendencies that were evident in the Durham Report. In fact, while in England, Robinson had many meetings and engaged in much correspondence on these topics. In the end, however, the tide of change was inevitable.

The captain turned toward the stables, which occupied the space to the west of the house. The stable master had also been up for some time and met him at the front door.

1.2 This picture of Beverly House from around 1885 shows the half-circle driveway as well as some taller buildings behind the house, which would be along Queen Street West. The Beverly Estate remained largely undeveloped until the land was sold in 1912.

"Good morning, sir," said Le Marchant, accompanied by an almost imperceptible nod of his head.

"Good morning, Captain. Are you ready for your trip today?" replied the stable master.

"Most certainly," Le Marchant replied in a slightly officious manner. "His Excellency is soon to rise and packing is almost finished. We will have breakfast shortly and Mr. Weller will arrive soon."

The two men walked into the stable and stood before two very fine bay horses. Le Marchant asked, "And how are the horses this morning?"

"Very well, sir. They appear to have slept comfortably. I fed them about an hour ago." As the stable master spoke, he reached over and patted the nearest of the two horses on its outstretched nose. "These are two of the finest animals I have seen in this country. Mr. Weller certainly knows horse flesh."

"Yes, that is certain," replied the aide-de-camp. "These two will carry us over the first stage of our trip with no problem at all. And it will be fascinating to watch the rest of the teams as they are hitched to the sleigh and pull their burden at each stage. I am looking forward to it." While he spoke, Le Marchant produced the carrot from his pocket, broke it in half, and offered a piece to each of the two horses.

The two horses munched contentedly on the carrot as Captain Le Marchant handed his sword to the stable master, asking him to stow it on the floor of the sleigh, within his reach, but well out of sight. The stable master nodded and took the sword, admiring the shining, highly decorated scabbard. "By all means, sir," he said, as he set the sword on a table, just inside the door.

The stable master followed Le Marchant onto the driveway and said, "I will have the team and coach ready in the yard at fifteen minutes to seven." The two men bowed ever so slightly to each other, and Le Marchant walked back across the driveway to the front porch and entered the house. He went back to his room to finish packing.

The sounds of activity increased in Beverly House as Captain Le Marchant finished packing his clothes and personal items in two small bags, which he left just inside the front door, so they would be handy to retrieve at the right moment. As he turned back down the hall, Le Marchant could hear the sound of conversation coming from the morning room. He also recognized the familiar breakfast aroma of pork, biscuits, and tea. Governor General Thomson was joking with the servants as Le Marchant entered the room and sat down across the table from his boss.

"Good morning, Captain, a fine day for a sleigh ride, wouldn't you say?" said the governor general.

"Yes, sir, a fine day, indeed. Packing is almost done. The horses Mr. Weller sent for are in the stable, and the stable master will have the team and coach ready at quarter to seven. We can expect Mr. Weller's arrival at any moment." Le Marchant never took time off, always the persistent organizer.

"Very well. I am most anxious to arrive in Montreal to take the situation in hand. I fear that the work will be much more difficult there than it was here." As he spoke, the governor general raised one eyebrow, in what passed for a frown on a normally impassive face. "The sooner I am engaged in the fight, the sooner we shall have our legislation passed. And the sooner you and I, Captain, can make passage back to England. Let us pray for success." With these words, the governor general raised his teacup in a toast, seconded by his aide-de-camp.

It had been a gruelling three months in Toronto. The objectives had been very clear on November 21st last year when the two had arrived at Beverly House for the first time. The governor general had been sent to Canada for the express purpose of passing legislation in the Parliaments of both Upper and Lower Canada that would change the structure of government for both provinces.[6] The old, obsolete style of government by the elites was to end!

After the job was done, he had presided over the prorogation of Parliament. In his speech on that occasion he hoped that, "It will be your endeavour to promote that spirit of harmony and conciliation which has so much distinguished your proceedings here."[7] These were fine words but did little to mend the divisions in the province. Mr. Thomson was accustomed to the barbs of indignant commentators and would chuckle a few days from now, when someone commented that his quick departure from the Upper Province resembled rats leaving a sinking ship.

Thomson had experienced first-hand the power and pervasiveness of the Family Compact during his direct and indirect negotiations with its members. Men of this sort would always yield a little bit if offered some perk or benefit, but it had to be something they felt important. You had to be inside their minds in order to negotiate with them. Thomson was a confident man who had the measure of his adversary. He had succeeded beyond his expectations in Upper Canada and could now press on to complete the second half of his work, hopefully with the same degree of success in Lower Canada.

1.3 Charles Poulett Thomson was known in England as a progressive public servant well before he came to Canada as governor general. While he was in Canada, this image appeared in a publication entitled Saunders' Portraits and Memoirs of Eminent Living Political Reformers.

In fact, many members of the Legislature of Upper Canada were at this moment very happy to see Mr. Thomson leave their province. They were angry and sullen about the legislative storm that had engulfed them. The governor general had come into their meeting rooms and salons with strong backing from the reform-minded ministry in London as well as the support of the queen. Like it or not, he had to be accommodated.

There were very strong opinions on all sides. The conservative members were dedicated to maintaining the existing structures of governance and administration, while the reformers were intent on breaking the monopoly of the Family Compact and opening the burgeoning community to more democratic methods of governing. The governor general had overwhelmed the members with reams of facts and figures, reports, and resolutions. He had been a key member of the Board of Trade in England for the last decade and knew the intimate details of trade, budgets, and government bureaucracies. It was a dominating performance never before seen by the members of the Legislature or the Executive Council of Upper Canada. They were amazed and a bit stunned by what had just happened.

Interestingly, members from both sides of the political spectrum were angry. Early in the process, Thomson had recognized that he must chart a course that sailed down the middle between the more entrenched conservatives, who wanted to maintain their power, and the wildly reformist group headed by Robert Baldwin, who constantly jabbered about responsible government. The fact that enough men on both sides had voted for Thomson's resolutions and were then unhappy with the outcome, spoke volumes about the delicate line of moderation he had followed all through these negotiations.

Governor General Thomson was certainly not going to give away responsible government at this time as that would seriously weaken the connection between Britain and the North American colonies, leaving annexation by the United States as a strong possibility and a serious threat. Besides, it would remove his ability, as governor general, to have any serious influence over the process of change.

Looking back on this position, the modern reader may be annoyed with Mr. Thomson for not following our basic desire for democracy. However, it is useful to consider that many of the measures put in place by Governor General Thomson in early 1840 resulted in the weakening of the power of the Family Compact. The new government of the Province of Canada would no longer allow positions like attorney general to include a lifetime tenure but would reserve the power to replace men in these positions when and if the governor general or the Colonial Office saw fit. More of these offices would be populated by professionals with appointments based on merit. This would transfer the power of patronage from the elites to the new government. In practice, these changes would help the reformers in that last push to gain the long-hoped-for responsible government. The result would be a landslide victory for the Reformers in the election of 1848 and the subsequent Great Ministry of Robert Baldwin and Louis-Hippolyte LaFontaine.

In Toronto, the governor general had succeeded on every score. He had managed to pass the bill to unite Upper and Lower Canada into one legislative body, effectively removing the current government and setting up a new one called the Province of Canada. The old Upper Canada would then be Canada West and Lower Canada would be Canada East. He had also managed to pass a bill to dispose of the Clergy Reserves, an old and seemingly intractable problem, strongly opposed by Bishop John Strachan, a close friend of Chief Justice Robinson. As a result, the primacy of the Anglican Church would be curtailed and a much greater degree of separation between church and state would begin. It was all very earth-shaking.

One way that Robinson and his friends coped with all this upheaval was to apply humour, in particular where they could ridicule the governor general, always in a civilized manner, to be sure. One joke that ran around at this time was the suggestion that the Union Bill had been passed partly because Thomson had installed a new and much improved kitchen range in the house soon after he moved in. We might guess that this was a purely practical matter in light of the entertainment involved in any home that became Government House. But it was a satisfying jibe nonetheless.[8]

Of course, all of these bills must be presented to Parliament in London for final approval. His bosses might also offer a recommendation regarding the actual date when these measures would take effect. Thomson had sent all the documents by courier to the Colonial Office and was waiting for a response from England. Indeed, some modifications to Thomson's bills would be imposed, mostly in the area of the Clergy Reserves, which would be fought over for many years. But, for the most part, Thomson was happy with his work.

As he sat in Beverly House on this February morning, anticipating a cold and bumpy ride for the next day and a half, part of him could smile contentedly and begin to look forward to the next great challenge. The other part worried over the time pressure he was under. His handlers in London expected results in a few months, something they could crow about in the next sitting of Parliament. They had no idea of the difficulties in the Canadian provinces, or even the stark realities of winter travel.[9] Oh well, he would do what he could. Lower Canada, here we come!

The trip to Montreal had been arranged about a week earlier, and the original day of departure had been set for Saturday, February 15th. However, the governor general had delayed the trip by a couple of days to deal with some pressing last-minute matters. Mr. Weller held himself in readiness, at the convenience of the governor general, and on Sunday it was decided that the trip would begin the next morning. At this point, everyone was simply anxious to get under way.

As the two men finished their breakfast, the clatter of wagon wheels came from the front of the house. Several vehicles had turned off Hospital Street and parked under the trees in the middle of the half-circle driveway. Two dozen uniformed figures scurried out of the wagons. Most of them, carrying various musical instruments, began forming themselves into a square facing the front door of Beverly House. Several of the figures who carried rifles and wore much more elaborate uniforms, moved quickly to stand on the porch beside the two sentries who had been there all night. These soldiers had done this job a dozen times for Governor General Thomson, but everyone knew that today was special. "Gentlemen! Ready!" commanded the band leader as he raised his baton.[10]

The governor general and Captain Le Marchant were at the front door, watching as the band formed up in the yard and the Military Guard took their places on the porch. At this moment, there was a clattering of hooves on the driveway. "Ah, that will be Mr. Weller," said Captain Le Marchant. The two men stepped outside and walked across the porch and onto the driveway. The governor general nodded to the members of the Military Guard and the officers saluted according to protocol.

A cab drove quickly up the western driveway and even before it came to a halt in front of the house, the occupant opened the door and began stepping out. As the cab stopped, the passenger was on the ground, taking several quick, long strides across the driveway. The governor general held out his hand, and the two men shook hands enthusiastically.

"Good morning, Guvner, and how are you this fine morning?" exclaimed Mr. Weller.

"I am very well, sir. It is wonderful to see you in such fine spirits this morning," responded the governor general.

William Weller turned back to the cab and waved to the driver. "We will be leaving soon, Lorenzo. I will see you in Montreal in a few days. Good luck!" Lorenzo was William Weller's oldest child and had just turned eighteen.[11] He was a smart and energetic young fellow, taking after his father in many ways. At this moment, he would return his father's good luck wishes and hurry back to the General Stage Office to finish preparing the sleigh he would drive to Montreal. Later in the morning, he would leave Toronto carrying the governor general's chief secretary along with much of his baggage. While they would press hard to arrive in Montreal in good time, they would not be included in the contract Mr. Weller had signed with the governor general, so they could travel at a more conventional pace.

1.4 William Weller sat for this portrait by Paul Kane in 1835. The budding young artist worked for a short time in his father-in-law's furniture factory in Cobourg, raising money for an educational trip to Europe. He painted portraits of local personalities in Cobourg and would go on to become a renowned Canadian artist.

"Are you ready to convey us to Montreal?" asked Mr. Thomson.

"Most certainly, Guvner. Captain Le Marchant has arranged everything, and we shall depart in short order."

The governor general was by now accustomed to Mr. Weller's more familiar greetings and actually found them charming. After all, William Weller was an American, and you had to make all sorts of allowances because of that. On the other hand, his reputation as a very successful stagecoach proprietor was pervasive in Upper Canada. He had been delivering the Royal Mail with his stage lines since the late 1820s, and everybody knew that his "General Stage Office" was in the Coffin Block on Market Street in Toronto.[12] Stages from all directions converged on this central hub of the transportation system of Upper Canada. Stagecoach travel had improved a lot due to the efforts of this man, and there was nothing Mr. Thomson appreciated more than a self-made man who built a business that was useful to society. And he made money doing it! This man was someone to keep an eye on.

In fact, the two men had met several times over the months since Thomson had arrived in Toronto. The most important meeting had been just a week ago when the governor general requested that Weller come to Government House to discuss a trip to Montreal. When this very unique venture was proposed to Mr. Weller, he did not flinch for a moment, but began explaining how his system of stage stops, stables, horses, and stablemen, which existed all along the Kingston Road, could be brought to bear on the operation.

William Weller was motivated by challenge and saw this as a ripe opportunity to secure a substantial fee from a reliable paying customer, as well as to gain publicity for his stage lines. Anything the governor general did was news, and Weller's stage line could use the publicity from this trip to drum up more business among the well-heeled passengers of Toronto. The business was doing well with the sound foundation of Royal Mail contracts, but he wanted to increase passenger traffic in order to tip the greater proportion of his business toward public transportation. He sensed that this was where the real profits would lie, once the public knew how reliable and safe stagecoach travel really was. What better way to help this along than to take the governor general on a very public and quite remarkable trip? He had seen the potential immediately and would do everything in his power to make the trip a success.

The governor general had insisted that a contract be drawn up and that an explicit time limit be included.[13] The two men agreed the trip must be completed in less than thirty-eight hours or else the contract would be null and void. Weller was comfortable with this and accepted it as a challenge to be overcome. In fact, he decided that he would drive the entire distance himself to make sure the governor general was provided with the very best service. William Weller was forty years of age at this time and had generally moved away from the role of driver, but he was happy to make an exception in this case.[14]

The biggest challenge would be the weather. He knew that there had been a series of thaws and freezing spells through the previous days, but he also assumed that some winter snow would be present along the Kingston Road at this time of year.

More importantly, frost would still be in the ground. Stagecoach travel over the very uncertain roads of the time was very difficult in spring and fall, but he had bet his reputation on winter stage travel, which was the only alternative when navigation on the lakes and rivers was closed. He was very confident he could meet the terms of the contract and was anxious to get started.

2

Departure

WHILE MR. WELLER WAS BEING GREETED BY THE GOVERNOR GENERAL IN FRONT OF Beverly House, a commotion to the west side of the house drew everyone's attention. In a very dignified and stately manner, the stable master drove the team and sleigh onto the driveway in front of the house. The people gasped in unison at the splendour of the fully harnessed team made up of the two fine bay horses that had been selected by Mr. Weller. The harnesses glistened in the lamplight and the horses pranced and snorted with excitement.

But the eyes of the spectators were soon drawn to the very unusual vehicle being pulled by the team. Few people in Upper Canada had seen anything like this before and the common first response was, "What is it?"

The governor general stepped forward as the stable master dismounted. Making a very solemn bow and unable to contain a wide grin, the stable master said, "Your Excellency, your conveyance awaits."

Governor General Thomson clapped his hands in delight, then grabbed the hand of the stable master and shook it vigorously. "Very good, sir, very good. Oh, it reminds me of my younger days in Russia. How splendid!"

Mr. Weller and Captain Le Marchant joined the governor general as the three men walked slowly around the team and vehicle. The horses were admirable, but the men's attention was concentrated on the amazing vehicle drawn by the team. A rectangular box sat nestled between two long sleigh runners, which were curved upward very elegantly at front and back. The impression was of a child's cradle suspended in a mother's arms. It was long and low and much narrower than a normal sleigh. In fact, it was a completely different model of sleigh, not seen before in Upper Canada.[1]

The governor general, with the delight of a schoolboy, described how he had travelled for many days in small sleighs like this while working for his father's merchant house in Russia and Eastern Europe. These sleighs were designed for long-distance travel over rough, snow-covered ground, ideal for one or two passengers in the context of the terrible roads and brutal cold of the Russian winter.

More comments came from the crowd when the side door was swung open and the interior of the cab showed what simply looked like a bed of buffalo robes over a thick mattress. It was intended that the governor general and Captain Le Marchant would ride together in the sleigh, reclining as in a lounge chair. They would be supported by a soft mattress and protected from the cold by buffalo robes, the most popular warm covering of the day. The passengers on this trip would not expect to sleep very much over the next day and a half, but they would at least be relatively comfortable in their constant motion.

On coming to Canada in the fall of 1839, Thomson had brought one of these sleighs with him and on the expert advice of Mr. Weller had agreed to have it modified for Canadian use. A cab was fashioned over top to form an enclosed space that would better shield the passengers from the worst of the cold and wind. In addition, stronger leather straps were added to cushion the ride.

Captain Le Marchant stopped at the rear of the sleigh and knelt down to inspect the runners more closely. He then stepped back and viewed both runners from a distance. "Capital job with the metal runners, Mr. Weller," he said, as much for his boss as for the stagecoach expert. Sure enough, Mr. Weller had installed iron runners down the middle of the wide wooden runners common on sleighs in those days.

The Weller Carriage Works in Cobourg had been experimenting with metal runners and found them very useful on rough roads, adding a measure of protection over ice and snow. It was found that the wooden runners would last much longer when metal runners were attached. They were a bit expensive, so not widely used, but for this particular trip, the addition of metal runners was just one more measure calculated to add speed and safety to the trip.

The only adornments on the vehicle before them were two wooden crests bolted to the doors on either side. The crests held the queen's coat-of-arms, which was not only readily identifiable for the people of Upper Canada, but revered in a growing sense as news came from the mother country of the young monarch who was now their queen. For the governor general, the queen's coat-of-arms was a powerful calling card, and in practice, as he galloped across the countryside, it acted like the siren of a police car in modern days.

The band started playing as the gathering admired the horses and voiced their amazement at the sleigh. Then the servants came out of the house with the baggage that would accompany the travellers on their trip. The baggage was stowed under the supervision of Mr. Weller, one piece for each passenger inside the cab and one piece each strapped into the boot at the rear of the coach. He had insisted that each traveller must take no more than two moderately sized pieces of baggage. Much experience had shown that the best personal luggage for a trip like this was a good quality leather grip (an old English term for our modern suitcase) that was flexible enough to withstand the pounding of the roads and water resistant enough to withstand the inevitable wet weather. The governor general was pleased to comply with Mr. Weller's sensible recommendations.

There were also several small food parcels, which had been prepared by the staff of Beverly House. Wheat-cakes, apples, and carrots were easy to store and might be easily accessed while the sleigh was in motion. There had been discussion of buttermilk in jars, but that idea was discarded in light of the potential for very rough roads along the way, to say nothing of potential freezing temperatures. Any glass items could be a problem and should be avoided. Of course, the elegant flask normally carried in a coat pocket by the governor general was considered an exception and would be a welcome companion as it carried his favourite port.

William Weller stepped up onto the front of the sleigh and surveyed the small bench where he would ride the full distance to Montreal. The driver's bench presented a very small space but was not unlike many he had navigated on all different kinds of conveyances. He opened his grip and pulled out a thick piece of fur, positioning it carefully on the bench. This would provide at least a measure of comfort during the long ride.

He pulled his favourite bugle out of his grip and then stowed the grip under the bench. He turned the horn over several times in his hands to make sure it was in good shape and then placed it securely inside the small wooden holder built for the purpose right in front of his seat. The horn would be used to signal his imminent arrival at the stage stops along the way. All the stable boys knew the sound of Mr. Weller's horn and would jump to life when they heard it.[2]

The stable master brought up the twenty-foot whip Mr. Weller had requested, and it was installed in a specially prepared hole in the floor just beside his bench. It would not be used very much, as Mr. Weller preferred to speak to the horses and not use a whip. In certain circumstance he might crack the whip over their heads as a warning, but for the most part, he deplored the extensive use of whips. The boss's habit was well known by the drivers who were employed by Weller's stagecoach lines, and some of them tried to follow along, at least in principle. However, it was a hard habit to break and in fact a bit unusual for the times. In any case, William Weller knew that the best he could do was set an example for others to follow.

The governor general and Captain Le Marchant positioned themselves in the cab of the sleigh, stowing the food items and arranging their baggage and the various cushions and coverings as seemed comfortable. They would be prisoners in this small travelling cradle for a day and half, so they needed to reconcile themselves to the space and figure out what the notion of comfort might be, in reality, once they were on the road. For now, it was all guess work along with some comical joshing back and forth about snoring and taking breaks. They would work it out as they went along.

As a finishing touch, the stable master carried a lighted torch to the right side of the sleigh and set it down into its holder to the right and in front of the driver's bench. They were starting out in darkness and would drive most of the trip in pitch-black night, so a torch was required. It would be December of 1841 before the Toronto Gas, Light, and Water Company would begin illuminating the streets of Toronto with gas lamps, but on this winter morning more than a year earlier, even the first steps of the trip on Hospital Street would be in almost total darkness.[3]

Mr. Weller had given instructions in this regard because he was concerned about the two-dozen stage stops they would experience – changing the horses every fifteen miles. He had requested that, at every stop, a fresh team be ready and standing on the right side of the road, positioned for a quick change. In order to assist the stable boys in performing these quick changes, he knew that a torch on the sleigh would be helpful. Of course, the torch would also light the way along the road for the driver and team.

The coachman took a few minutes to address each of the horses in the team, and then spoke to them as a group. When possible, he liked to establish a good rapport with the animals before asking them to run for him. This done, he stood up, took out his pocket watch, and announced that it was almost seven o'clock; time to be on their way. He took a small piece of paper out of a shirt pocket and with a short stub of pencil, recorded the departure time. This number would be critical when they arrived in Montreal, as it would allow him to calculate total travel time and determine if the terms of the contract had been met. He stowed the pocket watch, the paper, and the pencil back in the safety of his pocket and turned to the job at hand.

He jostled the reins lightly, speaking calmly to the horses, gauging their response to the touch of the reins. Amidst the band playing and the servants clapping, the horses snorted and stepped nervously, awaiting the anticipated signal and the glorious moment of departure. These beasts were born to run. This was their life's work. Let's get on with it!

The governor general and Captain Le Marchant were finally ready and signalled to Mr. Weller that they were in his hands. The military band played a lively tune, and the crowd of well-wishers clapped and yelled their goodbyes. Mr. Weller raised the twenty-foot-long whip and whirled it high into the air. He flicked it with a minimal twist of the wrist, and the whip responded with a crack like a pistol shot.[4] This signal was familiar code for the horses, and they started forward in unison. The coach slid over the snow toward Hospital Street as the three men waved goodbye to the gathering in front of Beverly House.

The trip had begun!

3

John Street to King Street

THE FIRST STAGE OF THE TRIP TO MONTREAL WOULD TAKE THE TRIO ABOUT FIFTEEN miles from Beverly House to the Rouge River Valley. But first, they must navigate the city of Toronto. The available documents show that they travelled the Kingston Road in general but do not tell us the route they took out of the city. That means we have to make an educated guess.

As William Weller drove down the driveway at Beverly House, it is likely that he would have been intent on finding the best road to travel on, even at this early point. He knew the streets of Toronto intimately and may have considered several options. He could have gone east down Hospital Street to Yonge Street and then south to King Street, turning east and going out to the Kingston Road. However, Hospital Street just to the east of Beverly House was interrupted by a ravine, which ran north and south in the area.[1] The road might not be in the best condition at this ravine. Besides, Hospital Street was not a very busy path. There were few commercial establishments here, and the city usually spent most of their road budget on keeping the primary streets in good condition.

Instead, it may be more likely that he saw John Street, just a few hundred yards to the west, as a better route. John Street was important because the Upper Canada House of Assembly was a short distance to the south, on the east side of John, between Market and Front Streets. There were some very important people living north of here who would travel down John Street routinely to their offices or to attend meetings. We already know about Chief Justice John Beverly Robinson, but we can also consider D'Arcy Boulton, farther north on John Street and the Hon. Alexander Macdonell, a member of the Legislative Council and Inspector of Licenses for the Home District, right there to the south of Beverly House. John Street was probably a better choice.

As William Weller turned south onto John Street, he ventured into a city of around ten thousand people. The old town of York had been incorporated as the City of Toronto in 1834,[2] and while there were signs of growth and improvement, archaic forms of government limited the funds available to make progress happen. The first mayor of Toronto, William Lyon Mackenzie, had tried hard to address the terrible condition of the streets in the city. Mud in the spring and fall bracketed the pleasant sleighing months of the winter. Choking dust and bone-jarring ruts were common fare for warm weather travel. The inhabitants were frustrated by the inconvenience, delay, and personal injuries that sometimes resulted.

In spite of poor funding and the political upheavals of the 1830s, some of the major streets in Toronto had been planked, and there were at least a few streets and public buildings with plank sidewalks as well. After the Rebellion of 1837 and 1838, more improvements were done, but it would take a serious upheaval at the higher level of government to make a big difference. The governor general who was riding in the odd-looking sleigh was planning to establish a Board of Works for the Province of Canada in order to provide a more effective system for funding and managing what today would be called "infrastructure projects".

On that February morning, the sleigh carrying the governor general skimmed along quietly on a smooth plank surface as the team trotted quickly down John Street. Plank roads had proven to be a good alternative to dirt roads although they were expensive in a world of limited financial resources. Several of the busiest streets in Toronto were planked by 1840, including John Street, the path to the Legislature.[3]

On his right, William Weller would see only a few small commercial buildings highlighted briefly by his passing torch. On the other side, on the east side of John Street, he could glimpse the lanterns in the stable area of the estate of the Hon. Alexander Macdonell, now a very old man but still living in his elegant residence, which faced south onto Newgate Street (later to be named Adelaide Street).[4] The house had a portico on the front and round columns the full height of the house. The gardens and fields to the north and east of the house provided the family with gardening and small-scale farming, and the larger field farther east would be used for animal exhibits during the agricultural fairs that became popular in the 1840s.

Macdonell's early history had been exciting as he fought for the Crown in many engagements during the American War of Independence, mostly before the age of twenty. He survived many skirmishes in the Mohawk Valley, where his family had settled and were forced to abandon significant holdings. He was with Butler's

Rangers near the end of the war and came with his family to Canada, obtaining land and position as a result of his war service.

The sleigh passed Newgate Street, and William Weller glanced in both directions to see darkness. It was early, but the city was waking up, bit by bit. As he looked down John Street, he could see shadowy figures walking quickly to their place of work, huddled against the February chill. Now on the right, he could make out the grounds of the hospital, with lanterns in front of the main hospital buildings, casting shadows through the trees. The main hospital building was large at over one hundred feet long and sixty feet wide with a rather flat-hipped roof; it faced south onto King Street.

Construction of the hospital had begun in 1820 after the Loyal and Patriotic Society of Upper Canada organized a trust fund to support construction and maintenance.[5] Dr. Grant Powell superintended the building and was associated with the institution for many years. However, it was 1829 before the hospital was open for patients, due largely to the fact that the building was used for meetings of the Legislature after the building that housed the Parliament of Upper Canada was destroyed by fire in 1824. This original hospital on King Street would be torn down after Toronto General expanded to Gerrard and Sumach streets in 1856.

By 1840, patients would number around one hundred with most from Toronto and area but some from other parts of Canada and even the United States. The hospital's reputation as a pleasant and well-operated facility was now well established. An immigrant's hospital was also established to the northwest of the main buildings, and this would be put to unprecedented challenges during the years in the late 1840s when Irish immigrants came by the schooner-load to Toronto and would die of fever or cholera before they could realize their dream of a better life in Canada.

4

King Street West

AS THE SLEIGH APPROACHED KING STREET, THE EAST SIDE OF JOHN STREET WOULD have been completely dark because there were no buildings at all in the west part of the lot between Graves and John Streets. However, William Weller was not surprised to see a lot more activity at King Street. He slowed the horses to a walk in order to avoid several pedestrians and sleighs that were going through the intersection. At the right moment, he tugged lightly on the reins, and the team swung neatly to the left, heads held high and trotting confidently on the firm, smooth, plank roadway.

William Weller always enjoyed looking down the length of King Street. It was the heart of Toronto at a time when its pulse was racing and a lot was happening. A quote from *Landmarks of Toronto* says: "King Street was the hunting ground for all that was fashionable in dry goods, tempting in groceries or exquisite in jewellery."[1] In just the last few years, commercial blocks had been built in several locations along King Street and they now housed every kind of store or tradesman you could imagine. To the delight of pedestrians and drivers alike, the street and sidewalks had been planked, making King Street in this downtown area one of the most comfortable and efficient pieces of road in the province.

At this time in the morning, most of the activity was well to the east of Yonge Street. In the block of King Street between John and Graves, there were two large properties, both with spacious gardens and woods blocking public view from the street. On the south side of King Street was Elmsley House, the home of the lieutenant governor of Upper Canada, which was at this time occupied by Major General George Arthur.

This property had been purchased by the government in 1814 with the intent that it would become Government House, the residence of the lieutenant governor of the province.[2] The earliest Elmsley House had been built by Chief Justice John Elmsley[3] in 1799 and was now expanded and duly outfitted for the pomp and circumstance of an English colonial governor. The previous occupant had painted the house loyal British orange in support of the Family Compact during the 1836 elections, and William Weller may have chuckled at this in-your-face example of partisanship, although he certainly would never say anything in public about it. He needed to be squeaky clean in these rancorous times; all he wanted was plenty of paying passengers in his coaches and both Family Compact and reformers needed the service.

As the governor general reclined in the sleigh and peered through the trees toward the elaborate buildings and gardens of Government House, he may have chuckled to himself. The current lieutenant governor had proven himself to be co-operative – to a point. George Arthur clearly feared reform in Canada, seeing it as a threat to the close connection with Britain and the precursor to annexation to the United States. He did not trust men like Robert Baldwin who kept talking about responsible government, which both Thomson and Arthur believed would be disastrous.

4.1 The Upper Canada "House of Assembly," where Governor General Thomson passed his legislation in 1840, was the third set of Parliament buildings, built in the early 1830s.

At this time, George Arthur was in a very difficult spot. His powers had been reduced in relation to the higher-ranking governor general, and he wanted very much to make everyone happy, or at least not annoy any one group too much. As a result, many of the things he tried to do were half measures that nobody liked. But after Governor General Thomson's work was done, he would have to admit that, while he had a poor opinion of the man, Arthur had supported his push for union of the provinces in Toronto and had assisted ably in the close-run election in Quebec. Of course, the union of the provinces meant that George Arthur would lose his job and become the last lieutenant governor of Upper Canada. On a happier note, when Arthur returned to England in March 1841, Governor General Thomson would recommend that he receive the baronetcy he craved, becoming Sir George Arthur.

On the north side of King Street, William Weller could glance up the long driveway to the main buildings of Upper Canada College, which at this time in the morning were beginning to come alive with students and teachers. Upper Canada College had operated for a short time on Adelaide Street, but the new buildings between King and Newgate Streets on the west side of Graves were opened to students in 1831, with the expectation that capable young lads from the province would obtain a higher level of education than was then available at the grammar schools. Sir John Colborne,[4] who was lieutenant governor of Upper Canada from 1828 to 1838, was instrumental in the success of the school and took pride in its role as a place for the sons of the gentlemen of the region.

4.2 *Upper Canada College became the incubus for leaders of the colony for decades to come. In 1890, the college moved to a new site in Deer Park at the head of Avenue Road.*

The sleigh crossed Graves Street and continued smoothly down King Street, still largely in the dark, as there were few establishments on either side of the street at this time. As they approached York Street, Weller could see more lanterns bobbing along the street as storekeepers came to prepare their goods for the morning opening. For the modern reader, it is hard to imagine how much the cycle of day and night, light and dark, controlled the habits of the population in 1840. Sure, there were lanterns and torches and fireplaces, which pushed back the dark so work could be done. However, fuel was expensive, especially whale oil, so only wealthier folks could afford to have lamps at their homes and in their businesses. As a result, opening times and closing times for businesses, even in the larger towns, followed very much the rhythm of sunrise and sunset.

At the corner of York and King Streets, there were two buildings that William Weller would certainly recognize. On the northeast corner of the intersection, a rather plain, white, two-storey frame building housed Mr. J. Jamieson's boarding house.[5] It was a very convenient location for a boarding house, very near the busiest commercial street and two blocks up from Front Street and the harbour. There were constant comings and goings of travellers, which in those days often meant travelling salesmen, carrying their cases full of books, watches, clothing or whatever it was they were hoping to sell.

The only unique feature of this structure was a gabled entrance at the corner of King and York. In 1843, this would become the main entrance for the Shakespeare Hotel, a name well known to Toronto residents for many decades. It was the haunt of actors, stage performers, and touring companies who came to town to perform at the Theatre Royal which would be located down a laneway on the east side of the Shakespeare Hotel. In this February morning in 1840, however, the building was quiet with only a couple of its boarders rousing in order to get to work on time.

On the south side of King Street, east of York, a large and stylish brick building at that time performed the mundane task of barracks for militia officers. The building was actually Toronto's first commercial block, built in 1835 and owned by William Chewett. It was one of many structures around the city in the middle decades of the 1800s that were designed by the architect John George Howard. Arriving from England in 1832, Howard initially worked as a teacher at Upper Canada College while developing his architectural business.

In the next several decades, J.G. Howard[6] would create a variety of structures in Toronto including the Home District Jail on Front Street, the Canada Company Office on Frederick Street, and Colborne Lodge in High Park. He owned significant property at High Park, well to the west of the city at that time, and he would donate part of that property to the city when he died. The result is the popular High Park that Torontonians love today.

William Weller would recall that for a few years before the Rebellion of 1837, the British Coffee House[7] had occupied the corner of this building with the entrance on the York Street side. It was a popular establishment with the residents of Toronto, until it was forced to close down owing to what *Landmarks of Toronto* described as "troublous times then brewing," meaning political turmoil that led up to the rebellion. The government then took over the building and used it as barracks for troops stationed in Toronto.

A little way up King Street on the north side, William Weller could see the front gate of Christopher Denham's brass foundry. On the south side of King Street, as they approached Bay Street, there were many small offices and tradesmen and stores in several brick buildings, and many older frame structures. John George Howard, the architect, had an office here, as did Jacques and Hayes and their cabinet business. On the northwest corner of Bay Street, the Wyman & French chair factory was already glowing with torches and lanterns as the workday began.

In more recent times, this was the location of the *Telegram* building, but it has a long history.[8] In 1840, much of the property at the corner of King and Bay was owned by Rebecca Richardson, who was a daughter of John Dennis. Mr. Dennis had acquired the property from Quetton St. George in 1813, who in turn had acquired it from William Smith in 1808. John Dennis is well known in York history as the ship builder for Lieutenant Governor John Graves Simcoe and, in that position, he gained wealth and status as well as much property around York.

Rebecca Dennis had married James Richardson, who later became a bishop but was earlier well known for his work as a ship captain during the War of 1812. His father, Captain James Richardson, had lost an arm in the raid on Oswego in 1814, while acting as ship master.[9] He was also the first owner of Lot 1, Concession 1, Cramahe Township, where the town of Brighton is located today.

Wagons and pedestrians were crossing Bay Street as the pace of business picked up in downtown Toronto. On the northeast corner, William Weller could make out the old Knott house where Mrs. Knott, now very advanced in age, still lived. On the southeast corner was Jordan Post's watchmaking shop, although Weller knew that the old man was now living in Highland Creek in Scarborough Township, and the shop was in the hands of his employees. Mr. Post would, in fact, play a role in the trip as the owner of the inn in Highland Creek where Mr. Weller would change horses at the end of the first stage.

Very soon, on the south side of King Street, Jordan Street appeared in the torchlight. Before Jordan Street existed, this was the location of the first Methodist church in Toronto,[10] but recently the old church, which had served as the Theatre Royal for a few years, had been torn down and replaced by a new three-storey brick building. A decade later, this location would be the first office of George Brown's *Globe* Newspaper, the liberal voice of the province for many years.

Now the sleigh was approaching the primary thoroughfare of Yonge Street. There were more people on the street here, indicating the presence of numerous stores and offices up and down Yonge Street, over on Bay, and down to Front Street.

On the immediate south corner of King and Yonge could be seen the sign for the Baldwin law firm, run by two of the most famous residents of Toronto, William Warren Baldwin and his son Robert Baldwin.

William Warren Baldwin had come to the fledgling village of York in 1799, first working as a doctor but then becoming a lawyer.[11] He prospered as a member of one of the elite families who helped York grow in those early years. Even though he had close connections with the other important families in the town, he was of a decidedly liberal frame of mind, and his son, Robert, developed along the same lines, also as a lawyer.[12]

The Baldwin law firm gained a well-deserved reputation for treating all clients fairly, even in conflicts with members of the Family Compact, which the Baldwins often won in court. Robert Baldwin had become the leader of the Reform Party in Upper Canada during the 1830s, and his political success and judicial reputation placed him in the uncomfortable position, in February of 1840, of being on Governor General Thomson's list of preferred men to assist in the restructuring of the government. Baldwin would acquiesce for a time, acting as solicitor general, but his strong principles and emotions would not allow him to support the governor general if he was not going to implement responsible government. When Thomson's true intentions became clear, Baldwin resigned in 1841.[13]

As the sleigh passed the Baldwin office, the governor general may have thought of the intense and sometimes emotionally charged discussions he had experienced with Robert Baldwin in the last few months. Baldwin had a serious following in the province and Thomson needed his support, but he also felt that Baldwin was unlikely to compromise. He would not be someone you could bribe with baubles. He was a tough, principled man, and this was another reason Thomson was happy to have accomplished his mission in Upper Canada and could now put Toronto behind him.

5

King Street East to St. James Cathedral

YONGE STREET WAS THE SECOND BUSIEST STREET IN TORONTO IN 1840, AFTER KING Street. It was being built up like the other streets in the city with houses and shops and offices. Even then, you had only to travel a few streets north before you were in the country again. In a broader context, however, the creation of Yonge Street was one of the most significant events in the very early days of Upper Canada.

In 1793, Lieutenant Governor John Graves Simcoe was motivated to build a road to the north by the threat of American incursion into Upper Canada. In fact, this would be a military road. Simcoe led a party of soldiers on the old portage route north from the Rouge River to establish a fort at Penetanguishene. Finding a different route that avoided the marshes and joined with the excellent natural harbour at York, he decided on this new route for his military road.

The next spring, Simcoe instructed his surveyor general, Augustus Jones, to blaze a trail for the new road. Actual construction of the road was initiated by granting land to settlers along the route on condition that they clear thirty-three feet of frontage on the road past their lots. A group of sixty-four families took up the challenge and construction of the road progressed, with fits and starts, over the next few years. The work was very difficult, but the road would be built up and then extended over the years, to result in what is sometimes called Main Street Ontario. Interestingly, no part of Yonge Street is a provincial highway.[1]

Just a few years before William Weller drove the governor general across Yonge Street, the main event of the Mackenzie Rebellion had taken place at Montgomery's

Tavern, just above Eglinton Avenue (today's Postal Station K), on December 4, 1837. Mackenzie set up a roadblock on Yonge Street, and a loyalist party tried to clear it, resulting in some shooting. The rebels scattered, and while there were other attempts by rebel groups to enter the city in the next couple of days, they were leaderless and confused. The rebellion, such as it was, petered out to nothing.[2]

On this February morning in 1840, the intersection of King and Yonge was yellow with torch light, which assisted two teamster wagons loaded with lumber on their way to the harbour. Several smaller wagons were parked in front of shops and stores, delivering products and supplies for the day's business. William Weller had to pull back on the reins and guide his team through the activity of this key intersection. Both the driver and the horses were anxious to get out on the open road so they could pick up speed, but right now, they had to deal with city traffic.

Just across Yonge Street, on the northeast corner, was a substantial four-storey, hip-roof, red brick building with the sign "Ridout Bros." on the front. This was the very successful iron mongering and hardware business of brothers Joseph and Percival Ridout. Old timers would remember the Dennis Cottage on this spot, the home of well-known boat builder John Dennis. In 1830, the old cottage had been torn down and this commercial building built to further demonstrate the growing importance of the business section of the city.

The north side of King Street from Ridouts at the corner of Yonge Street all the way to Toronto Street was filled with a variety of shops and merchants. Bethune and Blackstone were barristers; William Hall was a tailor; J.F. Saxon had another law firm; Samuel Caspar ran a general store; George Bilton operated a tailor's shop. Not quite on the scene yet, A. & S. Nordheimer's music store would be added to the street in 1844.

The most curious sight on the north side, just before Toronto Street, was The Checkered Store,[4] which had been built in 1831 by R.A. Parker for the purpose of selling what was then called "notions". A joke of the time was that this store sold "everything from a needle to an anchor". Certainly, the very distinctive checkerboard design painted on the front of the building gave an air of whimsy to King Street. Of course, that little bit of lightness was welcome in this area, because right across Toronto Street was the jail and courthouse.

The south side of King Street mirrored the north. E.H. McSherry was a hatter; Francis Richardson was a chemist and druggist; John Cornish was a shoemaker; Peter Peterson had dry goods; Rossin Bros. imported fine jewellery; P. Mullany was a butcher and Thomas Wallis was a grocer. Here one could see the commercial heart of the city of Toronto.

City maps from that period look much different than even a few years later. The block bounded by Yonge Street on the west, King Street on the north, Church Street on the east, and Market Street on the south was not broken up by Colborne Street running east and west across the middle of it, or by Victoria Street and Leader Lane, dividing it into three parts as we see today. In 1840, William Weller would have seen one long line of shops and buildings on the south side, all the way to Church Street.

After the Checkered House, the north side of King Street opened up to reveal the grounds of the jail and courthouse. Two large, two-storey, brick buildings stood back from the street, several dozen yards separating them. The building to the west, set back off Toronto Street, was the jail. Its partner to the east, close to Church Street, was the courthouse. An 1836 sketch of this part of King Street shows people, wagons, and horses along the north side of King Street, using the open area between the jail and courthouse as a promenade. It is an idyllic scene.

5.1 In 1840, the courthouse and jail buildings stood back from the north side of King Street.

The grounds had a different and much more ominous meaning to others. It was here, on the morning of April 12, 1838, that Samuel Lount and Peter Matthews were hanged for their part in the Mackenzie Rebellion. A double scaffold had been erected in between the jail and courthouse so that prisoners in the jail could see the hanging through the large windows, and the public could witness the spectacle standing in the yard along King Street.[5]

A large crowd of spectators was present on that morning to see the hanging. Many of them were in sympathy with the men but were not inclined to defy justice on this day. The rebellion that had ended less than two years before had spilt the country between loyalists and traitors, if you listen to the conservative description of events. On the other hand, from the other side you would hear words like reform, change, improvement, and repression. While the population of Upper Canada had doubled in the 1830s, the Family Compact still maintained a firm grip on government, with the support of conservative governors general and lieutenant governors sent over from Britain to keep the colony in check.

Much resentment had built up over the slow pace of change and the refusal of the elite to share power with the expanding number of worthy professionals, merchants, tradesmen, and prosperous farmers. It was a boiling pot that finally burst out when William Lyon Mackenzie[6] gathered his supporters at Montgomery's Tavern. The resulting skirmishes could hardly be called a rebellion. Certainly they were puny compared with the deaths and violence in Lower Canada. However, any violence used to defy the authority of the crown, however small, could not be tolerated.

After the rebellion, Lieutenant Governor George Arthur had struggled with the forces that bombarded him on all sides. The Family Compact saw this as an opportunity to demonstrate the power of the existing system and pushed for many more of the rebels to be put to death as a lesson for anyone else who might think of attempting violent acts against the state. On the other hand, he was being instructed by the more reform-minded ministry in London that any more deaths at the hand of the state would make matters worse. Local reformers were asking him to pardon all the prisoners. What was he to do?

Samuel Lount and Peter Matthews had been respected and prosperous men, part of a growing group that we today would call the middle class. Lount had been born in Pennsylvania in 1791 and was a blacksmith who had been elected to the House of Assembly to represent Simcoe County. Peter Matthews was the son of a United Empire Loyalist who had fought with Brock in the War of 1812. Both men had become supporters of Mackenzie and, because of their respected positions in the community, had developed into leadership roles.

Lieutenant Governor Arthur was inclined to make a bolder statement, but finally decided on a more moderate approach. He selected only the two most prominent leaders of the rebellion for the ultimate punishment. Lount and Matthews had been convicted according to the law, and he would make an example of them. Others were transported to Damien's Land and many would eventually be pardoned. Some would make their way back to Upper Canada in the next few years. In fact, William Lyon Mackenzie himself would return and be elected to the House of Assembly.

The challenge for the modern reader is to stand amidst the peace and prosperity at 1 Toronto Street and try to imagine that such an important execution took place right here, on this spot. A historical plaque appears on the wall on the northeast corner of the intersection of King and Toronto Streets to commemorate this important event in Canadian history.[7]

What was Governor General Thomson thinking as the sleigh sped along King Street past the jail? He may have pushed open the moveable slide in the door of the cab in order to catch one last quick glimpse of this notorious place. His job was to fix the mess left after years of mismanagement and failure to make necessary changes. If more reasonable men had been in charge in 1837, these unfortunate deaths could have been avoided. However, human nature being what it is, the outcome should not be surprising. Thomson closed the slide and settled back in anticipation of his long ride. He was anxious to finish the job of putting this colony on a sound basis for the future. No sense dwelling on the past.

In fact, this section of King Street would change very quickly. Plans were already afoot to construct a new jail at the bottom of Berkeley Street. The Cane Topological Plan for Toronto in 1842[8] shows the new courthouse and jail at the waterfront, between Berkley and Parliament Streets. It also shows the building that housed the old jail, but it is now the lunatic asylum. In contrast, the courthouse is still shown, just as it had been earlier.

The big difference in 1842 was that both buildings are hidden behind a full row of commercial buildings along King Street. An etching from 1846 in *Landmarks of Toronto* shows many different shops and trades in this area of new development, much like on the south side. That pleasant, open area in front of the jail and courthouse was a thing of the past because street-front property was so valuable. It was clear that the expansion of business was inevitable in downtown Toronto.

William Weller was more conscious of traffic in this area of King Street because he knew they were approaching the market. As he crossed Church Street, he slowed the team down and moved to the side to avoid a teamster wagon loaded with lumber and staves. A few steps more and the sleigh was opposite one of the most impressive structures in Toronto, St.

5.2 St. James Cathedral was brand new in February 1840, constructed in the previous year after the devastating fire on December 29, 1838. The new structure would be destroyed in the conflagration that engulfed this area of the city on April 7, 1849.

James Cathedral. Lanterns at the front of the church cast a faint yellow light on the solid stone structure, and the steeple stretched up into darkness, towering over the street below. In front of the church, a row of mature poplar trees lined the sidewalk, lending the grounds the feel of a garden, in contrast to the stately structure within.[9]

The church that William Weller saw from the sleigh on that morning in February 1840 was brand new. It was the third church on that site. The *Palladium* newspaper of January 4, 1839 informed the shocked community of the terrible fire a few days before: "Our city has been deprived of its chief ornament, as a public building, by the destruction of St. James' Church, on the morning of Sunday last, by fire, which was first seen at about half-past eight o'clock in the morning, bursting from the roof in such a manner as to show that it had been communicated by the stove-pipe. In whatever point of view it is regarded this is a great calamity, and is deeply lamented as such by every considerate and well-regarded mind in the community."[10]

The article goes on to debate the idea of building several smaller and less expensive churches around the city instead of continuing on the path of spending such large funds on one massive building. The second church had been built in 1833 and was designed as a neo-classical temple. It was a huge loss for the city, the parish, and for the members of the congregation.

The rector of St. James and the archdeacon of York at this time was John Strachan,[11] a man well-known over several decades of history in Upper Canada. After impressive work in Cornwall running one of Upper Canada's most prestigious grammar schools, he came to York in 1812, just in time to play a key part in the war with the United States. He showed great courage and energy in the crisis, in particular, assisting in the surrender of the city to the Americans after the small British force had left the city.

John Strachan would be, for the rest of his life, the strongest proponent for the Anglican Church in Upper Canada. He was absolutely certain that it was, and should be, the established church, meaning the exclusive church of the state. He would do much to develop the church and support its congregations and would not shrink from direct political activity if that was what it took. He became a member of the Executive Council and engaged in many battles against those who would countenance reform. In this role, he was allied with the Family Compact and was very close with many key figures in the government, especially Chief Justice John Beverly Robinson, who had been one of his students in the Cornwall Grammar School and would be a life-long friend.

Immediately after the fire, Archdeacon Strachan set to work garnering financial support from the many wealthy and powerful members of the parish for the construction of a new and better edifice on the same spot. Soon after putting this process in motion, Strachan left for England, where he would be consecrated as bishop of Upper Canada. He had lobbied long and hard for this elevated position and only managed to obtain it when he agreed to forego the salary. By the end of the same year, he was back in Toronto in time to open the new St. James Cathedral.

Bishop Strachan was much angered by Governor General Thomson's attempts to unify the Canadian provinces and spoke loudly against any change in the status of the Clergy Reserves. He insisted that revenue from the vast reservoir of land, which had been accumulated as Clergy Reserve land, must be used only for the benefit of the Anglican Church and for no other denomination. These funds had been earmarked for the support of what Strachan felt was the legitimate state church, and in particular, for building schools that were run by the Anglican Church. Any other suggestion was, in the mind of the bishop, next to treasonous.

Of course, Bishop Strachan was on the wrong side of history in this regard and was much disappointed in the last years of his life, in spite of being named bishop. He saw his church relegated, bit by bit, to the status of one of many denominations. Governor General Thomson and his backers in Britain had been very strong about this issue, although they tried to be moderate in an attempt to please everyone. That approach really did not work for someone as extremely partisan as Bishop Strachan.

In the end, John Strachan would live to see the new Dominion of Canada take shape a few months before he died in November 1867. In his long and active life, he had fought many battles and made many enemies in the process. However, a large body of people would remember his grammar school days, where many of the successful men of Upper Canada were nurtured and encouraged to enter public service. He had been a very effective rector and archdeacon in Toronto and had motivated much positive development in the church and in the education system.

6

King Street East to Market Square and East

ON THE SOUTH SIDE OF KING STREET, IN THE BLOCK BETWEEN CHURCH STREET AND Market Square, major development had happened in the years since the incorporation of the City of Toronto in 1834. The city owned the land at the corner of King and Market Street West, and several large commercial blocks had been constructed on both King Street and Market Street West to be leased and rented by businesses, merchants, and tradesmen.

This area of Toronto became the go-to spot for anything in the dry goods market. All along King and Market and down on Front Street were shops and merchants selling all sorts of clothing and bedding in endless varieties. In the early 1830s, word circulated that this area in downtown Toronto was as good as Montreal in variety and pricing. It was a tall order, which would take some time to be realized, but the objective was well established.

As the sleigh approached Market Square on the south side of King Street, William Weller had to slow down because there were many pedestrians, horses, and wagons on the street. They were in the intersection and going every-which-way, all hurrying to their places of work, delivering product, or obtaining merchandise for their own stores. This area came alive much earlier than the rest of the city, as there was so much to be done in preparation for all the shoppers who would come out during the day. One can imagine the sound of horses' hooves, wagon wheels on planks, shouts, greetings of people meeting on the street, and probably oaths of teamsters as they tried to manoeuvre their horses and wagons. There was a major buzz of activity around Market Square. It was the sound of money.

Suddenly, Weller had to pull the team up in order to avoid a wagon loaded with sacks of grain that was turning into Market Street West. As he steadied the team, a shadowy figure shuffled across King Street in front of the sleigh, hurrying so as not to be knocked down, but obviously having trouble with an old limp. In the light of his torch, William Weller recognized this mysterious figure right away and yelled out, "Well there, Martha, be careful you don't be knocked down again! Business waits for no one!"

The figure stopped on the sidewalk and turned toward the sleigh, a toothless grin evident from under her shawl. "Aye, Mr. Weller, will it be the guvner you have today?" Weller laughed and said, "To be sure, Martha, we are off for Montreal."

Martha gave a slight bow and turned down Market Street toward her stall at the fish market.

An engraving entitled "The Fish Market", which was produced by William Henry Bartlett[1] around 1840 shows the waterfront of Toronto in fine detail. The scene seems to pulse with activity and the unmistakable aroma of the fish market comes to mind; it is a wonderful work of illustrative art. At this time, this type of art was considered picturesque and sublime. It was very popular and sold well, allowing Bartlett to travel extensively and witness first-hand the places he wanted to portray. This image of the Toronto waterfront was not from someone else's watercolour or sketch but came directly from his experience, sitting to the east of the fish market and looking west across the harbour.

6.1 William Henry Bartlett's engraving of "The Fish Market" looks west along the shoreline, showing The Coffin Block, an odd-shaped building on the wedge corner of Market and Front Streets. The lower two floors of this structure housed William Weller's General Stage Office, and this area was known as the hub for stagecoach lines.

On the right side of the picture, we see the City Hotel and then, a bit farther west is an odd-looking building of three storeys. This was the Coffin Block, so-named because it had the unmistakable shape of a coffin, narrow at one end and wider at the other. The shape of this building was dictated by its location on the V of the angle where Front Street met Market Street, later to be called Wellington Street. The modern reader might marvel at the shoreline being in this location, but it illustrates how much fill has been deposited on the shoreline over the years, moving it constantly south.

The Coffin Block is very significant in our story because on the ground floor at the very easterly point of the Coffin block, the office for William Weller's stage-coach line was located. It was called "The General Stage Office",[2] and this is where stages from all directions converged with passengers who were coming to Toronto or were transferring to a stage headed to Cobourg, Hamilton, or Barrie. It was from this office that Lorenzo Weller would depart later that day, following his father to Montreal with the baggage and the governor general's chief secretary.

William Weller had arranged this trip to Montreal out of his office in the Coffin Block. Even at this early hour there were lanterns lit and people working there as he drove down King Street. They had been sending messages and doing everything they had been instructed to do in order to ensure a successful outcome for this enterprise. Mr. Weller was much respected and admired amongst his employees, and there was a common expectation that he would be successful this time, as in other challenges. Besides, Mr. Weller was known to be generous in his praise, demonstrating that he understood how important everyone in the team really was in accomplishing their goals. Oh, and he might be inclined to thank his employees in a tangible way, which would not be unwelcome, of course.

The building that stood in Market Square in 1840 was the second market in that location. Lieutenant Governor Peter Hunter had designated this property as a market space in 1803, and it would remain in this capacity to the present day. In 1831, the old wooden market building had been torn down, and the growing city had built a much larger and more robust market. *Landmarks of Toronto* describes the market building as "a quadrangular brick building with arched gateway entrances at the sides. Around it were set posts with iron chains dependent. This building filled the whole square with the exception of roadways on the east and west sides. Around four sides of this new market above the butchers' stalls ran a wooden gallery."[3]

The accompanying etching shows a large, solid building that would be easy for wagons to enter through archways on all sides. It would be difficult to list all the butchers that occupied the lower level along King Street, since the market was a primary exchange for meat products of all kinds. In the upper level, some of the larger auctioneers and wholesalers had offices, and the Commercial News Room shared space with the merchants.

6.2 Market Square had been designated as a town market space in 1803 and a wooden building constructed. In 1831, a new and larger brick building had been built to accommodate the growth in commercial activity in the town of York. In 1840, it was the centre of commercial activity in Toronto and also housed the City Hall.

When William Weller made his way past the market in February of 1840, the upper floor accommodated Toronto City Council. For eleven years, from 1834 to 1844, this was the location of Toronto City Hall. The population of the city doubled in that decade, so a new City Hall was built immediately south of Market Square on Front Street. Later, in the 1890s, City Hall would move elsewhere but the market stayed, evolving into the beloved St. Lawrence Market of today.

The mayor of Toronto at this time was John Powell, who had been elected mayor for an unprecedented third one-year term. Powell was not a particularly effective politician but had ridden a wave of fame for the part he played in the Mackenzie Rebellion. He had always been a staunch Tory, but he was also an alderman for St. Andrew's Ward. It was in this capacity that he and a companion rode up Yonge Street on horseback to meet Mackenzie's forces, who were reported to be marching south. At the slope between St. Clair and Summerhill, Powell was captured by rebels. Shortly after, he pulled a pistol from his coat and killed Anthony Anderson, the leader of the rebels who had captured him. He then tried to shoot Mackenzie, but the gun misfired, saving Mackenzie's life.[4]

John Powell was acclaimed as a hero and within a few months was elected mayor by a wide margin. The next year he was re-elected, although with a smaller margin. Then, just a month before William Weller's trip down King Street, Powell had been elected to a third term, but only after nine votes. Rebellion hysteria was widespread, and his attempts to strengthen local militia and increase the police force were loudly applauded by the conservatives in Toronto. This was the period, after some reform successes before the rebellion, when the Family Compact hunkered down and had their last period of electoral success. Governor General Thomson, riding by the office of Mayor Powell on this morning, would see to that.

In 1840, the east side of Market Square was bounded by New Street, so named because it had been the western extent of the first expansion of the city many years earlier. The Cane Topographical Plan for Toronto in 1842 still shows it as New Street, but it was soon renamed Nelson Street, the name we see in reports of the great fire in 1849.

Around the time of the governor general's sleigh ride, the property north of Lot Street in this area belonged to Samuel Jarvis, who was the chief superintendent of Indian Affairs. He had gained this and other positions partly on the reputation of his father, William Jarvis,[5] who had been part of Lieutenant Governor John Graves Simcoe's government in Newark. He had then moved with Simcoe when the capital was moved to York. William Jarvis had been the registrar for York County, but his career had stalled due to his argumentative nature, often resulting in challenges to duels that never seemed to take place.

His son carried on this tradition by his involvement in one of the last duels in Upper Canada in 1817.[6] Samuel Jarvis had been in a fight with John Ridout, a son of the powerful Thomas Ridout, and the two had arranged a proper duel with their friends as seconds in support. The story is that Ridout shot too early and, after a conference of the seconds, Jarvis was given a free shot. He took the shot and killed Ridout. In the trial that followed, Jarvis was acquitted because a properly conducted duel was still accepted by the courts. This would change, gladly, but Samuel Jarvis would carry this baggage for the rest of his life.

Unfortunately for Samuel Jarvis, some of the changes that flowed from the work being done by Governor General Thomson in 1840 would finally end Jarvis' position with the Indian Department, and he found himself without a job. In order to pay off some of his debts, he hired John George Howard to subdivide and sell property above Queen Street. In the process, the early Jarvis home, called Hazelburn, was torn down, and a street was laid out in the middle of the new town lots. It would be called Jarvis Street.[7]

On the southeast corner of King and New Streets, William Weller would have seen a long three-storey building stretching down New Street and containing several shops and merchant windows along the street level. On the second storey, in very large letters, was the sign "Mirror Printing Office". This building had housed

Thomas Moore's Crown Inn for a decade during the 183
office of George Gurnett's Tory newspaper called the *Co*

In January of 1837, Gurnett was voted mayor of To
vative city council that was intent on combatting the
hero of the rebellion for the Family Compact, would
the anti-reform efforts. Of course, George Gurnett
to learn that Charles Dunlevy was publishing his reformis...
the same offices where the Tory *Courier* had been printed.

On the north-east corner of King and New Streets, diagonally across from Market Square, Weller would have seen a building that contained several small shops and merchants. It had been built in 1833 by Daniel Brooke, and its strategic location would attract many tenants over the years. Before the rebellion, James Austin had been an apprentice of William Lyon Mackenzie and was unfairly labelled a rebel by the conservative element in the town. In order to protect himself, he had fled to the United States.

Austin would return to Toronto in 1843 and enter into partnership with Patrick Foy, creating a very successful wholesale business in the building at King and Jarvis. The building would survive the 1849 fire and, after much renovation and modernization, can be seen today at the north-east corner of King and Jarvis, one of the oldest surviving commercial buildings in Toronto. Today it includes shops at 150, 152, and 154 King Street East. James Austin would go on to found The Dominion Bank and build Spadina House.[8]

After William Weller had manoeuvred past the Market Square and across New Street, the activity on the street was reduced, and there would be fewer interruptions on the road. He was entering a part of Toronto that was still an active commercial area, but truth be told, was looking a bit worse for wear. This part of King Street, around the intersections of George and Frederick Streets, had been the centre of the early town of York. There had been stores and wholesalers on all four corners, and many of the institutions of the city began here, including the post office and the Bank of Upper Canada.

However, through the 1820s and 1830s, the centre of the city had gradually migrated west, and by 1840 was located in the Yonge Street area. A parallel move can be seen in the major government buildings. The early parliament buildings were at Front Street just south of the eastern part of the town. Now, rather than the city of York being seen as between Church and the Don River, the city of Toronto was seen to lie between Market Square and John Street. It was a shift that would continue.

As the sleigh drove down King Street in 1840, some of the old landmarks would still be evident. On the southeast corner of King and George Street, Mrs. Hughes ran a dry goods store in the building where George Duggan had been a merchant years. Diagonally across King Street, on the northwest corner, was a large building at this time occupied by the Nipissing House but until recently the tion of Gamble & Birchall, one of the most active wholesalers in the area. Just to he west of this had been another wholesaler, Bryce & Buchanan.

There were many firsts in this area. The first public school in York was called the Home District School, and it was conducted in a small stone building at the southeast corner of King and George Streets, where Mrs. Hughes had her dry goods store in 1840. The school had been started by Rev. Dr. Okill Stuart, who taught there for several years. His list of pupils is a who's-who of the early families of York. In 1813, Rev. Dr. John Strachan replaced the Home District School with the District Grammar School, which was located temporarily at King and Yonge, but later would be housed in The Blue School, located on the designated College Square north of St. James Cathedral.

The first brick building at York was built by Quetton St. George at the north-east corner of King and Frederick Streets. St. George was a French Royalist who came to Upper Canada around 1800 and was very successful in trade, bringing merchandise from New York for several stores he had set up, one of them in York. He was so prosperous that he was able to build a fine brick house at a time when all the bricks had to be shipped from Oswego. He lived in this house and carried on business on the ground floor. By 1817, Quetton St. George decided to leave York. He had been in partnership with James Spread Baldwin, who would continue to operate the business for many years.

William Weller touched the reins to ease the team into a trot. He was anxious to make better progress than had been possible in the city. Glancing back over his shoulder, he breathed a sigh of relief. It could have been a lot worse. Now they would be able to move along with little interruption.

As he crossed Frederick Street, Weller glanced to the north side of the street and saw the large, dark form of Quetton St. George's substantial two-storey brick building, which was still owned by the Baldwins, but had been rented for some time to the Canada Company.[9] It was dark and quiet right now, but later in the day it would be alive with officials, staff, lawyers, and land agents, all scrambling to take advantage of the huge resource of land that the government had set aside as Clergy Reserves and Crown Reserves since the early days of settlement. The company was formed in 1826 in order to manage and develop these lands, and after a few years of meetings in the Frank Hotel on Market Street West, the company had rented part of this spacious building for their offices.

One of the major complaints that had led to the rebellion was the unfair way all this undeveloped land was being handled. Large sections of road were left with no maintenance because the lots were reserved and nobody was responsible for the statute labour, which meant that people who owned the lots along the road were responsible for keeping that stretch of road smooth and unobstructed. Wealthy speculators took advantage of settlers by leasing or renting land to them and then pulling them off the property after they had done considerable improvements. Many people were very angry about this and some blamed the Canada Company, which was now in control of the disposition of the land. The company worked hard to help settlers find land and often provided transportation and other services to assist in the process. Major projects like the development of Guelph and the road to Goderich were extremely important for the growth of the country. However, it was the bad things folks remembered.

Across King Street, on the southeast corner of Frederick, William Allan had built a substantial brick building where he operated a grocery store. In 1822, Allan was also instrumental in founding the first Bank of Upper Canada, which would operate in this building for many years. In fact, the vault was still evident in the cellar in the 1890s.

Another first in this location was the first post office of York, which had been kept in a small log house on the east side of Frederick Street, just south of King Street. This was immediately across Frederick Street from D'Arcy Boulton's early house. The first postmaster was William Allan. The duties of postmaster were light enough in those early days to allow him to also hold the post of collector of customs and to carry on business as a merchant as well. But now, in 1840, the post office was a much more substantial operation and was located at the corner of Yonge and Front Street.

William Weller encouraged the team to increase their pace as the sleigh approached Caroline Street. This was another early street name that would change, in this case to Sherbourne Street in 1848, when the Ridout family wished to commemorate their heritage in England.

At Caroline Street, the sleigh would pass the Smith house. William Smith was an experienced builder who came to York with Lieutenant Governor John Graves Simcoe in the 1790s to help lay out the new town. Smith then chose a lot at the east end of town for his own residence, building a log house and later a more substantial frame house,[10] which his son, William Jr., would expand and occupy until 1832. *Landmarks of Toronto* includes a sketch of this building in 1821, where we can see that the Smith home was a substantial size and very close to King Street. In the 1843 *Toronto City Directory*, the British Exchange Inn is located on this spot, and we might expect that William Weller saw this establishment as he went by in 1840. In 1868, the hotel was rebuilt and called the Grand Central Hotel, and later would become the National Hotel.

6.3 *The celebrated York Hotel was run by John Jordan during the early decades of York when members of Parliament made the quick walk up from the parliament buildings for a meal and libations.*

After crossing Princess Street, William Weller saw another familiar sight. The south side of the block between Princess and Ontario Streets had been dominated for many decades by Jordan's York Hotel. In the early years of York, this was a classy place that drew clientele from the parliament buildings that were then a short walk south at the shore. A sketch of this establishment was provided by Henry Scadding,[11] who wrote about Toronto history. The sketch shows a stagecoach out front of the hotel, which would be a common sight in those days. When the parliament buildings moved farther west, the elite clientele moved with it. Even in the 1830s, the Jordan Hotel is mentioned as being run-down and a shadow of its former self.

The team received another signal from the driver to pick up the pace and, as the sleigh crossed Ontario Street, they could consider themselves outside the city of Toronto. There were a few buildings around this corner, such as Joseph Easton's saddlery and the boarding house of John Hay, but after that, the roadside was bounded by fields and forest. At Berkley Street, King Street swung north on an angle to head straight for the bridge over the Don River.

William Weller let the horses find their own rhythm and sat back a bit on the bench to relax after the intense activity of manoeuvring through the city. Daylight was beginning to extend into the fields and woods at the side of the road. Mr. Weller always felt more comfortable driving in the daytime. There were just too many things that could go wrong at night, and he had experienced many of them. There could be unseen obstacles on the road that could cause upsets or damage to the horses or vehicle, and it was not uncommon to encounter bandits in the unpopulated areas.

But this morning, everything was going fine, and the driver expected that to continue as the sleigh put mile after mile under its runners.

The road falling away under the sleigh runners was still decent plank road, but not as well maintained as the streets in Toronto. Once you ventured outside the main urban areas, the roads could be extremely bad. People complained to the government about it all the time and some improvements happened, but nowhere near enough to deal with the practical need. Most roads were still dirt trails maintained by statute labour. It was very much a hit-and-miss system. Many lots were not occupied by settlers, and therefore, the road received no maintenance at all. Here was one of the major complaints that led to the Mackenzie Rebellion, and as far as most folks were concerned, it remained to be addressed.

7

Across the Don

IT WAS STRAIGHT GOING ALONG THE EASTERN EXTENSION OF KING STREET, WITH only a few buildings along the road but lots of traffic heading the other direction, into the city. As dawn approached, farmers were bringing their grain to the market, and teamsters were coaxing teams of plodding oxen, dragging loads of lumber, staves, and shingles to the various builders and wholesalers in the city. The road was wide and flat and persistently straight, so meeting other vehicles was not a problem.

The next major obstacle was the Don River Valley. King Street had been heading northeast since Berkley Street, and it would meet the east end of Lot Street at the western edge of the Lower Don Valley. In 1844, Lot Street would be renamed Queen Street, so the modern reader can think of the current location of the Queen Street Viaduct as the general area where the bridge over the Don was located in 1840, but much imagination is required to conjure the landscape William Weller was approaching.

The straightening of the Don River happened in the 1880s, when a channel was cut down the valley, but in 1840, the Don River meandered through the marshes of the lower Don Valley. The location of the bridge had been chosen as the least difficult place to cross, way back in the 1790s, when barges and ferries began to take travellers across the river. Bridges were built but were constantly washed away and destroyed as ice and floods had their way.

In 1829, the lieutenant governor of Upper Canada, Sir John Colborne, personally shelled out £1,175 to repair bridges over both the Don and Humber Rivers, and then challenged the Assembly to reimburse him.[1] We don't know if he received any compensation for this, but it indicates that the situation was dire, and sometimes personal largess could make a difference.

Keeping a bridge over the Don River at the entrance to the Kingston Road was important for Toronto, but the local governments were hamstrung by laws that restricted how much money could be spent on a project before referring it to the Legislature. The limit was £50, and while this might grade a road or fix some plank, it would not build a large, permanent bridge over a river like The Don.

An article in the *Upper Canada Gazette* on September 22, 1827 explained the situation very clearly. The author of the article began by stating that: "The Don Bridge near this Town, is again in an impassable state – part of it gave way during the last week, and Horses and Carriages are now passed over, on a temporary floating bridge, on a toll being paid to the person who has erected that convenience…"[2]

The author also wished to warn those who were blaming the local magistrates for this debacle. In fact, the magistrates were simply following the existing law. If the job was estimated over £50, approval must be obtained in the Legislature where requests could take several years to work through all the political and financial issues. There was little concern for travellers. The article states: "If the system is bad, the fault lies in the Law, and should be amended."[3]

Here was an obvious example of the law not keeping pace with the degree of settlement and development that was happening in Upper Canada. The old rules were obsolete, and the gentlemen in charge had little incentive to make changes. And we wonder why there was a rebellion!

As fate would have it, the gentleman reclining in the sleigh as it approached the Don Bridge in 1840 knew all about this situation. In fact, he had already set legislation in motion that would help solve the problem. One of the important changes Governor General Thomson would implement was the creation of a Board of Works. This would be a major department of the government, led by professionals who had experience and knowledge in the building of roads, canals, and bridges. Soon they would also need to deal with railroads. Along with the Board of Works were new funding methods by which major projects could be financed. The roads would improve dramatically in the 1840s because of these changes.

William Weller knew the Don Bridge very well since he crossed it routinely and received constant reports of its condition. King Street had been planked out to the Don River a few years before and that work included a new bridge. On this day, the driver could be confident that the bridge would cause him no delays. The most recent reports from his network of messengers had confirmed exactly that.

This kind of reporting was part of Weller's large enterprise called The Royal Mail Line, which ran stages between Toronto and Kingston, carrying the Royal Mail as well as passengers. There was an extensive network of people, horses, and stables, scattered all along the route and geared towards running the stages efficiently. By 1840, steamboats had taken over much of the mail delivery, but stages were still required when navigation was closed on the lakes. In the winter, the conveyances were sleighs instead of wheeled coaches, but both did the same job.

Stage stops were roughly fifteen miles apart, which was considered to be the limit for running a team of horses at a good pace. The system required hundreds of horses and dozens of people, engaged every day to make the stage lines function effectively. All along the Kingston Road, there were taverns, inns, hotels, stables, and blacksmith shops that derived a good deal of their income from working with the Weller enterprise.

It was this system of resources that William Weller had in mind when he signed the contract with the governor general to drive from Toronto to Montreal in less than thirty-eight hours. He knew that he could make use of the people, horses, and stage stops that already existed for regular stage service. The conveyance and the cargo in this case would be a bit different, but the resources needed were the same.

We can expect that William Weller had sent messengers down the Kingston Road in the week after he signed the contract and right up until the day before they left. They carried instructions to the stable masters and hotel keepers along the way. Contractual relationships with other stage lines that operated from Kingston to Montreal would extend the reach of this network along the entire length of the trip.

There were explicit instructions that two of their stable hands would be on the road when the sleigh stopped, ready to unhook the tired and sweating team and move them off to the left and immediately out of the way. Another two hands would have their best two-horse team standing on the right side of the road, ready to move the team into place and quickly hook them up to the sleigh.

The expectation was that a stop should take no more than ten minutes. Many took less, partly because the hands knew their job very well, and to a man, wanted to help Mr. Weller succeed. We can imagine that this was an exciting and energizing experience for the fellows at the stops along the way, seeing themselves as a small part of something amazing and historical.

The sleigh came to Lot Street, and Mr. Weller swung the team to the right and down into the valley. Torches at each end of the bridge guided the team down the hill to the bridge, then across the bridge, and onto the road on the east side of the Don. This would be one of the best bridges they encountered on the trip, simply because it was relatively new.

On the east side of the Don River, the Kingston Road began. In this location, William Weller would have seen the substantial house and grounds of John Smith, who was the grandson of the builder who helped to lay out the town of York for

Lieutenant Governor Simcoe in the 1790s. In 1819, William Smith, Jr. purchased property on the east side of the Don River, south of the Kingston Road. The seller had been Mr. John Scadding,[4] who was the father of Rev. Dr. Henry Scadding, the well-known historian of Toronto and author of *Toronto of Old,* which has been useful as a source for this story. William Smith, Jr. built a tannery near the river and developed a substantial farm.

But wait, there is another connection to mention. John Scadding went back to England with Lieutenant Governor Simcoe in 1796 and then returned to York in 1817. Before he left York in 1796, he had put George Playter in charge of his property and installed him in a log house that had been built on the south side of the Kingston Road, on the east side of the Don River. In later years, this log house would be superseded by newer and larger homes, but the building would remain intact, used mainly as a storage shed for the farm.

Then, in 1869, John Smith offered the building to the York Pioneers,[5] an historical society that had recently been formed in Toronto. The York Pioneers were planning to participate in the first Industrial Exhibition in the summer of 1879, an event that would become the Canadian National Exhibition. They built a new pioneer cabin on the exhibition grounds where they exhibited pioneer household items such as furniture and cooking utensils. They also dismantled the old cabin from The Don and re-assembled it near the new cabin. In the early years, it was used to display military artifacts. At the time, the new cabin was seen to be much more important than the old one.[6]

Initially, the old cabin was called the Governor General's Cabin or Simcoe's Cabin because it was believed that Simcoe had built it and may have lived in it. Dr. Henry Scadding, the historian, researched the origins of the cabin and explained that the cabin was not related to Simcoe, but to the Scadding and Smith families. After Dr. Scadding's death in 1901, the cabin was named The Scadding Cabin in his honour. You can visit The Scadding Cabin on the CNE grounds today.

7.1 *The author visited Scadding Cabin during the 2017 CNE and found the York Pioneers busy greeting visitors and explaining the history of the building. Tanya Pitel, a University of Toronto student, graciously posed in front of the cabin with her lovely period dress and bonnet.*
It is worth a visit to see the oldest surviving house in Toronto.

8

East of the Don

MR. WELLER ENCOURAGED THE HORSES UP THE STEEP INCLINE, AND THE SLEIGH was soon back on flat ground east of the Don. The Kingston Road headed straight east from here, along the north edge of Ashbridges Bay. There was little development here due to the swampy conditions. Charles Coxwell Small owned extensive properties in this area, but the demand for land was low.

The planking of the Kingston Road in 1836 and 1837 changed the situation somewhat in that brick makers could now move their product into the city much more quickly. In fact, brick making would become a major industry in this area, taking advantage of the extensive clay deposits and proximity to the Kingston Road. However, it would be another couple of years before George Leslie leased twenty acres from Mr. Small along the south side of the road and began his Toronto Nurseries. A community would grow up around his business, and by the 1860s, would take his name to be known as Leslieville.[1]

Mr. Leslie had been astute in selecting the exact location of the property he leased for his nursery. Since he knew that most of the products he sold would be shipped down the Kingston Road to Toronto, he made sure to acquire property immediately west of the second toll booth on the Kingston Road. Besides being a smoother road, the planking of the Kingston Road had brought toll booths to collect fees from travellers. Mr. Leslie wanted to be located on the best patch of soil for growing fruit trees, but he was also able to locate himself very tactically related to the toll booths.

One might wonder how William Weller dealt with the toll booths that he would encounter at different places along the road between Toronto and Montreal. In fact, all government conveyances were exempt from tolls, so Mr. Weller did not have to worry about paying at the toll booths. However, some toll booths had gates across the road, which required someone in attendance to lift the gate and let the travellers through. The driver was concerned about the potential for delays at toll booths and had instructed his messengers to inform toll both operators to watch out for the governor general's sleigh and make sure they could pass without delay. The name "governor general" opened a lot of doors in those days, and it could be used effectively to clear the road ahead.

Past the toll booth, the road crossed three creeks that flowed into Ashbridges Bay. This body of water gained its name from the Ashbridges family who settled along its northern shoreline in the 1790s. Sarah Ashbridges' husband, Jonathan, had died in 1782, after the family had been disowned as Royalists in Chester County, Pennsylvania. Sarah brought her two sons, John and Jonathan, along with her three daughters to Upper Canada and was granted land as a United Empire Loyalist in the area east of the Don River, between Lake Ontario and the path that would later become Danforth Avenue. The Ashbridges Estate remains an historic site at 1444 Queen Street East, where two acres of the original estate and the second house built in 1854 were donated to the Ontario Heritage Trust in 1972.[2]

William Weller gave the horses their heads and settled in for the next part of this first stage of the trip. The relatively new plank road was still in decent shape, and he could make good time without jostling his passengers. The trip had gone well up to now, but it was early, and he felt the need to press ahead persistently.

Soon after crossing the last of the three creeks flowing into Ashbridges Bay, the Kingston Road swung northeast, moving away from Queen Street East. The modern Kingston Road follows this same route, swinging off Queen Street East just north of where Greenwood Race Track used to be, part way between Coxwell and Woodbine Avenues.

The next community along the road, known as Norway, was at the corner of today's Woodbine Avenue. An historical plaque at 320 Kingston Road[3] explains that a nearby building and cottage were built about 1825. A large steam sawmill was built here in 1835, and the community grew quickly, with a toll gate, hotels, and blacksmith shops.

The sleigh made it quickly through Norway, and soon the travellers would move out of the township of York East and into Scarborough Township. They were now out in rural country where the road cut through woodlands and farms. Blacksmith shops and taverns were to be seen along the road here and there, but most buildings were farm houses and barns, often behind the trees at the end of a long dirt path.

A short distance into Scarborough Township, the Kingston Road was met by the eastern extent of the old Danforth Road. Asa Danforth had built the first road east from York during the summers of 1799 and 1800.[4] He operated under contract from the government at ninety dollars per mile. The directions from the government at the time were to avoid obstacles and build the road as quickly as possible. Danforth was being paid by the mile, so the urgency to move along quickly was not lost on his sharp business mind. As a result, he picked the path of least resistance in many places, which meant that he kept back from the marshes and wide creeks at the lakeshore and tried to locate the road up on drier land.

Danforth was able to finish the road in 1800, but government officials were displeased with many aspects of it. They said it was not located in the right place, and many parts were not wide enough. There were few bridges over creeks and the foundation of the roadbed had been scraped over in such a cursory manner that in some places, it could not be recognized as a road after the first winter and spring seasons.

This criticism, combined with some other schemes that Danforth had been involved in, made him persona-non-grata with the government, and he was forced to leave Upper Canada. It was easy to complain about the new road but, in hindsight, it is also clear that the officials with the government had no idea of the scope and scale of the job of building and maintaining a road like this. Their expectations were not met, and they took it out on the builder.

Unfortunately, in those early years, there was so little settlement along the new Danforth Road that the conventional method of statute labour was ineffective in keeping the road maintained. It fell into disrepair in many areas, and enterprising local residents often responded by building alternate roads along the lakeshore where it served their needs. In 1817, the government was concerned about improving its ability to move troops and military supplies along the north shore of Lake Ontario in a situation where the American fleet threatened ships on the lake. It made sense to revitalize the old road.

The Kingston Road that William Weller travelled along in 1840 followed much the same route as the one built in 1817, sometimes on the same route as the Danforth Road, but most often closer to the lake to accommodate small communities that had sprung up on the lakeshore. Maintenance was still a problem, but the government was more aware of the need to allocate money for roads, and the planking of this section east of Toronto was one result. Of course, the tolls collected on the Kingston Road would never cover the full cost of construction and upkeep. The learning curve was steep as engineers and government officials alike gradually began to understand what it took to keep the roads in decent shape in the Canadian context of landscape, weather, and economy.

Scarborough Village[5] had obtained a post office in 1832, making it the first in the township. It was on the Kingston Road at the intersection of Markham Road and the eastern extension of Eglinton Avenue. William Weller guided the sleigh through the small village as he had done many times in the last decade. As early as 1829, Weller had partnered with Hiram Norton of Prescott to operate a mail stage line between York and Kingston. The advertisement said that stages were "…leaving Kingston and York Mondays and Thursdays at noon, arriving on Wednesdays and Saturdays, A.M."[6]

This had been one of William Weller's earliest attempts at running stagecoach lines along the lakefront. In a few years, he would own the line himself and improve it dramatically with more comfortable coaches and more reliable drivers. The roads were exceedingly bad in those days, and the Weller coaches were often mired in mud or upset in creek beds. However, this was the best service the people along the Kingston Road had experienced, and they welcomed the Weller coaches.

9

Highland Creek and the Rouge River

WILLIAM WELLER KNEW THAT THEY WERE APPROACHING THE END OF THE FIRST stage of the trip. Up ahead was the village of Highland Creek. The horses were running easy, and he knew this pair could probably go farther, but the men at the Post Inn at Highland Creek were waiting for them, and they must keep to plan. The village was named for the waterway, Highland Creek, which ran southeast from the middle of Scarborough Township to the lakeshore in the area of today's Port Union. The area was a prosperous farming community, and Highland Creek village was on the Kingston Road with several mills and commercial enterprises.[1]

Jordan Post's inn had been William Weller's choice as the stage stop for the first stage of this trip. He had known Jordan Post for most of a decade. Mr. Post had been a well-known watchmaker in Toronto during the 1820s and had moved to Highland Creek in 1832 to operate a store and inn. Mr. Post was seventy-three years old when he pulled up stakes in Toronto and moved to Scarborough, a move that demonstrated the enterprise and persistence of the man. Weller knew that Post was a good manager and would make sure everything was ready and done properly during this critical first stop.

Highland Creek village was spread out on both sides of the creek and the Post Inn was on the east side. William Weller guided the team down into the valley and along the plank road to the bridge over the creek. Here was another example of a waterway and a bridge that had presented serious problems for stages many times in the past, but today the bridge was in good shape, and the sleigh ran over the bridge and up the valley to the east side with no trouble.

As soon as the sleigh was on flat ground again, William Weller reached down and pulled his horn out of its holder, took a deep breath, put his lips to the mouthpiece, and gave three loud blasts on the horn. He waited a few seconds and then repeated the same sequence. This was the signal that the men and boys at the Post Inn were waiting for. This told them that William Weller would be in their midst in a few minutes with the governor general, and they must make themselves ready to do a quick change of horses, according to instructions Mr. Weller had provided.

It was daylight now, and many people were on the Kingston Road on foot or on horseback along with many wagons and sleighs. Everyone looked up when they heard the horn blasts. The traffic on the road halted in anticipation of the mail stage coming through. This was a common habit of the times. People were anxious to see the arrival of the stage any day, but this was a special stage, carrying the governor general. You did not see the governor general in Highland Creek very often, so there was some movement toward the Post Inn to catch a glimpse of their exalted guest.

As the sleigh came within sight of the sign for the Post Inn, the driver gave another blast on the horn and placed it back in its holder. He took the reins carefully in hand and began to talk to the horses. They responded by slackening their pace and moving over to the right side of the road. The inn was on the south side, so the fresh team of horses was standing right there in the driveway at the side of the road, perfect for a quick exchange.

The sleigh moved in smoothly, slowed down, and came to a halt just ahead of the fresh team of horses. Two young men sprang into action, detaching the sweaty and excited team from the sleigh and quickly moving them to the left, across the road, and out of the way. Almost simultaneously, two other fellows moved the fresh team into place and hooked them up to the sleigh.

While this was happening, a jug of water was handed up to the driver and Mr. Weller took a healthy drink. When he handed the jug back down, it was passed through the open window of the coach to the passengers inside. Just as the passengers finished with the water, the last check of the harnesses was complete and several men shouted "Ready." The jug was quickly handed out of the coach, and the window closed.

Mr. Weller pulled out his whip and gave it a crack over the heads of the horses, just like he had done in front of Beverley House in Toronto. The sleigh surged ahead, and Mr. Weller yelled out, "Good work, gentlemen, we are off to Montreal!" At this the men cheered and clapped as the sleigh headed down the Kingston Road.

The first change of horses had been executed perfectly, exactly as planned. Mr. Weller was a man who loved to see a plan come together, and he was grateful for the participation of everyone who helped. The fellows who were slapping each other on the back and shouting encouragement to the sleigh as it disappeared down the Kingston Road knew this very well and were delighted to be able to help. It was not hard to work for William Weller.

The Kingston Road continued straight northeast from Highland Creek. William Weller knew this was a section of the road where they could make good time since the planking would continue to Rouge Hill,[2] and there would not be a lot of traffic in this rural area. The terrain undulated more here, and this team would have to deal with hills more than in the first stage. No problem, it was all perfectly manageable.

That is, until the Rouge River. For the next several miles, William Weller contemplated the most difficult and potentially dangerous river crossing on the Kingston Road. The Rouge River crossing had been a serious problem since the first Danforth Road was built. The Rouge Valley in its lower reaches is deep with very steep banks on both sides, which made the building of a bridge across the river an expensive enterprise and the maintenance almost impossible. Every spring, the ice and floods of the river would wash away the bridge. It seemed like a losing battle.

It may be difficult for the modern driver to understand the direct physical challenge this problem presented to travellers more than one hundred and seventy years ago. As we whiz by in our quiet and cushy automobiles, on a wide, high, and long bridge over the 401 or Kingston Road, we might never consider today's scenery at the Rouge Valley, which consists of the tops of trees. It is not an issue for us anymore. The wonders of modern technology have solved this problem completely. But in 1840, it was an existential threat. One had to be very careful crossing the Rouge.

The Rouge River crossing was a particular problem for stagecoach drivers, and William Weller had plenty of experience with this location over the last decade while running the Royal Mail between Toronto and Kingston. In fact, Mr. Weller had taken matters into his own hands at one point. A few lines in the *Cobourg Star* of April 20, 1836, say that a bill was passed in the Legislature in Toronto "... granting the sum of £600, to remunerate Mr. Weller, of this town, for losses sustained by him in improving the hill at the river Rouge, and erecting a bridge over that river."[3]

William Weller was a businessman who would lose money if his coaches were delayed for long periods of time at any one place on the route. If he took the initiative, he could easily hire local men to do the work of improving the hill, as the article says, even to the extent of building a bridge. The government was slow to act and would dither about irrelevant issues, but he needed to get things done. He also may have been fairly sure that his costs would be covered eventually, since his partner in an earlier stage line, Hiram Norton, was a member of the Assembly from Prescott. Weller would always cultivate positive relationships with the powers that be, and his growing reputation as a businessman went a long way in smoothing over actions he might take that could be seen as impertinent and maybe a little rash. He could get away with it.

Reports from his network indicated that the planking on the road was fairly good right up to the Rouge, and that the relatively new bridge was in decent shape. William Weller had this information in mind as he came to the edge of the Rouge Valley and saw the steep incline in front of his team. He stopped at the crest of the hill and took stock. There was snow on the dirt road leading the last few hundred yards down to the bridge, which he could see clearly at the bottom of the valley. While there might be some slippery places, this would be better than mud.

His mind swirled with all the stories he had heard of mishaps at the Rouge. His own Royal Mail coaches had been delayed and in some cases damaged after sliding off the road. He recalled a particular incident that Mr. Courtice of Darlington Township had described to him. Courtice had been taking a load of lumber to Toronto, and the wagon and team were forced off the edge of the road by another wagon that was out of control. Luckily, there were no injuries to man or beast in this case, and he eventually made it to the lumber dealer in Toronto with most of his load intact. It was a dangerous place.[4]

Before starting down the steep hill, Mr. Weller asked his two passengers if they would disembark for a short time, just until they were across the bridge. Captain Le Marchant exited the coach and assisted Governor General Thomson to the side of the road. They would follow a few steps behind the coach just to make sure they were not caught up in any unfortunate incident. The passengers were well rested by this time, having enjoyed the trip so far and were not in the least concerned by their driver's method of handling this difficult situation.

Mr. Weller eased the team down over the crest of the hill. The horses were very unsettled about the scene that lay before them and with a less experienced driver might have taken fright. Many accidents happened on the approach to this crossing, evidenced by the remains of broken sleighs and wagons along the side of the road. Mr. Weller kept his focus on the horses and their immediate behaviour, speaking quietly to them and easing them down the steep incline. This was delicate work.

Soon they reached the flat road before the bridge and proceeded across the solid wooden bridge where the metal sleigh runners skidded along on the wet planks. Luckily, there were no other vehicles crossing at the same time, and the horses remained in good order. Once they were on the other side, Mr. Weller pulled the team up at the side of the road and beckoned his passengers to board once more. His experience had been that the trip up the east side of the valley would be less dangerous, and he did not want to force these particular passengers to climb up the long and steep road to the crest of the valley.

Once the passengers were on board, Mr. Weller encouraged his team to proceed slowly up the hill. He was more concerned with other vehicles having trouble coming down the hill towards him, than moving up the hill himself. There was little traffic on the road at this time, and the slow and arduous slog up the hill was accomplished without incident. At the top, Mr. Weller pulled off the side of the road where there was a water trough. While the horses drank, he spoke softly to them, patting them on the neck and letting them catch their breath after this difficult pull up the hill. He needed them to maintain their strength since they were only at the beginning of the second stage.

10

Pickering Township

ON CROSSING THE ROUGE RIVER, THE TRAVELLERS MOVED FROM SCARBOROUGH into Pickering Township but were still in York County. It was not until 1852 that York was divided into three counties – Peel, York, and Ontario. The first community they encountered was the small village of Rouge Hill, which would gain a post office in later years, but at this time was a small scattering of buildings along the road.

The Kingston Road continued in a northeast direction, keeping its orientation with the shore of Lake Ontario. The smooth and comfortable plank road had ended on the other side of the Rouge Valley, and now there would be an unpredictable variety of conditions, changing mile by mile. Planking would appear only occasionally along the length of the Kingston Road, and William Weller knew he had already passed the best patch they would see during their trip. After that, dirt roads would prevail in whatever form they might take.

The next town on the road was Dunbarton, founded in the early 1830s by William Dunbar. The decade of the 1830s would see a major influx of settlers along the shoreline of Lake Ontario. Many would take farms but others were tradesmen who would flesh out small villages with blacksmith and carriage shops. William Dunbar and his sons would be well known tradesmen in Dunbarton into the late 1800s.

When the Mackenzie Rebellion was bubbling in Upper Canada, this area of south Pickering Township was seen as a hotbed of reform. One of the most notorious participants in the rebellion came from Pickering. That was Peter Matthews, who along with Samuel Lount, was hanged at the Toronto jail in April 1838. In fact, William Dunbar and his two sons, Alexander and William, were apprehended by one of the parties sent from Toronto to track down traitors. The Dunbar men endured the humiliation of being marched down the Kingston Road to Toronto and spent several days in jail, but they were allowed to come home when no evidence of any treasonous activities came to light. It was not an unusual event during that troubled time.

Governor General Thomson may have pondered these events as the sleigh progressed eastward through Dunbarton, but it is more likely he was thinking ahead, worrying about the challenges he would face once they arrived in Montreal. Now that the passengers were in their second hour of the trip, the novelty had worn off, and they reclined in silence, deep in their own thoughts.

Governor General Charles Poulett Thomson[2] was a long way from his roots as he rode along the Kingston Road towards Duffins Creek. He had been born at Waverley Abbey, Wimbledon, Surrey, England on September 13, 1799, which made him forty years of age, the same as his driver, William Weller. His father was a partner in J. Thomson, T. Bonar and Company of London and St. Petersburg, one of the most successful merchant houses in England. For several generations, this enterprise had operated in the lumber trade as well as general merchandise, primarily in Russia and the Baltic.

Charles was the youngest of nine children and was known as "the youngest and prettiest of the family…the spoilt pet of all."[3] Very early in his life he projected an air of self-confidence and arrogance that could make him appear vain and self-centred. As a young man, he developed a reputation as a lady's man and would often ape the manners of the aristocracy. It seemed he appreciated the trappings of nobility more than his own family's practical business lifestyle. In this regard, Charles Thomson could be tiresome, even to his own family.

At age sixteen, Charles was sent to Russia to learn the family business, but after two years, ill health forced him back home, prompting the young man to embark on a prolonged tour of southern Europe. Then, in 1821, he travelled extensively in Eastern Europe, returning to London in 1824. He loved to travel and continued to visit the continent routinely. In fact, Charles Thomson was not a very good businessman and in 1825 avoided financial disaster only after the intervention of an older brother. The young man had difficulty finding his true calling.

In the same year, he entered the political world, when Joseph Hume secured the liberal nomination for him in Dover. Young Charles did not have the advantage of noble parentage, so he could not automatically slide into the civil service. Besides that, his family had made it clear that they would not foot the bill to buy him a seat in Parliament. However, it was seen that he had potential.

In the end, he won a slim victory at an outrageous cost. On top of that, he would generate a good deal of distress among family members with his decidedly liberal views. In fact, he was not a good politician. His voice was weak and halting when he did occasionally speak in Parliament. It was said he presented the appearance of a barber's apprentice.[3] He did not excel in this world either.

The skill that young Charles Thomson did develop was the ability to find mentors and work his way up the ladder. He was a very confident young man, but also very cautious, always conscious of the behaviour that would most impress his associates and put his career on a positive trajectory. His family did not support his choice of public service, but he persisted, clear in his own heart that he would not make a very good merchant.[5]

As time went by, he was able to demonstrate a natural ability in finance and administration. Soon he had become one of those smart young men on the way up. His very liberal views found powerful supporters in this period of reform, and eventually he became vice-president and then president of the Board of Trade. In this capacity, Charles Poulett Thomson became the nuts-and-bolts financial expert in the areas of taxation, trade, and regulation. He developed a reputation for garnering massive amounts of details, using charts and lists to argue his case. In this way, he distinguished himself from most of his peers and competitors. He was the fellow who would do the grunt work in support of an issue. Gentlemen of noble birth might look on him with disdain in terms of his lineage, but they respected his effectiveness as an administrator. He had found his place.

After ten years in the Board of Trade, Charles Thomson was looking to step up to the Chancellorship of the Exchequer. However, he was bypassed for this position and decided to quit the Board of Trade, in a bit of a snit. Then, to the surprise of most of his colleagues, he accepted the offer to be governor general of the British North American colonies in Canada. Thomson had served briefly on a committee that had looked at the possibility of a union of the two larger Canadian colonies, so he was familiar with the problems.[6] However, in the eyes of many, it seemed like a sideways move or even a demotion.

His primary supporter in this position was Lord Durham, who had produced the Durham Report, which analyzed the situation in the Canadian colonies in view of the Mackenzie Rebellion of 1837 and 1838. The two men agreed on many points regarding the reforms that were critical in the Canadian colonies. They felt it was critical to make changes that would allow progress to occur, and that this would reduce the likelihood of another rebellion. They might differ on methods, but they were both solidly on the liberal side of the scale. Even then, they both drew the line at the idea of responsible government. That would give away too much. When he went to Canada, Charles Poulett Thomson knew he was going to initiate many reforms, but he was not going to go any further than his bosses in London would allow.

And now, here he was, jostling along in one of those old familiar sleighs from his Russia days, happy with his success in passing important legislation in Toronto and anticipating with some trepidation the struggles he would have in Lower Canada in accomplishing the same job. It was good to have a day or so to sit and think without all the hassles and interruptions of official government work. He watched out the window as the trees and farms passed by. It was almost like a holiday for the governor general.

Only a few miles east of Dunbarton, the Kingston Road swung northward a little and brought the travellers to the Duffins Creek Valley and a bridge over the creek. The road here was not as smooth as the planking west of the Rouge, but the time of year meant the ground was still frozen, even though most of the snow had melted in the previous few days. The valley was not very steep, and the bridge proved to be discouraging in appearance but solid in function, as it supported the sleigh across to the other side.

Less than a mile east of the creek was the small village of Duffins Creek. The name was derived from an Irishman named Duffin,[7] who had built a cabin on the north side of the Kingston Road, just east of today's Church Street, way back in the 1780s. He was self-sufficient in his lonely home, trading with the natives and pulling many salmon from the waterway, which was then known as the Salmon River.

One day, Mr. Duffin was not to be found, except for a lot of blood in his cabin. He was never seen in the area again. Nobody really knows what happened to Mr. Duffin, but the creek took on his name, and the small community that grew up just east of the creek was also known as Duffins Creek, well into the later 1800s. The village had gained a post office in 1829, which was given the name Pickering in deference to the township, and eventually the official name of the community would become Pickering Village.

The modern Kingston Road through Pickering has been straightened and a section of the Old Kingston Road can be seen on maps to the north of the current road. Turn right off Elizabeth Street, and it is like stepping back in time with numerous heritage buildings and a traditional, small-town atmosphere.

William Weller encouraged his team straight east down the Kingston Road, out of Duffins Creek. Not far along the road, they came to the well-known Old Post Inn. If he had been closer to the end of the second stage of his trip, he would have gladly stopped here, as he knew this traditional stage stop would provide excellent service.

The Old Post Inn was a substantial brick building, built in 1815 by George Washington Post to serve the local community, as well as the east-west traffic along the Kingston Road. Inns would become the family business for the Posts.[8] One of

George Washington Post's sons, Hiram, would later operate another Post Inn not far east down the Kingston Road. His father, Jordan Post, had developed a successful watch-making business at King and Bay in Toronto in the early 1830s and then, late in life, had moved to Highland Creek to operate a successful inn on the Kingston Road, which William Weller had selected as the first stage stop of this trip.

Today, the modern appearance of the Old Post Inn[9] can be seen at 365 Kingston Road East in Ajax, near the northeast corner of the town, on the south side of the road. The building was designated under the Ontario Heritage Act in 1992, and in 2012, underwent a careful and extensive renovation, which was able to preserve most of the interior and a good portion of the exterior of the building. Today it serves as a daycare centre.

10.1 The Old Post Inn was built in 1815 and became a very popular inn on the Kingston Road east of Ajax. In 2012, the building underwent careful and extensive renovation, which preserved the character of the structure. It now houses a daycare centre.

11

Perry's Corners

THE KINGSTON ROAD RAN ALONG A CONCESSION LINE FROM JUST WEST OF DUFFINS Creek, and the sleigh followed it straight across the Pickering Township line into Whitby Township. By this time, William Weller was anticipating the end of stage two of the trip and was targeting a well-known stage stop in the relatively new village of Perry's Corners. This small gathering of stores and blacksmith shops had once been called Windsor, after the substantial Windsor Harbour, just a little way south on the lakeshore. Many settlers had created homesteads in the concessions north of here, but it was only in 1833 that the first shipment of grain went out through the harbour.

In 1836, Peter Perry had come to Whitby Township and decided to begin a general merchandising business. He picked a location at the intersection of the Kingston Road and the main road from the north down to the harbour, called Brock Road. This small village would take on his name for a time and would be the nucleus of the town of Whitby, which like many towns along the Kingston Road, would later take on the name of the township.

The 1840s would see some major improvements in this area, mostly due to Perry's work and influence. The road to the north was built soon after Mr. Weller came by, and Peter Perry would soon begin another settlement on the south shore of Lake Scugog, which would take the name Port Perry.

Peter Perry[1] was an exceptional man for his times. He was part of a very large United Empire Loyalist family that had settled in Lennox and Addington County and then expanded out from there. His uncle, Ebenezer Washburn, had been a member of the Assembly and held several public posts, providing his young nephew with a solid example of public service. Peter Perry would take his uncle's moderate position to the left of the political spectrum and become a very strong advocate of democracy and egalitarianism. He believed that the rural farmers and small tradesmen were the source of all sovereignty in Upper Canada, and he would deny the right of the elites to rule, whether they came from England or were members of wealthy local families.

The decade leading up to the Mackenzie Rebellion was a turbulent time, and Peter Perry was in the middle of the political fights, being a member of the Assembly for twelve years until he was defeated in 1836 and decided to get out of politics. We don't often hear his name in the history books, but he was very active, along with the major figures, Robert Baldwin and Marshall Spring Bidwell and, of course, William Lyon Mackenzie. Unlike all of these men, Perry was uneducated, could not read or write, and was a poor public speaker. However, he was a passionate advocate for the regular folks in the countryside, which were the majority in numbers. When he did get up to speak, they knew what he meant, even if the language was halting and often profane. The effect was that people kept voting for him, and he was able to assist his more academic compatriots in moving forward on some issues, even though they were most often stifled by the strongly conservative elites. Peter Perry was an important part of the movement that would achieve responsible government long after his political career was over.

After his defeat in 1836, Peter Perry saw the writing on the wall. This last election had been brutal and unfair. The result was that the extremists in his party gained prominence. He distanced himself from Mackenzie and was a law-abiding businessman in Perry's Corners as the rebellion swirled around him. While it is probable that he acted as an advisor at a political level, he avoided taking any direct part in the tumult.

Perry's attention had been drawn to the potential of Windsor Harbour as a trading hub on Lake Ontario, which could be used to funnel the massive amount of lumber and wheat produced in the northern concessions down to the lake for shipment. Other movers and shakers all along the north shore of Lake Ontario were thinking the same way, and they would, over the next couple of decades, compete with each other to build roads into the north and to improve their harbours in order to lure all that lucrative trade through their own four corners. At every point, stores and shops were developing in support of the increased traffic and trade. It was a heady time, with nothing but more development, more trade, and more money to be made, mostly at some point in the future.[3]

William Weller knew Peter Perry and was well aware of his store and stables there at the corner of Brock Road. It seemed like the ideal place to make his second stage stop. His Royal Mail coaches were always accommodated well at this establishment, and Perry was known as a good proprietor, who treated everyone fairly.

As he approached the four corners, William Weller pulled out his horn and gave several blasts, so the people at Perry's Corners knew he would be there shortly. The two passengers stirred themselves to witness the second change of horses. They were learning that their own curiosity regarding the folks on the street was more than matched by the fascination those folks felt about the gentlemen driving through their town. The sleigh came to a halt in front of Perry's store, and the fresh team was fastened to the sleigh in short order. A cold drink was passed around, and the sleigh lurched forward with much waving and clapping from the spectators. For the three men on the sleigh, it was on to stage three.

The fresh team took to their task enthusiastically, and the driver gave them their heads. The road to the east of Perry's Corners was often some of the worst on the Kingston Road in the spring and fall, but the mild weather had not yet pulled the frost from the ground and some snow remained. The horses splashed through puddles and ruts in some places, but for the most part, it was easy going. They needed to persistently push ahead to make good time regardless of conditions, and the straight stretches in this part of the country provided some opportunity for moving quickly.

The next village on the Kingston Road was called Skaes Corners at this time, but would later be named Oshawa. Unlike many of the towns that would develop along the Kingston Road, this small collection of stores and shops had a long history. Well before settlers began to clear the land for farms in this area, the coureurs de bois transported furs down the substantial creek to the natural harbour on the lake at this location.

In 1760, a trading post was built near the harbour, and later, that abandoned building would be used as the home of Benjamin Wilson, the first settler in the area.[4] Many more United Empire Loyalists would come to the area, and the harbour came to be called Windsor. When the Danforth Road was built and later upgraded to the Kingston Road, the settlement at the four corners, on the road north of Windsor Harbour, took on the same name.

An important development was the building of a colonization road north from Windsor Harbour in 1822, following more or less the ancient Nonquon Road to Lake Scugog. The new road was named Simcoe Street, after the first lieutenant governor of Upper Canada, John Graves Simcoe, and it was at this corner that the small settlement of Windsor appeared.

Then, in 1836, Edward Skae moved his store to the four corners of Windsor, and it became a popular meeting place, acting as post office and stage stop. It was so well known that popular opinion turned the name of the place into Skaes Corners. However, the village would have another change of name soon after Mr. Weller drove the governor general through. In 1842, a post office was established here, and the people were asked what official name they wished to apply to the postal station.

A long-time resident, Moody Farewell, was asked to sound out his native friends on this topic, and the name Oshawa was suggested. There have been many discussions about the real meaning of this name, but generally speaking, it means portage or variations on "where you left your canoe." Considering how the harbour and lower Oshawa Creek had been used for so long, it made perfect sense. Of course, the modern reader might appreciate the irony that the name of a place that became a major producer of motor vehicles represents the idea of getting out of your vehicle and walking for a while. Seems somehow fitting.

William Weller hardly slowed down as he left Skaes Corners and approached the next village of Harmony. There was a well-known tavern at the corner of Harmony Road, which had been run by Acheus Moody Farewell until just a few years before the governor general passed through. He had acquired the land in this area in 1804, and the Farewell name became synonymous with Harmony.

There is a fascinating note of historical trivia here. A.M. Farewell and his brother William had been involved in fur trading at the south end of Lake Scugog for a few years before 1804. They had established a fur-trading house where the natives brought furs and traded them for guns, clothing, food, and many other items.[5] In the spring of 1804, a man they hired to tend to the trading house, John Sharp, was murdered by Ogetonicut, an Ojibwa man of the area. A.M. Farewell was considered a witness and was expected to accompany the lawyers and the prisoner to Newcastle, the new village on Presqu'ile Point, which was the county town of Newcastle District. Apparently, the murder took place just inside the border of Newcastle District, and the trial had to be held in the courthouse for that district.

Mr. Farewell was unable to catch the ship at York or at Annis Creek, now called Port Oshawa, and had to make his way to Newcastle in a canoe. As it turned out, a terrible storm came up, and the government schooner H.M.S. *Speedy* was lost with all hands and passengers the next night.[6] Nothing was found after the storm subsided and nobody knew what had happened, except the obvious story of the ship sinking in the storm. After waiting at Newcastle for a few days, A.M. Farewell paddled back to Annis' Creek and began his new life, including his tavern at Harmony.

Just east of Harmony, the Kingston Road left the concession line and veered southeast to follow more closely the contour of Lake Ontario. This change in the road happened at the farm of Acheus Hudson, whose parents were Reuben Hudson and Sarah Farewell. In those days of limited travel, neighbours were often connected by marriage.

12

Darlington Township

VERY SOON THE TRAVELLERS CROSSED THE BORDER FROM YORK INTO DURHAM County and entered the township of Darlington. Durham County was among the original counties along the north shore of Lake Ontario, and while the extent of it would change over time, the three shoreline townships would remain as Darlington, Clarke, and Hope, until various realignments in more recent times.

Just inside Darlington Township, William Weller came to the small hamlet of Prestonvale, which in earlier times was also known as Black's Hill. This was the first post office in Darlington Township, named for the first postmaster, Colonel James Black. Another small village just a short distance east, at the corner of Courtice Road, was called Short's Corners. These villages are now included in the village of Courtice.

Christopher Courtice, Sr.[1] had brought his family to Canada from Putford Bridge, Devonshire, England in 1833 and settled on land south of the Kingston Road. The family included sons Thomas Courtice and his brother Christopher. They acquired a good deal of land centred around the corner of Courtice Road and Bloor Street, also near the Ebenezer Church. In fact, Courtice was called Ebenezer for a time until the official post office name was applied in the 1880s.

The Kingston Road ambled slightly southeast across Darlington Township, toward the town of Bowmanville. In 1840, the town of Bowmanville was centred on the area around the Kingston Road, from Scugog to Temperance Streets. It was a growing and dynamic place with several stores, hotels, and shops. Mr. Weller knew

Bowmanville very well because there were several very good taverns and hotels that acted as stage stops for his Royal Mail Line. On this day, he would not be making use of them, but would tip his hat as he went by.

The town owed its existence and prosperity to Mr. Charles Bowman,[2] who had come to this location in 1824 and recognized the potential for a major business, commercial, and transportation centre. Initially, Bowman purchased a store that had operated sporadically for several years at the northwest corner of Kingston Road and Scugog Street, where Tim's Rent-All is located today. He revitalized the building and the business and added others along the street. By early in the 1830s, people were calling the place Bowmanville, after the primary benefactor, although the name would not be official until 1853.

Down at the lakeshore, there was a small but thriving village called Darlington Mills, right beside Port Darlington, which had been the home of the first settlers to the area in the 1780s and 1790s. The port was critical to Mr. Bowman's plans. If you could move all that lumber and wheat down from the back concessions into the port, then a lot of people at each end, and all the way along the line, would make money. It was the most common recipe for prosperity along the north shore of Lake Ontario at this time.

In addition, Mr. Bowman purchased three hundred acres of land to the west of the store and began to lay out the street plan for a much larger and ambitious town. During the 1830s, he donated land and money for a meeting hall and several of the major churches of the town. There is a local legend that he gave a plot of land to the eldest daughter of each family, under the premise that when she got married, a house would be built there, and the town would naturally expand. Whether that story is true or not, it is repeated because it fits the man and his habits. He treated people fairly and was much appreciated by the town folk. His business always extended credit, which was vital to new settlers. An example of his approach is that during the financial crisis of 1839, Bowman gave out his own script in order to keep commerce flowing. Today those bills are rare and valuable.

Charles Bowman owned a company in Montreal called Bowman and Company, which had interests in many different places in Upper Canada, including Colborne, Port Hope, Goderich, and Trois-Rivière in Lower Canada. He was obviously very astute and had a good sense for the potential of a situation. While he never lived in Bowmanville, his name was certainly on the minds of many people who lived there for many years.

As William Weller guided the sleigh through the busy main street of Bowmanville, he kept an eye out for Mr. Alphonzo Hinds and his Waverly Hotel, which was well known as one of the best hotels on the Kingston Road between Toronto and Kingston. Two of the features that made the Waverly Hotel so favoured by the public were clean linen on the beds and real soap! Imagine that! Historians suggest that these were the reasons why the Waverly Hotel survived the terrible cholera epidemic of 1832, unlike most public establishments. Mr. Hinds was certainly ahead of his time.

William Weller tipped his hat graciously towards the Waverly Hotel as he spurred the horses on down the Kingston Road. They had made good time so far, although it was still very early. The roads had been relatively good, and even though they had encountered some muddy and wet spots, their progress had not been impeded very much. He was satisfied with the trip to this point.

However, he knew that they were approaching rougher country, where stretches of the Kingston Road were badly maintained. In a few weeks, some places between Bowmanville and Belleville would be impassable, even for travellers on horseback. Creeks would wash out in the spring freshet, and boggy areas would leave the road under water for long stretches. In the back of his mind, William Weller was racing down the Kingston Road, praying that those terrible spring conditions did not appear early this year. If they did, he would be very hard pressed to meet his contract with the governor general. It had been a risk worth taking, but here, in the midst of the process, the stark reality of bad roads ahead was hard to ignore.

13

Clarke Township

THE SLEIGH WAS APPROACHING THE BORDER BETWEEN DARLINGTON TOWNSHIP and Clarke Township, and the driver was preparing himself for his third stage stop. He was happy to avoid traffic and delays at the popular hotels and taverns in the major towns, which is why he had tipped his hat to Mr. Hinds in Bowmanville. On the other hand, he was eager to patronize the small taverns out in the country, which he knew had good horses and could provide the quick service he needed.

One of the instructions he had sent down the Kingston Road in the preceding week was for the stable near the border between Clarke and Darlington to be ready to assist him. This was a small, rural crossroads in the area of the extensive properties of Samuel Street Wilmot. He had purchased land in the west side of Clarke Township, near the lakeshore, where a considerable creek emptied into the lake. This waterway would take on the name Wilmot Creek and Samuel Wilmot would go on to gain a solid reputation as an effective farmer and good neighbour.

In 1840, the Wilmots had a good tavern on the Kingston Road, but later, during the 1860s, Samuel Wilmot, Jr.[1] would work hard to create the first fish hatchery in Canada West, with the purpose of recovering the salmon population, which had declined dramatically with increased farming and drainage of marsh lands at the mouth of the creek. His efforts in creating techniques and equipment to manage a fish hatchery would be used as the foundation for this industry in the future.

Mr. Weller sounded his horn, and the fellows at the tavern changed the teams quickly, sending the travellers on their way with another drink of water. The road was straight ahead, pointing in a southeasterly direction. Farms were evident on both sides of the road, and the potential of the countryside was evident. Soon, however, the sleigh came to an intersection where the Kingston Road met the second concession line. Mr. Weller turned left and followed the concession line straight east into the town of Newcastle.

Modern maps show that Number 2 Highway west of Newcastle dips a bit south to come across Highway 115, and then goes straight into Newcastle. It is evident that today's Number 2 Highway does not follow the path of the old Kingston Road. Looking more closely, we can see segments of small roads that run north of the current Number 2 in this area. On the west side is Browview Road, and on the east is Given Road. It is clear that the most easterly section of Given Road swings down to meet Number 2 Highway, which demonstrates the route that William Weller would have followed in 1840. There is a clear representation of this in the *Beldon County Atlas Map* for Clarke Township, which is dated 1877.[2] Yes, the roads have changed over time.

The small cluster of stores and shops on the Kingston Road at Mill Street had just recently been named Newcastle when our travellers entered the town in February 1840. Since 1833, it had been called Crandell Corners after Stephen Crandell,[3] who had set up a store at this location in anticipation of business from the increased traffic in all directions. A small village called Bond Head had already formed at the lakeshore, near the southern end of Mill Street, and there were high expectations for development of the port to take produce from the north. As we can see, all the towns along the lake had a similar idea at this time.

As the sleigh crossed Mill Street and quickly headed back out into the countryside again, Mr. Weller's thoughts wandered to a location about five miles north of Newcastle, at the village of Orono. This is where his father, David Weller, lived with his second wife and several of William's younger siblings and several half-siblings. David Weller had been in this location since 1831, which was around the same time that his eldest son, William, was becoming deeply engaged in running stagecoach lines in Upper Canada.

David Weller purchased land south of Orono in 1837 and then, in 1838, he bought property at Concession 5, Lot 29,[4] which in plain terms could be described as the western half of Orono, north of the mill pond. His wife at this time was named Susan, and she was his second wife. In effect, David Weller had two families, an early family with his first wife, of which William was the first child, born in 1799, and a second family with his second wife, whom he married around 1815.

David Weller had been born in Fairfield County, Connecticut in 1772, but the family moved to Hinesburg, Vermont in 1787, where he would be married for the first time. It is also where William and three other children were born to his first wife. Sometime before 1815, David Weller's first wife died. He then married Susan and moved his family to Canton, New York, which is not far south of the Saint Lawrence River, near Prescott.

William Weller married Mercy Wilcox in Canton in 1820, and then he attended law school in New York City. Their first four children were born in Canton and then, around 1825, he moved to Prescott, Ontario. It appears as if his father did not accompany him to Prescott, since records show that David Weller's last three children were all born in Canton, New York. However, we can speculate that both father and son may have been travelling back and forth a good deal, since it was during these middle to late years of the 1820s that William Weller was able to build his resources and reputation enough to start engaging seriously in the stage-coach business.

In the Prescott area, one of the most active men in transportation and commerce was Hiram Norton. In those days, Prescott was positioned very well at the top of the rapids in the Saint Lawrence River. Tons of goods needed to be transferred from wagons and small boats into schooners for the trip to Kingston, Toronto, and points west. This was called the forwarding trade, and it created a lot of wealth in the Prescott area for many years, until the canals in the Saint Lawrence allowed ships to avoid the rapids.

Hiram Norton was involved in many enterprises, and by 1827 had become a partner in a stagecoach line with Jonathan Ogden. This line had begun as a summer service as early as 1825, running initially from Port Hope, where Ogden had a livery business, to Carrying Place, where the steamboat Charlotte landed routinely. In 1827, a new line was advertised by partners H. Norton of Kingston and J. Ogden of York. It said specifically that the stage books were kept in Howard's Hotel in York and the Mansion House Hotel in Kingston[5].

Then, in December 1829, an announcement[6] in the *Upper Canada Gazette* proclaimed a "New Arrangement of Stages," which would provide a twice-weekly service from York to Kingston, with the proprietors William Weller working out of the Steamboat Hotel (formerly Howard's) in York and H. Norton at the Kingston Hotel in Kingston. Norton and Weller had purchased the line from Jonathan Ogden, and William Weller set out to make this the best stage line in Upper Canada.

William Weller began to make his reputation as a stage line operator at this time. Everybody, including Weller, knew very well how difficult it was to run stages routinely, with the terrible roads and unpredictable weather. However, Weller learned how to select the best horses and drivers and to change the design of the coaches for greater reliability and comfort. He made arrangements all along the line so that performance at stage stops would be predictable and consistent.

He also pursued a marketing approach that was aggressive and practical. For example, in January of 1830, we see an announcement in the *Kingston Chronicle* that tells the proprietors of newspapers in York that their papers could be taken on the York–Kingston stage the next day after the governor general's speech in Parliament. In this way, this important and anxiously awaited speech could be in Montreal by the next Monday, rather than in the normal week or two. And this service would be free of charge![7]

By 1840, there had been a lot of water under the bridge regarding his stagecoach enterprises, but at this moment, William Weller was more interested in his family as he sped away from their home in Orono. He thought about how his younger brother, Chauncey, was twenty-four years of age now, and taking over much of the farm work from his father, who was close to seventy. Don't ever tell the old man he should slow down, unless you wanted a good cuff up-side the head. In reality, however, David Weller was slowing down, and the farm was growing.

William Weller considered this for a moment. His father and his step-mother would need a comfortable place to live once they retired from farming. He expected that Chauncey would carry on with the farm at Orono, and they could live there, of course, but William had different ideas. His financial situation was much improved in recent years, and he hoped that he might share some of his wealth with his father who had been such a staunch mentor and supporter. When the time came, he might be able to obtain some property near Cobourg so his father could live comfortably and be close to William Weller's home and all those grandchildren. Oh well, a topic for another day.

Right now, there was a significant piece of road to navigate. For some distance east of Newcastle, the Kingston Road kept to the concession line, and the land was relatively flat, so the going should be easy. But his experience in driving coaches along this road caused him to be sceptical about the road west of the small village of Clarke, which would later be named Newtonville. The road would swerve south and then north to the village, and then go north of the concession line, before coming back to the line just before the Hope Township border.

The concern in this location was the various marshy spots where the road might be very soft, and in the mild weather they were seeing today, very muddy. As he approached this area, William Weller noticed a few spots where his cohorts had been repairing sections of the road. In these low and wet sections it was common to build corduroy roads, which would keep horses and vehicles out of the water and mud.

Corduroy roads were being built in parts of Upper Canada as early as the time of the War of 1812, and more were built during the next two decades. Construction was rather simple because, most often, little care was taken to prepare a roadbed, other than to level it as much as possible. Logs would be laid down across the road, snugged up to each other and dirt placed on top to make a more or less flat surface.

However, it was usually a matter of days or weeks after being laid down that a washboard effect was evident to travellers. Horses' hooves and wagon wheels were met by the round edges of logs and some logs became misplaced resulting in gaping holes. This presented horses and vehicles with a considerable challenge. Sure, it was helpful to provide a solid base on which to run, especially in boggy places, but the surface, if not adequately filled in with dirt, or not maintained over time, made for a hellish ride and was dangerous for horses.

Some of the most extreme language we see in the history books about the roads in Upper Canada in the 1830s comes from travellers trying to describe their horrific experiences with corduroy roads. It could take many hours to travel a few miles as the driver had to go very slow, bumping over every log, and often having to manoeuvre around broken logs, which could easily break a horse's leg. Of course, winter travel with a good sleigh over corduroy roads could be much better, as long as there was some snow remaining and the frost had not yet come out of the ground. Luckily, the travellers were able to continue with no delays, at least for now.

14

Hope Township

SOON AFTER CROSSING THE BORDER BETWEEN CLARKE AND HOPE TOWNSHIPS, THE Kingston Road straightened to run along the concession road once more. There were numerous prosperous farms along the road here as occasional marshy spots became less frequent, and the long sloping hills inched higher every mile. The horses were strong and persistent in their efforts, but the long inclines, coupled with some rough sections of road, would take their toll.

As the sleigh moved easily over the straight road approaching Roseberry Hill, Mr. Weller's mind turned to an incident with one of his Royal Mail stages, which had happened here a couple of months earlier. Around ten o'clock on the evening of Wednesday, December 4th, 1839, the Toronto and Kingston Mail Stage stopped at the top of the very steep Roseberry Hill, about eight miles west of Port Hope, to let the passengers back on after they had walked up the incline.[1]

It was customary for passengers to get out and walk in places where the road was considered particularly dangerous. It was thought to be a means of protecting the passengers from accidents that were common on steep hills, but also a way to save the horses from expending a lot of effort pulling half a dozen passengers as well as the stage loaded with baggage up a steep hill.

The modern reader might find it difficult to visualize the roads of those early days before equipment and technology allowed for the cutting of hills and filling in of swamps. We are so accustomed to smooth, straight roads. However, in Mr.

Weller's day, the road followed the lay of the land, and stage drivers simply had to cope.

As was his habit, the driver of the stage checked the baggage that was strapped onto the rear of the vehicle. Surprisingly, he found the straps had been cut, and three pieces were missing. He had seen them safely stowed only a mile or so back so knew that someone had made off with them just recently and was probably still in the neighbourhood. A horse was removed from the team, along with one of the coach lamps, and the driver, accompanied by one of the passengers, headed back along the road to see if they could apprehend the culprits and recover the lost baggage. This activity alarmed the folks in the neighbourhood, and a patrol was kept up all night in the vicinity.

With daylight, the trunks were found near the road only a few hundred yards from the scene of the crime. One trunk had been forced open, and several items of clothing lay strewn on the ground. The thieves appeared to have sensed danger and fled before they could take advantage of the booty. A quick survey determined that nothing had been taken.

An article in the *Cobourg Star* newspaper described the details of this attempted robbery and made a point of praising Mr. Weller for his quick and aggressive action in offering a reward.[2] It also added some commentary by asserting that this kind of event was all too common, and every measure must be taken by the local constabulary and stage operators to prevent such despicable events. In those days, constables were few and far between, and the stages were easy game for bandits.

William Weller and his passengers experienced no such mishap on Roseberry Hill on this day. They were driving in daylight, and the passengers did not disembark to ascend the hill, relying on the skill of the driver and the smaller and lighter nature of the sleigh to minimize the problem. After they passed Roseberry Hill, the driver was looking forward to the next stop. It would be just three miles west of the small village of Guideboard (Welcome) and another couple of miles from the larger town of Port Hope.

Marsh's Tavern[3] had been a popular stage stop on the Kingston Road for decades, operated by the Marsh family, who owned the land south of the road. William Marsh held the property at this time. He was a grandson of Col. William Marsh, a well-known United Empire Loyalist who had followed a path similar to the Wellers, being born in Connecticut and then moving to Vermont. After the war, the Colonel had acquired significant land grants in Upper Canada, although he returned to Vermont after making sure his sons were established. His son, Mathias, settled in Sidney Township, and the others in Hope Township, including Samuel, who was the father of the current innkeeper.

Marsh's Tavern was renowned for good service and better-than-average facilities. William Weller knew he would be looked after well at this stage stop. He blew the horn on approaching the tavern, and the stable boys scrambled to make the fresh team ready. When the sleigh came to a halt, there were many folks standing outside of the tavern, hoping to catch a glimpse of the illustrious passenger. The governor general opened the curtain and waved to the crowd, glad of a break from the monotony of travel.

Mr. Marsh came out to shake the hand of his friend, Mr. Weller, as a water jug was passed around. The two men knew that they were related in some way, although they would be hard pressed to explain exactly how. Research has shown that Hannah Marsh, a sister of old Colonel Marsh, had married Asa Weller, the famous merchant and bateau railway operator at Carrying Place.[4] The father of Asa Weller, Eliakem, was a brother of David Weller, who was William Weller's grandfather. Not exactly kissing cousins but, for those who do genealogy, a connection to savour.

Very quickly, the travellers were on the Kingston Road again, heading straight east into the small village of Guideboard, where the Kingston Road turned south and headed for the thriving town of Port Hope. The village that is labelled in the *Beldon County Atlas* in 1878 as Welcome P.O.[5] was, even in the 1850s, still known as Guideboard. It straddled a major four corners that had gained hotels and taverns, as the traffic on the Kingston Road increased through the 1830s.

While the sleigh carrying the governor general would turn south at Guideboard, the passengers could see that there was a very good road continuing due east, passing on to the village of Dale. This had been the route of the original Danforth Road and represents one of the places where the priorities of the government in 1800 caused Asa Danforth to keep his road up on higher ground, away from the marshy land at the mouth of creeks near the lakeshore. Later, when settlement grew at Smith's Creek, the Kingston Road was extended into the village and would follow closer to the lakeshore to the east, serving the new population centres.

At Guideboard, William Weller turned the team south onto the Toronto Road. This would be a familiar name that they would encounter again and again in the towns and villages in this area of Upper Canada. Any road heading out of a town going west, toward Toronto, would often be named the Toronto Road. In most cases, the same road was called the York Road until 1834 when the newly incorporated city took the name Toronto.

The Toronto Road struck southeast in a straight line toward the town of Port Hope. William Weller may have considered taking the old Danforth route through Dale and avoiding the busy streets of Port Hope. However, on this day, he preferred to stick to the best road, which was the main street of the town. As the number of buildings along the road increased, the travellers came to Ridout Street and turned left, coming soon to Walton Street, where they began the descent into the river valley and Port Hope's main business district.

The town had grown slowly from the initial settlements in the 1790s. However, in the decades after the governor general's sleigh came through town, it would be known as "The City of Bricks" due to the extensive number of brick homes and buildings that were built in the era after the harbour was improved and the railways came to town. In modern times, much of that built heritage is still evident due to the considerable efforts of the Heritage Port Hope Advisory Committee, which recognized the Walton Street Heritage Conservation District in 1997.[6] Other districts have been added since then, ensuring the preservation and promotion of one of the best-preserved heritage streetscapes in Ontario.

But in 1840, the buildings were still rather scattered and made of wood. There were mills and tanneries as well as stores, shops, and hotels, on both the east and west side of the river. The harbour had been improved somewhat with the addition of wharves, but the true potential of the town as a trading centre, bringing goods from the north to be shipped across the lake, was in the future.

Human settlement at this location can be traced back to a substantial village of the Mississauga people, situated at a convenient spot beside the Ganaraska River, near the shore of Lake Ontario. A settlement had been there for many generations before 1778 when Peter Smith, a fur trader, built his cabin at the mouth of what came to be known as Smith's Creek, and began business in the area. Around 1790, Smith left the area, and Lawrence Herkimer took over the trading post. He also had a trading post on Rice Lake in partnership with his brother, Jacob Herkimer. By a quirk of fate, Jacob Herkimer was a passenger on H.M.S. *Speedy*, which was lost in a storm off Presqu'ile in 1804.

A group of four families came to Smith's Creek in 1793, along with some surveyors, and situated themselves at the mouth of the creek. In the next year, Elias Smith and Captain Jonathan Walton made arrangements with the government to obtain land in Hope Township, in exchange for bringing more settlers to the area and building a mill at the mouth of Smith's Creek.[7] The mill was built with the help of a mill-wright, Captain John Burns, as well as Joseph Keeler, who was building a settlement to the east at Lakeport. Captain Walton would return to his home in New York State, and Elias Smith would settle in Smith's Creek, becoming the patriarch of a large family and a respected founder of the community.

The settlement around Smith's Creek grew as good agricultural land to the north was settled and became productive. In 1819, efforts to improve postal service meant that duplicate names must be reduced. George S. Boulton, who lived in Smith's Creek at the time, suggested Port Hope[8] as the new name, and the community approved. G.S. Boulton was a son of D'Arcy Boulton and would carry on in his father's footsteps, becoming a barrister and then a member of the Executive Council of Upper Canada. He became one of the most prominent citizens of Cobourg. At the time of the trip, he was a neighbour of the Weller family in the east end of Cobourg and had recently sold property to Mr. Weller in downtown Cobourg for his stagecoach business.

During the 1830s, many important changes had occurred in Port Hope. In 1832 the town had been incorporated, and in 1834, a Board of Police had taken over governance of the town, with J.D. Smith as the first president.[10] There was talk of a canal from Lake Ontario to Lake Simcoe, and for a time, the Port Hope and Rice Lake route was under consideration, but nothing came of it. The Port Hope Harbour and Wharf Company had been incorporated in 1829, but serious disagreements would prevent any significant progress in developing the harbour in these early years.[11]

William Weller was very familiar with the hotels and taverns in Port Hope, but would not be patronizing any of them on this trip, since he had stopped at Marsh's Tavern not too long ago. However, as he crossed the bridge over the river and turned right onto Mill Street, he may have seen some familiar faces around the Hastings House, which was at the foot of Walton Street.

This very important location had been a popular stage stop for many years; a previous establishment being known as the Old Inn. Now it was a routine stop for the Royal Mail Line run by Mr. Weller. The Hastings House was located in a building that had been built in 1823 by John Brown and was the first brick building in the town. In 1840, the Hastings House was run by Thomas Warren Hastings, and it was widely held that he ran a first-class operation.[12]

The sleigh turned left at Peter Street, and the team churned up the soft ground, as they pulled up the hill, out of the river valley. Peter Street ran along the concession line and was the path for the Kingston Road from Port Hope to the east. Soon the travellers were out of town and into the countryside again. In a few minutes, they crossed the border between Hope and Hamilton Townships and entered Northumberland County. William Weller was now very close to home.

15
Cobourg

AS THE TEAM SURGED ON TOWARD THE TOWN OF COBOURG, WILLIAM WELLER'S thoughts turned to his family. His wife, Mercy, was at home with their six children, and he would dearly love to stop and see them, but not this time. He had spent a lot of time away from home in the last decade, struggling to build his stagecoach business. To his great joy and pride, his wife was very understanding and acted independently in running the house and taking care of affairs in Cobourg. It had been a long and difficult process, first making a home in Prescott, where he was in partnership with Hiram Norton, and then living by himself in Toronto as he developed toward his own full ownership of the line.

In 1834, they had finally been able to move to Cobourg, where his stage business was set up and the family made a permanent home.[1] At first they had rented a home in the middle of town, but soon he had arranged with George S. Boulton for the lease of a house on the north side of King Street, east of the town. William Weller would apply the name Cottesmore to the house, which was spacious and comfortable, with extensive grounds that gave the children space to run and play in gardens and orchards. They were happy in Cobourg.

But it had not always been happy, by any means. The six children that William and Mercy cared for at this time had four other siblings who did not survive. There were the twin girls who died at birth in Canton, New York in 1823, and then the two-year-old boy, Albert Freeman Weller, who had died in Prescott in 1827. More recently, in the midst of the joy at the birth of the latest addition, George James Weller, in May of 1838, four-year-old darling Helen Marie Weller had passed away.

Of course, William Weller could not think of his children without worrying about his sons and how they would make their way in an increasingly complex world. He would try to provide them with opportunities, but they would have to grab the opportunity and run with it. While he tried not to spoil them, it was hard for him to discipline the boys, and impossible for the girls, so he left that kind of thing to Mother.

Lorenzo was the oldest and had turned eighteen recently. He was a hard worker and loved the outdoors like his father. More importantly, he had developed into a reliable hand, riding with him or running errands in support of the business. Right now, he was preparing to depart from the General Stage Office in Toronto to follow his father down the Kingston Road and all the way to Montreal. Was this too much for an eighteen-year-old? Maybe, but then the father recalled how he had felt at eighteen when nobody would give him meaningful work to do. The boy would be fine.

The second son, William Henry, was fifteen and much more bookish than his older brother. While quiet, he could hold his own on a horse and treated all his friends fairly, often acting as arbiter between bickering chums. He would go on to be a barrister and assist his father a great deal with legal matters. Charles Alexander was only ten and the most ambitious of the bunch. He would make the second barrister in the family and go on to a distinguished career as a judge in Peterborough.

After family, William Weller constantly ruminated over the complex operations of his stagecoach lines. Today he was engaged in a very unusual, one-off project, but at his stage manufacturing and repair facility on Swayne Street in Cobourg, the spring work was in full swing. They were preparing the coaches that would hit the road once the snow cleared up. He had a contract for carrying the Royal Mail from Toronto to Kingston and, while he had benefitted from the instalments from this contract to cover expenses, bonus payments for performance were hovering over his head like ripe fruit to be picked. All he had to do was make sure everything worked perfectly, and the post office people were happy at the end of the season. He needed that cash flow to keep the business going.

A smile came over his lips as he recalled a recent event in Cobourg that had given him great joy. In December 1839, he had driven a shiny new coach out of the carriage works, into the yard behind the Albion Hotel.[2] A crowd of several dozen people were there for the occasion. He had been so proud of this new model of coach, which contained some of the latest technology, all focussed on providing his customers with a safer and smoother ride.

Of course, the people in the yard were most fascinated by the very unique paint job on the coach, which featured a light-yellow body and black trim. In the years to come, people would learn to recognize a Weller stage long before it rolled up to the tavern, due to the bright and unusual colours. It was all part of Weller's persistent marketing campaign, which was intent on making the stage a familiar and common part of everyday life.

This new and specially designed coach was not for the normal Toronto-to-Kingston line, but was created specifically for the Telegraph Line, which ran from Toronto to Hamilton. He had recently purchased this stage line and had worked hard to make agreements with hotels, taverns, and stables along the way to support the running of the stages. These new coaches were larger than previous models, designed to provide comfortable seating for six adults and their baggage. New attachments on the boot made it easier to store baggage of all types, and additional leather straps would decrease the jolting of the terrible summer roads.

Several other features pointed to the type of clientele William Weller expected to entice into his stages. There was a collapsible writing desk, which could be folded out in front of a passenger or folded back into the side door. His best clients were among the merchant class or government officials who were happy to pay a good fare for a better experience. Everybody knew how dangerous and uncomfortable it could be to ride a stagecoach, and William Weller had set out to change the public's attitude and hopefully make some money in the bargain.

For basic safety, there were strong leather loops hanging from the inside of the coach for passengers to grab during a rough ride, something like subway riders might use today. On the ceiling of the coach, several pieces of thick padding were installed, designed to prevent injury should a passenger be tossed in that direction by a particularly big bump in the road. A common joke of the day was that you should always keep your hat on when riding in a stagecoach, so as to keep your blood off the ceiling. All of these features would not be installed immediately in all of the smaller and less elaborate coaches, but many of them would come into common usage as a matter of competition. This stagecoach proprietor was responding to the public need and, in the process, became known as The Stagecoach King!

But his recollection of that day went quickly to the horses. He had decided that the Telegraph Stage Line would run six-horse teams. On that morning of the turn-out, he was piloting an impressive team of six spirited bay horses, and he revelled in the sight, the feel, and the emotion of such a spectacle. The crowd clapped and cheered as he turned the stage around the yard. In those days, people appreciated a good horse put to work in an effective way, and Mr. Weller was known as one of the best at this part of the business.

The Cobourg that William Weller approached that Monday morning was one of the most prosperous and dynamic towns on the north shore of Lake Ontario. In some ways Cobourg resembled its close neighbour, Port Hope. For one thing, the history of the main road was similar in the two towns. The town of Cobourg grew at the lakeshore, but the original Danforth Road passed well north of the town, the same as it had done at Smith's Creek. Later, the Kingston Road would approach Cobourg from Port Hope, then, at its northwest corner, dip southeast to the middle of town, and continue east out of town along the lakeshore to Grafton. All these years later, it is interesting to see how similar the route of Number 2 Highway looks on a map for these two towns.[3]

As with two brothers near the same age, competition sometimes taints the relationship. Basic geography determined that Port Hope and Cobourg would compete with each other through the middle of the 1800s, as each town struggled to gain dominance in the region as a trading and transportation centre. The vast resources of the northern lands must come down to the lake to be loaded onto schooners. Whichever town could provide the best road to the lake and the best harbour to handle the ships, might gain more business and grow prosperous.

The settling of two thousand Irish Catholics by Peter Robinson in 1825, in the area north of Rice Lake, would stimulate this competition, although Cobourg seemed to have a leg-up on the early benefits. For one thing, Peter Robinson was a brother of John Beverly Robinson, Solicitor General of Upper Canada. It did not hurt at all to have direct support from wealthy and powerful people in the government of the time. One of those who helped was George Strange Boulton,[4] who happened to be Peter Robinson's brother-in-law. G.S. Boulton was an extremely active businessman, speculator, and promoter of new enterprises. As a member of the government, he had direct impact on decisions and could move projects forward without worrying about that modern pest we call conflict of interest.

As the sleigh moved quickly over the straight road approaching Cobourg, the first cluster of buildings that came into view was the village of Amherst. This small village had developed along Burnham Street, which linked the old Danforth Road, located just south of the current 401 interchange, to the newer Kingston Road. Land in this area had belonged to early settlers Asa and Zacheus Burnham. In 1807, Asa Burnham had donated two acres on the east side of Burnham Street, north of Elgin Street, for a new courthouse.

The District of Newcastle had built a courthouse and jail in 1802 on Presqu'ile Point at what Lieutenant Governor John Grave Simcoe had designated as the "county town" of Newcastle District. However, when H.M.S. *Speedy* was lost in a storm on October 8, 1804, the tragic loss of the attorney general of Upper Canada and several members of the Legislature caused the government to label that location as "inconvenient."[5] They took the drastic step of revoking the status of county town from Newcastle. A search was then conducted to find a new location for the county town, in a better location.

The Burnhams were influential in York, and Asa Burnham took advantage of the situation to offer his land for the courthouse, therefore bringing the benefits of a county town to Amherst. The courthouse and jail were opened in 1807, and over the years, the small village prospered due to its location on the Kingston Road and its status as county town for the district.

By the late 1820s, the building needed repairs and was considered inadequate, so plans were made to build a new courthouse and jail. Officials at Cobourg went ahead and built a much more substantial building on the west side of Burnham Street in the vicinity of today's Golden Plough Seniors Residence. They were later accused of using public funds without the proper approvals from York, but the building was there and the dispute, while loud and long, eventually faded away.

15.1 The Cobourg courthouse and jail stood on the west side of Burnham Street, just north of Elgin, in the area of the current Golden Plough Lodge. The imposing structure had been built in 1831 with a view to predicting growth and prosperity for the community, and it served until being replaced by Victoria Hall in 1861.

This large, two-storey building, with majestic pillars on the front, would later be famous as the location of the only hanging ever to take place in Northumberland County. Dr. William Henry King had poisoned his wife in Brighton and was incarcerated here, with the sensational trial held in April of 1859. Ten thousand people were said to have attended the hanging, which took place on the east side of the courthouse, near Burnham Street.[6]

All of that was of no concern to William Weller as he turned right in Amherst to follow the Kingston Road into Cobourg. He did recall that in 1837, Amherst had officially become part of the town of Cobourg, so over the next few years, the name Amherst would fall away and become a footnote in history.

William Street was the route that the Kingston Road took into downtown Cobourg, angling southeast and eventually meeting King Street West. William Weller knew that the road was fairly good through the town, and that he was not going to stop, so he urged the horses to a rhythmic gallop and watched for traffic that might impede his progress.

The most important building along William Street in 1840 was the Old Stone Kirk.[7] William Weller was very familiar with this church since it was the Weller family place of worship. This church opened in 1834, the same year that the Wellers permanently located in Cobourg, and they had been strong supporters, both financially and by their routine presence. There were also some very strong emotional ties to the church because the cemetery on the east side of the church already provided resting places for friends and family. William Weller did not like to be reminded of the loss of his precious little girl, Helen Marie, who took ill suddenly and died in July 1838, to be laid to rest in the Old Stone Kirk Cemetery.

Unfortunately, there would be more Wellers interred in this cemetery in the decades to come, including his first wife, Mercy, and William himself. However, today we can find no moss-covered memorials in a grassy vale. The Old Kirk was replaced by the magnificent St. Andrew's Presbyterian Church, which was opened at 200 King Street West in 1862. After that time, a tangled legal dispute made the Old Kirk property off-limits for many decades. The building eventually fell down, and the cemetery reverted to a wilderness of weeds and bushes. Some elderly Cobourg residents recall playing there as children.

In more recent times, an attempt was made to preserve what little was left of the cemetery, and as a result, several memorial stones from the Old Kirk Cemetery can be seen within a small fenced area behind St. Paul's Lutheran Church. While none of these memorials are for William Weller or his family members, research has uncovered a snapshot taken in the 1960s of Mercy Weller's memorial, standing amidst trees and bushes in the Old Kirk Cemetery.[8] The picture is blurry, but it is all we have to recall the Weller burials in their family cemetery.

The sleigh sped past the Old Kirk and its cemetery and soon turned left onto King Street West. The town of Cobourg that the travellers entered was a thriving, prosperous, and growing community. In the earliest days, settlers had avoided the low and marshy land near the lakeshore. Multiple creeks entered the lake, and none of them was large enough for navigation, so settlers went north to the higher ground to find workable farmland.

The first settler in the immediate downtown area of what became Cobourg was Eliud Nickerson, who had a log hut in the area of King and Division Street in 1798. His original grant included all the land between Division and College, and from Elgin Street to the lakeshore. Joseph Ash settled, at the same time, to the northeast of Nickerson. Elias Jones is said to have opened the first store in the village in 1802 and would be an important figure in the town until his death in 1836. In those early years, the settlement at the lakeshore was called Hamilton, in recognition of Hamilton Township.

To the north, however, progress was spurred by the presence of the Burnham family. The Burnhams had been directed to this area by a relative of theirs, Aaron Greely, who was an agent in a settlement scheme designed to bring more settlers to the Newcastle District. Zacheus Burnham first acquired land to the northwest of what would later become Cobourg, and along with his brothers, Asa, John, and Mark, would become the largest landowner in the area.

Zacheus built Amherst House near the Danforth Road, and a small settlement developed around this area, which would be called Amherst. The addition of the courthouse and gaol for Newcastle District in 1807 improved the status of this little settlement because it was now a county town. Zacheus Burnham[9] developed the art of land acquisition and by 1821 would own 1,780 acres in Hamilton Township. He would continue to speculate in land all around Newcastle District until his death in 1857.

Elijah Buck also settled in the immediate town site near the lakeshore in 1808 and operated one of the first taverns in the area, at the location of the Capital Theatre. He also engaged in manufacturing wagons and was so well respected that people started calling the settlement Buckville for a time in the 1820s. The first issue of the *Cobourg Star*, in 1831, has a notice from Elijah Buck, saying he was disposing of his tavern stand and other buildings and property, along with twenty village lots.[10]

During the years 1817 and 1818, a significant influx of settlers came to take up residence at, or near, the little village of Hamilton. In 1819, Rev. William Macaulay, a Church of England clergyman, applied the name Cobourg to the village, and it stuck. The name came from Prince Leopold of Saxe-Coburg in Germany, who had married Princess Caroline. The extra "o" was added over time.

Along with the new name, Cobourg was now on the main road between York and Kingston, as the new route of the York Road, also called the Kingston Road, came closer to the lakeshore and ran through the developing village. This change was critical as Cobourg now became a stopping point for travellers on the Kingston Road, and businesses would grow along King Street to service the traffic. Stores and hotels and blacksmith shops brought in customers as well as ambitious entrepreneurs, who were looking for opportunities.

One of the most active businessmen in Cobourg was James Gray Bethune,[11] who opened his first store in Cobourg in 1817. Soon after, he built a sawmill and distillery and became the first postmaster for Hamilton Township. He was aggressive and progressive, and soon became a champion for the economic development of Newcastle District, and in particular, the village of Cobourg. His objective in this pursuit was to ensure that the growing traffic in trade goods and people from the rich hinterland north of Rice Lake came through Cobourg, and not through chief rival Port Hope.

In 1826, Bethune opened a branch store in Peterborough and began wholesaling to the storekeepers in that region. He became an agent with the Canada Company and was very active in the real estate market in Newcastle District. Determined to provide better facilities to support his vision, Bethune was treasurer of the new Cobourg Harbour Company, which succeeded in building an excellent harbour in Cobourg. In 1830, he opened large warehouses at Cobourg and Peterborough, and the next year launched a steamboat on Chemung Lake.

The growing reputation of James Gray Bethune led to his appointment as an agent for the Bank of Upper Canada and cashier of the branch in Cobourg. Unfortunately, this led to his downfall. So anxious was he to encourage and facilitate growth and development that he chafed at the restrictions on credit that the bosses in York imposed on him. He arranged loans that were not approved by the bank's Board of Directors, and eventually, his books did not add up. There was an audit, and by 1834, James Gray Bethune was ruined, along with many small businessmen and merchants in the area.

Even with this failure, James Gray Bethune left a legacy of economic development that would be carried on by many others in the community. Cobourg would be known in the 1830s as one of the most progressive towns in Upper Canada, and the movers and shakers in town were not finished. The improvements to the harbour in 1831 were instrumental in bringing business into town, and the bustle along King Street increased apace.

William Weller became a major addition to this dynamic business activity in 1834, when he decided to establish the head office for his stagecoach line in Cobourg. It was a central location along the Kingston Road, half way between Toronto and Kingston, and the progressive business climate would have made Cobourg an obvious choice. We might also speculate that William Weller could imagine all of the wealthy and successful folks in Cobourg, paying full fare to ride in his coaches on their business trips to Toronto or Kingston. This was the clientele he would target as the years went by, and with some success. Give them a reliable service with more comfortable coaches, and the seats in those coaches would be filled.

16

Five Hours from Toronto

THE ARRIVAL OF WILLIAM WELLER AND THE GOVERNOR GENERAL DID NOT GO unnoticed in Cobourg. A small piece in the *Cobourg Star* on Wednesday the 19th would provide its readers with the basics: "His Excellency the Governor General passed through on Monday last, at full gallop, on his way to Lower Canada; having performed the distance between this place and Toronto – seventy five miles – in just *five hours*."[1]

The italics are from the original. Mr. R.D. Chatterton, editor of the *Cobourg Star*, was as impressed as everyone else at the enterprising spirit of Mr. Weller, and he tended to express his appreciation in subtle ways. In this case, he comments that Mr. Weller always achieves his objectives, and the road would have to be very bad, indeed, to keep him from accomplishing what he set out to do.

The trip was starting to drag for the passengers inside the coach, who could do little but chat and snooze. It was not a particularly rough ride, and the features of their customized conveyance minimized the effects of the road. They had been travelling for five hours when they galloped through Cobourg, which means that their overall speed was slightly under fifteen miles an hour. The trip was off to a very good start.

Up on the driver's bench, William Weller was thinking in similar terms. They had made very good time from Toronto, and he was pleased with their position at this time. He knew that the worst of the roads would be ahead of them, so fifteen miles an hour was not likely to continue. He felt that if he could maintain thirteen miles an hour over the trip, he could meet the conditions of his contract. With no major interruptions or obstacles, this could be achieved. A little luck was in order.

In 1840, the skyline of Cobourg was highlighted by two distinctive spires. William Weller could see both of these landmarks as the team galloped down King Street West, toward the middle of Cobourg. On the left, up the hill, was the spire of the Upper Canada Academy and straight ahead, on the north side of King Street East, was the steeple of St. Peter's Anglican Church.

The Upper Canada Academy was opened in 1836 by the Methodist Conference as a college for both boys and girls. In 1833, Egerton Ryerson had gone to England and managed to achieve his objective of a Royal Charter for the planned institution.[2] This was the first Royal Charter ever granted to a non-Anglican establishment and was an important step along the road to non-denominational education in Upper Canada. The Academy had struggled in its early years due to the economic and political turbulence, but soon, in 1841, it was to be granted a provincial charter as Victoria College, with full degree-granting powers and Egerton Ryerson as its first president. The building serves in a different capacity today, but the classical columns of the façade of the building still stand guard over the town and look calmly out over the harbour and Lake Ontario.

St. Peter's Anglican Church was founded in 1819, around the same time that its first rector, Rev. William Macauley, named the village. At that time, a large, wooden building was built on the north side of the new Kingston Road. As the town of Cobourg developed, this part of the Kingston Road would be called King Street, and St. Peter's Anglican Church would have a dominant position on the eastern edge of the busy downtown business area.

Many of the wealthy and powerful in Cobourg were members of St. Peter's and helped to grow the congregation and its ministry. In 1854, a much larger and more modern St. Peter's Anglican Church was built around the old wooden building, and when the new church was ready, the old one was removed.[3] The story goes that in the last few weeks of construction, use of the old church was deemed unsafe, so services were held in a local distillery, no doubt causing some snickers and raised eyebrows. Along with additional structures, St. Peter's is still a dominant presence in the downtown, just across King Street from Victoria Park.

Both of these early Cobourg landmarks can be seen clearly in a watercolour by Lieut. Philip Bainbrigge, painted in 1840, the same time as William Weller galloped through the town. Upper Canada Academy, with its tower and columned façade, is evident on the left, and St. Peter's Anglican Church is there to the right side, on the north side of King Street.

Lieut. Bainbrigge painted and sketched many scenes in Upper and Lower Canada in the years 1838 to 1840, and many are available as tangible records of the towns and byways of the time. In this case, Bainbrigge was on a schooner in the harbour, looking north into the main part of Cobourg. The substantial wharf can be seen with the schooner *Cobourg* tied up, its two tall smoke stacks spewing black smoke into the air.

The *Cobourg* had been launched in 1833 by a group of enterprising Cobourg businessmen and merchants, hoping to take advantage of the growing trade going through the Cobourg harbour, destined for other harbours all around Lake Ontario. This particular side-wheeler had an inauspicious launching and was out of service more than in during its life. It was soon replaced by newer and more powerful boats.

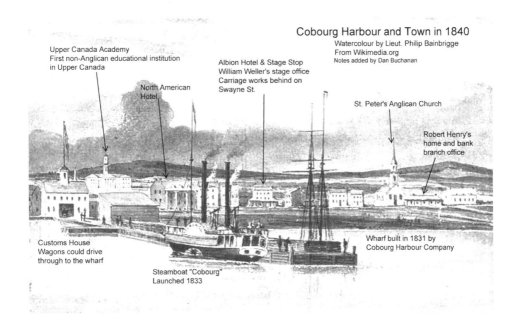

16.1 Cobourg Harbour, 1840

On the far left of the painting, we see the Customs House, which had an opening under the building through which wagons could be driven onto the wharf. This was an extremely busy place in these years of massive lumber shipments and hot demand across the lake for wheat and other products from the northern concessions. Cobourg harbour was meeting the expectations of the investors, and the businesses along King Street were buzzing with activity as a result.

To the left of the smokestacks of the *Cobourg* can be seen the North American Hotel. The Cobourg *Star* had gushed, "It gives us great pleasure to announce, that our deserving townsman, Mr. Strong, who has long had the reputation of keeping the first Tavern in this village, has shifted his quarters to a handsome new building, in the immediate vicinity of the Wharf…"[4]

Oren Strong had taken over this brand new and very handsome establishment in 1836, after more than a decade building a good reputation as a tavern and hotel keeper. However, in April 1840, he would sell the property to James Hagerman. The hotels were constantly changing hands, being renovated and improved to meet the growing public desire for travel accommodations and for entertainment. By the late 1830s, we see more mention of a fully stocked bar and supplies of wine and liquor, as the bar in a hotel became a major source of revenue.

As the sleigh approached Division Street, William Weller could see a gathering of people in front of the Albion Hotel, on the north side of the street, just past the intersection. Word of his unique sleigh ride had spread around town very quickly as the messengers had rushed around the stage office in the Albion, making sure everything was ready. They knew that Mr. Weller was not stopping in Cobourg, but they had to make sure they could offer any help that might be required. Several crews of men had gone up and down the road between Marsh's tavern and Grafton to make sure that this stage of the trip would be trouble-free.

The governor general pushed aside the window covering so that he could catch a quick glimpse of Mr. Weller's place of work. Captain Le Marchant commented to his travelling companion that he could see a sign along the street for the *Cobourg Star* newspaper, and this solicited a snort from the governor general. He offered the suggestion that Mr. Chatterton should be cautious with his language when commenting about issues he knew nothing about. Besides, said the queen's representative, with a smirk, "Changes are afoot that will deprive poor Mr. Chatterton of his coveted position as a magistrate in this fine town."

As predicted, word would come just a few days later that Mr. Chatterton would be compelled to step down from his position as magistrate, an event that generated a good deal of warm copy for several weeks.[5] The term "conflict of interest" would not be widely used for many decades, but that was one of the basic concepts that informed the changes Governor General Thomson was making in the Canadian provinces at this time. He believed that a man should not hold a position of governance in a community while gaining income from a powerful tool like a newspaper. It makes common sense to us today, but it was a developing idea in 1840. Mr. Chatterton was not amused.

At this time, the Albion Hotel contained a small rented office used by the Royal Mail Stage Line, and there was an arched driveway leading back to the stable area behind the main hotel. This was the public face of the Weller stage business, but much of the operations were behind the Albion, along Swayne, and over towards McGill Street. There was a large carriage and wagon works managed by Alfred

Munson, William Weller's nephew. In a couple of years, this establishment would grow and be taken over fully by Mr. Munson, whose father, Linus Munson, had married Weller's sister Laurene before they came to Upper Canada in 1834.[6]

16.2 Albion Hotel

The Albion Hotel is shown in Lieut. Bainbrigge's watercolour from the harbour, although the shape and form does not match well with the most elaborate image we have of the Albion from this time period. There is a sketch of the block of buildings at the corner of King and Division Streets that contains the Albion Hotel. The work is signed at lower left by "F.P. Rubidge, Surv." Frederick Preston Rubidge[7] was a well-known civil engineer who was involved in many developments in Upper Canada, from the proposals for locks and canals up the Trent River, to the expansion of Cobourg harbour. The image is more of a diagram than a work of art, but it shows the function and charm of this important establishment in Cobourg.

We can see, in the middle of the hotel section, the arched driveway into the stable area behind the hotel. To the right, the sign "W.S. Conger" demonstrates that Wilson Seymour Conger operated the store beside the stage office. There is a standard Royal Mail stage, with four-in-hand, standing in front of the hotel, waiting for the moment of departure. It could be that the gentleman in the long coat and floppy hat is Mr. Weller, so common a sight was he at the stage office.

There had been a popular hotel in this location since the 1820s, called first the Cobourg Hotel and then the Steamboat Hotel, operated by Oren Strong for many years. At this time, in 1840, this establishment was near the end of its life, as the much larger and more modern Globe Hotel would be built not far to the east in 1845. The old Albion would suffer the indignity of a public auction sale to dispose of its contents. A newer Albion would be built here a bit later, but the heyday of the Albion had passed.

As the sleigh raced by the Albion, Mr. Weller stood up and waved to the gathering of cheering faces and waving hats. He was delighted to greet his fellow townsmen and receive their support, but was happy he had decided not to stop in Cobourg. The critical thing right now was speed, and he was fairly sure that a stage stop in front of the Albion Hotel would have been delayed one way or the other due to the size of the crowd and the intensity of feeling of his friends. He sat down as the cheering crowd receded to the rear of the sleigh, and set his sights along the Kingston Road.

On the south side of King Street, soon after passing the Albion, the travellers would pass one of the first brick commercial blocks in Cobourg at 35 King Street East. This red brick structure was built by William Graveley around 1837, and initially hosted Graveley's drug store and F.G. Callender's dentist office. The habit of building a large building that contained several units designed to house storefronts below and offices above would become the norm in downtowns all across Upper Canada. This building represented a trend that would continue in Cobourg.

Very quickly, on the left, was College Street, which sloped gently up to Upper Canada Academy, and on the northeast corner of King and College Streets were the lovely grounds of St. Peter's Anglican Church. A little farther along, on the south side of King Street, at the corner of Henry Street, was the home of one of Cobourg's most revered citizens. Robert Henry[8] was a nephew of the famous fur trader and explorer, Alexander Henry. He had worked as a trader in the north with the upstart North West Company, during some of the most dangerous years of the conflict with the Hudson Bay Company. In 1816, he decided to leave the tensions of the fur trade and settle in Cobourg. Very quickly, he established a partnership with James Gray Bethune in a grist mill and several other commercial enterprises.

Robert Henry was hit hard by the financial disaster resulting from Bethune's banking irregularities but was able to survive and live an active life in Cobourg. He was a justice of the peace for many years, and in the 1830s, became an agent for the new Commercial Bank of the Midland District, an alternative to the Bank of Upper Canada, which was controlled so closely by The Family Compact. His home on King Street East in Cobourg would be known as a branch of the bank where local folks might find an opportunity to finance a business or commercial enterprise, outside of the pervasive force of the conservative elite of the province.

It was the perceived presence of a safe full of cash that made Robert Henry a target in July of 1839 when "The Cobourg Conspiracy"[9] was hatched. In the aftermath of the Mackenzie Rebellion, a group of dissidents operating from the United States cooked up a scheme to rob and murder several prominent Cobourg residents, including Robert Henry, D'Arcy Edward Boulton, and George Strange Boulton, who all resided on or near King Street East.

However, before an attack could be carried out, one of the conspirators alerted the authorities when it became clear that the objective was more than robbery. As a result, the perpetrators were caught, and no damage was done. During the trial, the prosecution was able to describe Robert Henry, one of the victims targeted by the plan, as one of Cobourg's "most respectable and inoffensive inhabitants".[10]

The Boultons, who were targeted along with Robert Henry, represented a concentration of wealth and power in this new suburb in east Cobourg. George Strange Boulton was a son of Judge D'Arcy Boulton of York. His brother, D'Arcy Edward Boulton, had built The Grange in York in 1817; that famous large residence is now part of the Art Gallery of Ontario. G.S. Boulton was called to the bar in 1818 and practiced as a lawyer in Port Hope for a time, before he was appointed Registrar of Northumberland County in 1824, which prompted him to move to Cobourg. He became very active in local politics and commerce, investing heavily with James Gray Bethune and suffering the consequences.

G.S. Boulton was also a member of the Legislative Assembly during the 1830s and represented his conservative family and friends very effectively. In Cobourg, he was a powerful advocate for development of resources such as the harbour and roads. He was one of the primary investors in the first Cobourg Railway Company, which suffered the same fate as many large enterprises when political upheaval caused financial recession at the end of the 1830s.

The G.S. Boulton home on James Street would become an important heritage site in Cobourg, along with the home of his nephew, D'Arcy Edward Boulton,[11] on the west side of D'Arcy Street, just north of King Street East. The younger Boulton was also a lawyer and would be very active in the next few decades, especially in the story of the Cobourg and Peterborough Railway Company. The street by his home would be named D'Arcy Street in his honour.

For the driver of the sleigh, there was only one attraction worthy of note on the Kingston Road east of Cobourg, and that was Cottesmore, his home. It appears as if William Weller leased or rented a home at this location since he is not mentioned in any transactions in the Land Registry records for this location. Later in the 1840s, after more than a decade in this location, the Wellers would move to the west side of town, near the south end of Tremaine Street. The land around and including the Cottesmore lot would, in the 1850s, be owned by George M. Clark, William Weller's son-in-law. In 1861, the land was divided into town lots, and a street was run up the middle of the property. That street is called Cottesmore Avenue.

As the sleigh approached the Weller home, the driver could see a cluster of figures standing at the side of the road. His wife was there, holding the baby, George. Sixteen-year-old William Henry was prancing about waving his arms and shouting.

The younger ones, Caroline, Charles, and little Dabbie, gathered around their mother's skirts, waving timidly, glad for a chance to see Daddy in action.

William Weller was extremely proud of his family and stood waving as the sleigh sped by at a gallop. He would have dearly loved to stop and grab each one of the little group in his arms for a big hug. However, there was the matter of a contract, and William Weller knew better than most the sacrifices a successful enterprise demanded. He would be back in a few days and would be able to kiss his wife and kids and spend some time at home. At least that was the plan.

17

Grafton

WILLIAM WELLER SETTLED ONTO HIS BENCH AND GAVE THE HORSES THEIR HEADS, holding the reins lightly. They were nearing the end of stage four of their trip, and he knew that most of the best roads they would see had already gone under the sleigh runners. The smaller towns and rural areas along the next part of the trip would offer fewer miles of well-maintained roads and maybe some surprises. Travellers had to be ready for anything.

While the Kingston Road followed the concession road and was relatively flat moving out of Hamilton and into Haldimand Township, this experienced driver knew that the next team of horses was in for a challenge. Up ahead lay the rolling hills of Northumberland. For the modern driver, the hills and wonderful vistas they provide are most often a pleasure, but for the traveller in 1840, the heavy loam clay soil covering the long, rolling hills represented much more of a challenge. Numerous marshy areas and the occasional narrow, deep creek bed presented obstacles as well, and delays were inevitable, even for the simplest trip.

Certainly, Mr. Weller's crews had been down the Kingston Road from Cobourg to Trent Port, so any major problems should have been dealt with. However, these roads were unpredictable, especially at this time of year. The weather was mild, right around freezing, and precipitation was holding off for now, but rain or snow could come down any minute. Snow would be best, of course, since rain might cause the frost to come out of the ground in places, leaving mud holes that could cause a problem.

Just east of Hare Road, the Kingston Road swerved north to avoid some difficult terrain near the lake. The team did not flinch at the long slope ahead and, even though they were tired from running persistently from Marsh's Tavern, the pace remained at a high level. Down the long slope and on flat ground again, the driver began anticipating a quick stop at Grafton.

A mile west of the village of Grafton, the sleigh passed Barnum House,[1] a very popular tavern and hotel that had been operating at this location since before the War of 1812. Eliakim Barnum had come to Upper Canada in 1807 and quickly demonstrated his enterprising nature by turning a pretentious old log house, called The Poplars, into a thriving tavern. During the war, British soldiers were billeted at the tavern during their retreat from York. Unfortunately, the house did not survive these particular guests, as a fire was started, which completely destroyed the building.

Barnum showed his Tory leanings by refusing any remuneration from the British government, and proceeded to build a lovely new home on the same site. That house still stands along the north side of Number 2 Highway. Barnum House was designated a National Historic Site in 1959, and in 1982, ownership was transferred to the Ontario Heritage Trust. Major restoration has taken place both inside and out, in order to show the nature of the home in the 1820 to 1840 period. This structure represents one of the finest examples of Georgian architecture in this area. The land to the north as far as the 401 is now a conservation area.

East of Barnum House, the Kingston Road began a long curve, which would bring it back down to the concession line for a straight run through the village of Grafton. William Weller was not much concerned with heritage buildings as he took up his horn and prepared to make a quick stop at Grover's Inn. However, the modern reader might be fascinated to learn that the small town of Grafton has preserved an extremely significant number of structures that William Weller and the governor general may have noticed on their brief run through the town in 1840.

From the west end, Barnum House is a mile out of town, but is a very important part of Grafton's built heritage. Closer to the village, on the south side, the modern traveller can see two lovely two-storey, brick houses, designed on the Georgian theme. Our travellers in 1840 would have seen only the first one, as they passed Spalding's Inn, which was built around 1834 by Thomas Major Spalding[2] and used as his home and a very popular tavern and hotel for many years.

Long before this brick building was built, in 1834, Spalding's Inn was well known as a halfway house between York and Kingston. It is mentioned in records as early as 1816, mostly related to fees due for inn-keeper licenses.[3] The second building, on the corner of Brimley Road, was built a few years after Mr. Weller made his trip through Grafton, the occupants to be John Steele and his wife, Mary Spalding, a daughter of Thomas Spalding.

William Weller pulled out his horn and gave a couple of blasts for the folks at the Grafton Inn. As he did, he sped past the home of Dr. Elam Burr Ives. Dr. Ives was well respected as an excellent doctor who travelled on horseback around the country dispensing medical assistance. He came to Grafton around 1815, and this house was built sometime after that. It has been much changed over the years, but it was there as the governor general passed by, and the modern traveller can enjoy its charm today.

The most important building in Grafton in 1840 was The Grafton Inn, on the north side of the Kingston Road, at the intersection with the Old Danforth Road, which originally went south to the harbour. The original owner of this very popular inn was John Grover,[4] one of the earliest settlers in Haldimand Township. In fact, the village was known as Grover's Corners until the decision was made in 1832 to name it Grafton, after John Grover's hometown in Massachusetts.

The substantial frame building that William Weller would see here in 1840 had been built in 1833 to replace a very old log structure, and the fine new building only enhanced the reputation of this establishment. John Grover was almost seventy at this time and had sold the property to a Mr. Pepper, but the quality of hospitality and service was not diminished. Today, the Grafton Village Inn is widely known as a delightful example of neo-classical design, with hospitality commensurate with its heritage value.

Arrangements had been made to change horses at the Grafton Inn, and William Weller could see the fresh team standing off to the south side of the road in front of the Lawless store. A crowd had gathered on both sides of the road, and there was clapping and shouts of encouragement as the sleigh stopped. A very quick swap of the team was accomplished. A jug was passed to Mr. Weller and to his passengers, and we can speculate on whether it contained fresh water or something more energizing, but in any case, the three men were grateful. The driver gave the team a crack of the whip, more for public show than anything else, and they were off again on their journey east.

The modern traveller will see an attractive grey building on the south side of Highway 2, right across from the Grafton Inn. This structure was originally built in 1837 of one-inch planks stacked and nailed on top of each other. It was built for James Lawless,[6] who conducted an active business from this site. Over the years, many residents of the area would recognize the Lawless wagons on the roads, delivering products for customers. Also, just behind the Lawless store, on the Old Danforth Road, is a commercial building that has housed many different businesses and services since it was built around 1820.

No sooner had the sleigh surged away from the Grafton Inn than a young man on horseback came up the Kingston Road from the east, waving his arms and shouting loudly. "Mr. Weller! Is that you, Mr. Weller?" he shouted over and over as he approached.

William Weller drew up the team and stood up to answer the young man. "Yes, young fellow, I am Mr. Weller. What is all the fuss about? Is something wrong?"

In between gulps of air, the young man explained to Mr. Weller. "Yes. There is a lumber wagon stuck on the bridge over Shelter Valley Creek, and I'm afraid you will not be able to cross. Some men are coming to unload the wagon, so the broken wheel can be pulled out. It has damaged several planks on the bridge, and it may take some time to fix!"

The driver thought for a brief moment and asked the young man, "Is there another way across the creek? Maybe an old ford we can approach from here?"

The young man turned his horse back to the east, stopped to think for a moment, and then he turned back to Mr. Weller. "Yes, sir, there is an old trail down into the valley. I know the place. The creek is slower there, so the ice should be strong enough to cross." He stood up in his stirrups and said to Mr. Weller, "I'll take you there if you like."

Mr. Weller responded, "Lead the way, son. We will stop where the trail leaves the main road so that my passengers can get out and walk to the other side."

With that, the young man spurred his horse and started quickly down the Kingston Road, with the sleigh following close behind. They sped up the long incline out of the village of Grafton, and soon they passed Cherry Hill Road. Mr. Weller could see the roof of the Campbell & Co. distillery to the north, as well as the neat row of cottages that stood along the north side of the Kingston Road, providing homes for the workmen.

At the top of the hill, on the north side, was the local cemetery, and immediately east of there, the road turned sharply south and started down into the valley. Today, the road that runs south, off Number 2 Highway, is called Benlock Road. In 1840, our travellers would have identified the village of Benlock, which contained a mill, blacksmith shop, carpentry shop, and several homes. It was centred around the water power of Shelter Valley Creek. The traffic of the Kingston Road went through this growing and thriving little village.

Today, Fairview Cemetery holds the plain but dignified memorial of Benjamin Ewing, who died in 1852. Seven years before Mr. Weller came by, Benjamin Ewing[7] had called a meeting at his home and, acting as secretary, presided over the naming of the small settlement. It would be called Benlock. The optimism in the room was palpable, as we can see by a report in the *Cobourg Star* of February 6, 1833. The "valuable and never failing powerful stream of water" would power the ambitions of Benlock to become "the mart of this and the back adjoining townships."[8] Where have we heard this sentiment before? It seems that every community along the north shore of Lake Ontario had visions of greatness.

A little farther along, the young man stopped his horse and pointed to an opening along the south side of the road. Mr. Weller stopped the sleigh and addressed his passengers. "Gentlemen, we must navigate a difficult path. For your own safety, I suggest you cover the next short distance on foot. We will meet you on the other side of the bridge. Is that to your satisfaction, gentlemen?"

As he spoke, Captain Le Marchant and Governor General Thomson exited the coach and stretched their legs. The governor general responded, "Yes, that's fine, Mr. Weller, whatever you need. We are agreeable passengers, you can count on that!" With that, the two men started walking down the road toward the bridge.

Mr. Weller gestured to the young man and said, "Come sit with me on the bench and tell me where to go. We will take it slow and careful. This is a fine team but let's keep calm and try not to spook them."

The young man jumped onto the sleigh and extended his hand to Mr. Weller. "Master Tom Sinclair, at your service, sir!" he exclaimed with all the pomp and circumstance he could muster. Mr. Weller shook his hand, noting the broad smile and firm handshake. Tom Sinclair pointed to an opening between some trees at the side of the road and said, "That is where we can meet the trail a short distance into the woods."

Mr. Weller spoke calmly to the horses and eased them off the road and between the trees. In a few minutes, they came upon the remnants of an old road and turned east to follow it until they came to the creek. The ice seemed solid on first glance, but before the driver could speak, his young companion was off the sleigh and out onto the creek, slipping on the ice and stomping his feet at intervals to make sure it was hard. "The ice is hard, Mr. Weller. It should hold us all with no problem. Shall I lead the team?

Mr. Weller blanched a little at this, but he could see that Tom was already in front of the horses, speaking kindly to them and tugging lightly on their bridles. They responded by gingerly stepping onto the ice, uncertain and annoyed, but stepping forward nonetheless. There was rough snow on the surface of the ice, so the horses had something other than slick ice to step on. Mr. Weller was relieved to see that the horses were moving across under the guidance of young Tom Sinclair, and before he knew it, they were stepping onto the bank at the other side of the creek.

"Nicely done, Mr. Sinclair!" said Mr. Weller as Tom jumped back onto the sleigh. "You have a way with horses, it seems."

Tom Sinclair grinned from ear to ear as he climbed back onto the sleigh, then responded quietly, "Well, that's what my pa says."

Tom pointed out the trail to Mr. Weller, and in a few minutes, the sleigh found its way back onto the Kingston Road. Captain Le Marchant and the governor general were close at hand, and Mr. Weller could see, back on the bridge, the lumber wagon, resting at an odd angle, with several men around it.

As the two passengers climbed back into the sleigh, Mr. Weller thanked Tom Sinclair, saying that he would look up his father once he was back in this part of the country and offer him proper compensation for the services rendered. Then, as the young man turned to walk back up the road to his horse, Mr. Weller reached into his pocket and pulled out a large coin. "Mr. Sinclair," he shouted. "Thanks so much for your help!" With that, he flipped the coin and Tom Sinclair caught it deftly in one hand.

He stared at it briefly and then put it to his mouth, and bit on it sharply. Raising the coin in the air, he smiled and shouted, "Thank you Mr. Weller. Your money is always good with Tom Sinclair!"

With that, Mr. Weller laughed out loud. Turning to the job at hand, he flipped the reins and started the team back on their way along the Kingston Road. As he drove on, he thought, *That young man will have a job in my stage business one day, mark my words!*

18

Wicklow and Colborne

NOW THAT THE TRAVELLERS WERE FREE OF THE PROBLEM AT THE BRIDGE EAST OF Grafton, the driver was intent on making good time to their next stage stop near Brighton. Not far along the road, the sleigh passed quickly through the thriving little village of Wicklow, and then hurried along towards Colborne. On the north side of the road, just east of Wicklow, Mr. Weller would have seen the old Baptist Chapel, which had been built in 1824.

The Kingston Road in this area demonstrated the nature of the rolling hills of Northumberland. Ancient glacial moraines lie back from the lake, and the waterways have made their way through at various points. The road curves sharply around the end of ridges or edges up long slopes, then runs down into marshy areas, with occasional bridges across the creeks. It was a varied landscape, and the driver had to keep his wits about him.

Soon after the Baptist Chapel, William Weller would prepare himself for Herriman Hill.[1] He had navigated Herriman Hill many times in his stagecoach travels and knew it could be a serious challenge. His thought on this day was that frost would still be in the ground, so they could avoid the terrible muddy morass that would greet travellers in a few weeks. As he approached, he could see that his theory was largely correct. The sleigh would glide harmlessly over this dangerous spot, with only a few signs of mud splashing up from the horses' hooves.

Herriman Hill was notorious as one of the worst mud holes on the entire Kingston Road. This was common knowledge, as we can see in an article in the

Colborne Chronicle in 1974, which contains information dictated by well-known local resident Susan Burnham Greeley. "There was a place between Colborne and Grafton called Herriman Hill, from the name of the first settler there, which was said to be the worst place between Kingston and Toronto, and the terror of the stage drivers. This arose from the nature of the soil, for it was not much of a hill and, in fact, a "brick yard" was worked so close beside the road for some years." [2]

It was not a steep hill, as even modern drivers on Highway 2 can see just east of Knight's Appleden, but the soil here had a particular composition that caused it to break down into mire when it was wet. It may have made good bricks, but many a traveller, including Mr. Weller with his Royal Mail stages, had spent much time and energy extricating vehicles from the mud at this place.

It was in places just like this, that the term "carrying a rail" originated. When the stagecoach became stuck in the mud, passengers were expected to leave the comfort of the coach and find a fence rail heavy enough to assist in prying the vehicle out of its predicament. C.W. Jefferys, one of Canada's best-known historical illustrators, provides a graphic demonstration of carrying a rail. A finely dressed gentleman is up to his knees in mud, carrying a fence rail, ready to assist the driver and the team in navigating this mud hole.

18.1 Carrying a Rail. C.W. Jefferys was one of Canada's most prolific historical illustrators. His sketch of a stagecoach mired in a muddy road demonstrates one of the very common practices of the stagecoach era. If we look closely, we might speculate that the scene of this activity could be Herriman Hill. The hill is not steep, and there is cleared land across the rail fence. Also, the stagecoach has the appearance of one of William Weller's standard Royal Mail coaches. It could be his name on the door.

Nathaniel Herriman[3] had come to Haldimand Township in the 1820s and settled on the south side of the Kingston Road, at Lot 9, Concession A. By the time he moved to Grey County in 1839, his name had been associated with the mud hole in front of his farm. For generations afterward, local residents and provincial travellers would vie with each other for the honour of telling the most spectacular disaster stories from their experiences in the mud of Herriman Hill.

Of course, the modern driver sees nothing of this today. Even in the 1890s when Susan Burnham Greeley[4] dictated her story, elderly residents could only imagine the hills and vales and their muddy characteristics in those early years. Plank roads and then gravel roads would remove the worst of the mud holes in the 1840s, at least on the main roads, and we can expect that Herriman Hill was one place the road contractors targeted when they were charged with improving conditions for travellers on the Kingston Road.

At the border between Haldimand and Cramahe Township, Mr. Weller would notice the road down to Lakeport, which was one of the very earliest settlements in these parts. Joseph Keeler[5] brought several families from Vermont, along with Aaron Greeley, a surveyor, to this location on Lake Ontario in 1793. They established a settlement, built a mill and a wharf, and assisted the others in settling on their own homesteads in the area.

The original Joseph Keeler was called "Old Joe" and his son, who was called "Young Joe", carried on his father's tradition of enterprise by establishing a store on the Kingston Road. This store, along with the shops and houses that grew up around it, would become a thriving village that would take on the name Colborne in honour of the beloved Sir John Colborne, who was lieutenant governor of Upper Canada from 1828 to 1839.

William Weller guided the sleigh over and around the hills and soon came to the curve just west of Colborne, where the road heads south to meet King Street by the public square in the middle of the village. The public square had been included as a feature in the initial plans for the village in 1815 and continues to serve that purpose as Victoria Square.

The driver may have glanced to his left as he drove by the square, noticing the Wesleyan Methodist Church, which was built in 1823 on the north side of Church Street. The sacristy would be built on the south side of the old church in 1862, resulting in the lovely structure that served as the Colborne United Church until recent times. On down Church Street, he would have acknowledged Keeler House, which was built in 1812 by Old Joe Keeler. Mr. Weller may have recalled that the old gentleman had passed away just a few months earlier, in July of 1839. Today, the Keeler House remains an important part of the built heritage of Colborne and is the home of two recipients of the Order of Canada: Tony and Jane Urquhart.

Just before William Weller turned left onto King Street, right in front of him were two homes he would recognize. At 3 King Street West was the oldest house in Colborne, called the Thornton Residence. The next house to the west was built in the 1830s and would be occupied by Cuthbert Cummings from 1844, when he retired from the stresses and dangers of the fur trade to enjoy a life of leisure in the more civilized Colborne.[6]

Not far along King Street East, the imposing St. Andrews Presbyterian Church stood majestically on a rise, back from the street. It had been built of limestone, on land donated by Young Joe Keeler, with the stipulation that a seat be reserved for him. Today this building represents another of Colborne's most important heritage sites.

The travellers would not be stopping in Colborne but, if they were, it would likely be at the Keeler Tavern in East Colborne. Young Joe Keeler had built this substantial building in 1832, at the corner of a road to the farms in the north concessions, now called Parliament Street. For many years he operated a popular tavern, hotel, and stage stop. An artist's rendering of the Keeler Tavern is available in a watercolour by James Pattison Cockburn,[7] who was an English soldier talented with the brush. He had been posted in Quebec from 1826 to August 1832, and travelled around Upper and Lower Canada, sketching and painting interesting scenes. His watercolour of the Keeler Tavern shows a substantial building on the main road, with carriages and people out front. We can see that the private home at that location today, in spite of major renovations, maintains the character of the original building.

18.2 Keeler Tavern, East Colborne, by James Pattison Cockburn

William Weller knew that the next few miles would be challenging because of the hills and valleys, and a few bridges that he hoped were in good shape. Any thought of planked roads was in the future for this part of the Kingston Road, so travellers accepted the risk of dirt roads, well aware of the conditions they would meet at any particular time of the year.

The travellers proceeded at a gallop, up the long slope from East Colborne and then down a steeper grade into the little hamlet of Salem. A substantial creek crossed the road here, a creek that provided enough water power to support several mills that would be the lifeblood of the village. The bridge, while not in the best shape, had been repaired recently and did not slow down the pace of the trip.

Just after the creek, on the right, Mr. Weller would notice Salem Cemetery, which contained memorials for many of the earliest settlers in the area. Brothers Nathan and Seth Burr Gould had settled here about 1800, selecting good land along the lakeshore and near the new Danforth Highway. They would produce large family trees, linked with Gould ancestors back in Connecticut, to keep genealogists busy.

A precarious bit of road led through a sharp valley to the east of Salem, leaving the concession line to avoid the hills that edged closer to the lake in this area. The Kingston Road would come very close to Lake Ontario along the next pleasant and relatively flat piece of road to Brighton, providing glimpses through the trees of the dark and cold expanse of the lake. It would be another month, at least, before navigation was opened on the lake, and until then, the lake was to be avoided. A sleigh ride along the Kingston Road was the best alternative.

19

Brighton

ON COUNTY ROAD 2, THE MODERN DRIVER WILL SEE A SIGN INDICATING THE BORDER between the Township of Cramahe and the Municipality of Brighton. The road that leads north at this point is fittingly called Boundary Road. However, in 1840, William Weller would not have seen any sign here. In fact, at that time, Cramahe Township extended all the way to the village of Brighton, meeting Murray Township at Prince Edward Street in Brighton.

The history of Brighton Township presents an unusual situation. The townships of Cramahe and Murray had been surveyed in the 1790s, and settlers had come in to settle on these fertile lands. Near the border of the two townships, two settlements developed along the Kingston Road. At the intersection of Ontario Street, the settlement was called Bettes Corners. To the east, at the corner of Prince Edward Street, was Singleton's Corners.

In 1831, a meeting was held in Simon Kellogg's tavern to discuss the need to form one village, in order to avoid the confusion of two post offices so close together. A committee was formed to decide on a name, and the new postmaster, Nathan Lockwood, proposed the name Brighton, which was his parents' home in England. The name seemed to suggest a glorious future for the rough little village on the north shore of Presqu'ile Bay, so Brighton it would be.[1]

There was another town meeting at Simon Kellogg's tavern in January of 1836. This one requested that the village be granted a constable and magistrate of their own, since the closest police and court was in Colborne or Trent Port. Their petition

says, "...we view with deep regret the many disadvant
part of Murray and the east part of Cramahe have for

Unfortunately, the request landed on deaf ears. Th
until the Reform Party gained its landslide victory
1848. Finally, legislation was passed in Toronto and
Township was created, from the west part of Murray
along with Presqu'ile Point. Brighton would have its
the people wished.

This would have been unknown to William Welle ——————— galloped along
the Kingston Road, with a cold breeze blowing off the lake. He had decided to stop
at Proctor Inn, at Huff Road, and not in the village of Brighton. This tavern was
owned by Isaac Proctor, a son of Josiah Proctor, who had brought his family from
Vermont to Cramahe Township in 1810.

*19.1 Proctor Inn. The white house we can see on the north side of Number 2 Highway at Huff Road
not far west of Brighton was built in the 1820s by Isaac Proctor. It was a very popular stopping place
on the Kingston Road for many years.*

Isaac Proctor had operated a tavern just west of Huff road since he purchased
land there in 1818. In 1825, he purchased a half-acre lot on the northwest corner
of the Kingston Road and Huff Road, where he built a substantial building, which
would be known far and wide as the Proctor Inn.

eller pulled out his horn once more to sound the alert for the tavern
stable boys at Proctor Inn. He swung the team and sleigh up to the
the building, and the fresh team, which had been standing in position, was
pped in. The obligatory jug was passed to the driver and passengers, and the
travellers were on their way in less than five minutes. It had been another good stop.

The sleigh moved along the Kingston Road, toward the village of Brighton. A
little west of Brighton, on the left, the driver recognized the Simpson homestead,
tucked neatly under the ridge to the north. This property was now in the hands of
John Simpson, a son of the old settler, Obediah Simpson, who is considered the
first settler of Brighton. Obediah Simpson had grown up in plantation country
near Cape Fear, North Carolina. He had fought for the British during the War of
Independence and ended up here in Cramahe Township, after brief stays in Nova
Scotia and Adolphustown. At the entrance to Presqu'ile Park, there is a memorial
cairn in the grassy area beside the road, dedicated to Obediah Simpson and his wife
Mary and their family.[6]

As the sleigh passed the Simpson farm, the driver made sure to watch for traffic
turning onto the Kingston Road from the Percy Road. In 1840, the Percy Road was
the primary north-south road in this area, reaching through the concessions to
the north all the way to Percy Township. This road had developed very soon after
Obediah Simpson and other early settlers had come to Cramahe Township, and
would provide critical access to the north for people and goods moving between the
excellent protected harbour at Presqu'ile Bay and the rich farmland in the northern concessions.

The modern driver might be curious about this Percy Road. In fact, the Old
Percy Road[7] (so-called as early as the 1850s) was replaced in the middle of the 1850s
by the Brighton and Seymour Gravel Road, which would develop into what we
know as Highway Number 30. The author grew up on Number 30, half way between
Brighton and Campbellford, at the village of Codrington, which came into existence
because of the new road.

The sleigh dipped into the narrow valley where Butler Creek ran under a decent
bridge and meandered south and then east to empty into Presqu'ile Bay. As the team
pulled the sleigh up the hill out of the valley, they passed the intersection at Sand
Street, later to be called Ontario Street. Hotels and stores would proliferate around
this busy corner over the decades. In recent times, the property on the southwest
corner has been transformed into the lovely Rose Ellery Park, named after a revered
local citizen.

A little farther along, on the north side of Main Street, William Weller would
see the Ira Hodges tavern, which was built in the 1820s, along the same lines as the
Keeler and Proctor inns. This building still stands today, east of the YMCA, as a

private home. The Hodges Inn was a popular meeting p
1850s and was another reminder of the close connectio
the early settler families. A sister of Ira Hodges had ma
brother of Isaac, the hotel keeper.

19.2 Hodges Tavern. The house behind the trees at 156 Main Street, Brighton shows the same pattern of tavern construction as the Proctor and Keeler taverns to the west of Brighton.

One of Isaac Proctor's sons, John Edward Proctor, would have a profound impact on this community. Beginning around 1844, he would parlay his family real estate holdings into significant business enterprises, trading in lumber and wheat and operating general-merchandise stores. In the 1850s, he took ownership of the main wharf on Presqu'ile Bay, at Gosport, and became engaged in shipping over several decades, eventually owning his own schooners.

In the late 1860s, John Edward Proctor built a large, two-storey brick house on the west side of Young Street, up on the hill north of town. The new structure was added to the smaller frame house his father had built on the site in 1853, and the result was a large, modern home for his growing family. This structure has been preserved, and today proudly overlooks the town of Brighton as Proctor House Museum. The public can tour this excellent example of the home of a wealthy merchant in the mid-eighteen hundreds. In 1999, an old barn on the Simpson property was torn down and rebuilt just west of Proctor House, to be called The Barn Theatre. These two facilities support events and activities that celebrate Brighton's history and culture.

ngston Road passed by a scattering of wooden houses and shops, although
still separated the two original hamlets. As he approached the intersection at
in and Prince Edward Streets, William Weller was intent on negotiating this odd
three-way corner in the middle of the afternoon, when traffic was at its peak. The
road edged north a bit to follow the old route of the Danforth Highway, which went
directly to Smithfield along what today is called Dundas Street.

Why do so many towns along this old road have a Dundas Street? Henry Dundas
was a good friend of John Graves Simcoe back in England. He was the War Secretary
in the Pitt government from 1794 to 1801, around the same time that Simcoe was
trying to build a loyal British colony in Upper Canada. Simcoe envisioned a King's
Highway linking York, the new capital of the province, with settlements along the
north shore of Lake Ontario, as well as points to the south and west, into the Niagara
district. For a time, the official name for this important future route was the Dundas
Road, although parts of it were never built and many parts that came into being
were called by other names. Over time, the name Dundas would be used for many
streets in towns along that early route, all the way from Windsor to Quebec.

To his left, William Weller could see Sanford's Hotel, often called the Brighton
Hotel, which sat back seventy-five feet from the road, leaving a spacious yard for
turning stages and changing horses at this popular stage stop. Weller had stopped at
Sanford's Hotel many times because it was a Royal Mail stop and was probably the
best outfitted accommodation in the area. On this day, there were several sleighs in
the yard and a dozen people standing outside the hotel, which made him glad he
had changed horses back at Proctor's Inn.

He slowed down in front of Simon Kellogg's tavern, which stood at the southwest
corner of Main and Prince Edward, and then made a quick right turn, then a left
turn, to speed out of Brighton on Elizabeth Street. Now the travellers had moved
from Cramahe into Murray Township. The road from Brighton to Smithfield would
demonstrate once more that the original route of the Danforth Highway had deliberately kept to the higher ground. From the place where Brighton would spring up,
it had followed Dundas Street along the crest of the ridge, directly east to Smithfield.
Then, just east of Smithfield, it had turned south to Carrying Place. It is important
to remember that the original Danforth Road did not go to Trenton, but went into
Prince Edward County and on to Picton and the Glenora Ferry, which crossed the
water to meet the road to Bath and Kingston.

Mr. Weller had a more practical concern. He would have been worried about
the low ground east of Brighton, which he knew often presented a challenge. It had
been improved with an installation of corduroy, if one can say that a corduroy road
is an improvement at all. In any case, with the frost still in the ground, even this
notoriously bad piece of road did not deter the travellers.

A few miles farther along, and the village of Smithfield appeared on the left. John Drummond Smith[9] had come from New York State as early as 1793 and made his home in this area, where the creek and the village would take his name. He had married Mary McDowall, a daughter of Rev. James Robert McDowall, the famous saddlebag preacher.

Mr. Weller kept up the pace with this fresh team, as he wished to continue to make good time. Several long stages were behind them now, and the plan was to have two shorter stages through Trent Port and into Belleville, where they would stop for an hour to have a meal and let everyone, including the driver, stretch their legs.

20

Trent Port and Belleville

AT SMITHFIELD, THE MODERN DRIVER WILL SEE THE SIGN FOR THE CITY OF QUINTE West. This reflects the border between Brighton and Murray Townships, which was established in 1852, when Brighton Township was created. In recent years, Murray Township has become part of the City of Quinte West.

William Weller urged the team along the road approaching the village of Trent Port. Strategically located at the mouth of the Trent River, the village of Trent Port, also called Trent River, would later be called Trenton. From the earliest days, the Trent River would define the town, but when a bridge over the river came into service in 1834, the town took on a much more important role.

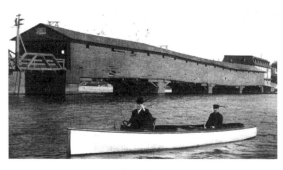

20.1 Covered Bridge at Trent Port

Squire John Bleecker[1] had established a trading post on the west side of the river before 1790, and he operated a ferry, a job that was carried on by his son, John Bleecker, Jr. In the late 1820s, an ambitious young Irishman named John V. Murphy acquired land on the west side of the river, where the ferry crossed, and he took over the operation of the ferry for many years. Then, in the early 1830s, the authorities decided that the crossing was important enough to warrant the cost of a bridge. The civil engineer Hugh Nicole Baird[2] was engaged to design the bridge, and it went into operation in 1834. The bridge was an impressive structure. It was 750 feet long, 32 feet wide, and 26 feet high and covered for two-thirds of the distance. This bridge represented a major improvement for the general travelling public but in particular for the stage drivers.

When William Weller approached the river in Trent Port in 1840, he recalled being involved in the situation at this crossing for more than a decade. He had supported Mr. Murphy in his application for a license to operate the ferry, which the government let for three years at a time. Before a bridge was available, the smooth, reliable operation of a ferry was critical to Mr. Weller because he was running his stages on a schedule, especially regarding the delivery of mail. John V. Murphy had built buildings and organized the ferry in a very efficient way, so he deserved support.

He had also commiserated with Mr. Murphy when the contractors who built the bridge, beginning in late 1833, ignored the presence of the ferry and obstructed the route of the ferry crossing, causing Mr. Murphy to incur significant extra costs in operating the ferry for the period of several months before the bridge was opened. Mr. Murphy's petitions[3] to the government included William Weller's name in support of his request for compensation.

Cyrus Weaver[4] had established an inn on the west side of the river in March of 1835, soon after the bridge was in place. This would be a popular and well-known inn at a strategic location at the river crossing. William Weller had decided that he would stop here to change horses because it was midway between his last stop, west of Brighton, and the next stop in Belleville. He also wanted to make sure, before he crossed the bridge, that there were no vehicles on the bridge, and he would have a clear run across. His people on the spot would make sure of that.

Coming down the hill into the river valley, Mr. Weller pulled out his horn and gave several blasts to alert the innkeeper and stable boys at Weaver's Inn. The sleigh passed a cluster of wooden buildings near the river and pulled up outside of the inn. Mr. Weller waved to Mr. Weaver and the horses were changed in the normal efficient manner. In less than ten minutes they were on their way.

The sleigh approached the bridge, and a young fellow stood at the entrance, waving them through. The horses entered the regular open bridge at the west end with no problem, but they hesitated as they approached the unfamiliar barn-like cover overhead. The driver provided calm words and deft handling of the reins, and they moved forward. Hooves clattered on wooden planks, and the sound echoed around in the enclosed barn. Soon, they were on the other side, now in Sidney Township, speeding down the Kingston Road toward Belleville.

When the travellers crossed the Trent River, they entered into Hastings County and the Midland District. From 1792 until 1849, Midland District was a high-level administrative structure that included the counties of Hastings, Prince Edward, Lennox, Addington, and Frontenac. Its western border was the Trent River, and its eastern border was the Gananoque River.

The road follows close to the shore of the Bay of Quinte between Trenton and Belleville, and the travellers were able to make good time, since the terrain was mostly flat. Despite a few low spots, where broken corduroy logs poked above the mud, the sleigh moved quickly past the prosperous farms and fertile fields. This area had been among the first settled after the War of Independence due to its proximity to the bay, and by 1840, many families had farmed here for several generations, giving the area a lived-in look.

After the travellers were well out of Trent Port, they would see on the right, along the shoreline, the Old Sidney Burial Ground, which provided a resting place for the early settlers of the area. The Bleeckers from Trent Port were here, along with Reuben White's family, including himself in 1858, prompting the name of Whites Cemetery. The famous early settler of Belleville, John Walden Meyers,[5] is also here, with many of his family and associates.

The sky remained dull grey and the temperature around freezing as the sleigh approached Belleville. Mr. Weller pulled out his horn and sounded the alert. He had arranged something special for his passengers in Belleville, which was seen as a practical midpoint of the trip. They would spend an hour in Belleville, time to obtain a good meal and take a rest from the sleigh. The passengers could stretch their legs after confinement in the coach, and the driver could rest himself in a soft chair. The team would be changed and Mr. Weller had also arranged for a thorough cleaning of the sleigh, along with a careful examination of the livery and the vehicle's suspension and runners. He wanted to ensure that everything was ship-shape for the long hours of travel ahead.

Arrangements had been made with the owner of the Mansion House, the most prestigious public house in Belleville. The owner and operator of the Mansion House[6] was Mr. Royal Munro. His establishment was known far and wide for its clean and commodious rooms and its excellent table with the best of wines and liquors, as well as a very efficient stable with the best horses found in the region. Its location was also very convenient, sitting at the four corners where Front Street and Bridge Street met, where the Kingston Road crossed the Moira River. This was the center of the growing business and commercial area of Belleville.

20.2 Belleville Bridge. A substantial bridge is shown crossing the Moira River at Belleville in a watercolour by Thomas Burrowes around 1830, illustrating some of the development at the centre of the town.

Another blast from the horn was heard as the sleigh came to the western edge of the Moira River valley. The driver made his way down to Bridge Street and across the bridge to Front Street. From here it was only a few yards to the entrance to the Mansion House. A crowd of people had gathered at the front of the building and along the street. Curious onlookers had come over from Billa Flint's store, interrupting their gossip and tobacco spitting, to see what a governor general looked like. It wasn't every day you could catch a glimpse of the most powerful man in the British North American colonies stopping in your town. This was a big event in Belleville.

Soon after the sleigh came to a halt, Mr. Munro was at the forefront of the crowd, clasping Mr. Weller by the hand and greeting him like an old friend. In fact, they had been in business together for almost a decade. Munro had come to Belleville in 1829 to engage in hotel operations. Within a few years he was a partner of Mr. Weller, acting as agent for carrying the Royal Mail on stagecoaches between Trenton and Kingston, while Weller handled the section from Trenton to Toronto.[7] This had been very lucrative for both men and would continue into 1837, when Mr. Weller took more complete control of the enterprise.

When William Weller was looking for a place to make his mid-trip rest and needed assurance that he could provide the governor general with appropriate accommodations and hospitality, he looked no further than his old partner, Royal Munro. And Mr. Munro would not disappoint. The three men were whisked into the dining room where a substantial meal awaited, with staff in well-pressed uniforms and serious faces. Governor General Thomson was not a stickler for pomp and ceremony, but he did appreciate a good table and was quick to praise Mr. Munro for his excellent choice of wine.

Settlement at the mouth of the Moira River had begun soon after the end of the War of Independence when Captain George Singleton[8] and his partners, Lt. Israel Ferguson and Col. Alexander Chisholm, built a warehouse to store the furs they would collect from the natives in the area and to the north. The settlement would be called Singleton Creek for a time. Singleton had married Israel Ferguson's sister, Nancy, which connected these men even more closely. The three had served together during the war and were the best of friends.

Captain Singleton had been badly injured in the battle of Oriskany in the Mohawk Valley in 1777. After he recovered and the war was over, he planned to be a fur trader in Upper Canada and his military buddies would accompany him. They were an interesting trio, particularly with the aggressive young commissariat officer, Chisholm, who had a propensity for writing petitions to government officials. All three had been with Burgoyne in his failed campaign in New York State, Chisholm being held captive for some time.

Unfortunately, their successful fur trading business was interrupted in 1789 when Singleton died suddenly of fever in the town of Bath while the group was on its way to Montreal with a load of furs. His wife, Nancy, had recently given birth to a son, John, and with the passing of the breadwinner the two were left in the care of friends. Her brother died soon after this, and a few years later, she married Alexander Chisholm, and they set about making a home. [9]

Alexander Chisholm[10] obtained thousands of acres of land due to his military service, but the land he really wanted, at the mouth of the Moira River, eluded him. He wrote many fawning petitions, hoping to gain favour with the authorities. However, John Walden Meyers had much more currency in these affairs due to his exemplary service to the British as a spy during the war. The village and the waterway would soon be called Meyers Creek, and Alexander Chisholm would move his attention to land at the mouth of Butler Creek on Presqu'ile Bay, where he built a saw mill and grist mill in 1797. His wife, Nancy, would outlive three husbands and become a revered member of the new village of Brighton, with a street named for her son, John Singleton.

Meyers Creek became Belleville in 1816, and by 1840, the town had experienced a rush of development and improvement and had the look of a community with great potential. The large and imposing court house and gaol had been completed in 1838 and dominated the sandy hill on the east side of the river. The spire of St. Andrew's Presbyterian Church pointed skyward nearby, and more substantial buildings were being built along Front Street, joining the merchandising business of

Billa Flint, a young and aggressive businessman who had come from Brockville at the same time as Mr. Munro.

Belleville had been incorporated as a Police Village in 1836, with Billa Flint as the first president.[11] In this capacity, Mr. Flint had motivated many badly needed improvements, including the installation of flagstone sidewalks on Front Street, between Dundas and Bridge Street. Of course, there were several reasons for making this happen, not the least being improved access for the public to Flint's store on Front Street.

Flint's largest enterprise, begun in 1837, was a steam-powered saw mill at the mouth of the Moira River, which would grow dramatically both in size and technical complexity. Massive amounts of lumber would be produced at this mill, most of it loaded onto schooners for export, and the harbour was much improved to accommodate this trade. Flint would also become deeply involved in development in the northern townships of Hastings County where raw materials could be found. Billa Flint would have a dramatic impact on Belleville and area for several decades, with his own unique approach to the mixing of private enterprise and public service.

Billa Flint may not have been very happy to see the governor general in Belleville, especially so close to his store on Front Street. He may have grumbled as his patrons removed to the Mansion House to catch a glimpse of royalty, or the closest they might ever see of it. Flint had no sympathy with the reforms that Governor General Thomson was implementing in Upper Canada, since they went counter to his strong support for the established order.

It was only a couple of years ago that Flint had been a magistrate during the rebellion and worked diligently to track down every rebel he could find and bring them to justice.[12] The courts had been frustratingly lenient with the reformers, and even strident letters to people in high places did no good. He hated the idea of the Rebellion Losses Bill, which would lead to such trouble in the next decade, but he would hedge his bets by maintaining relationships with members from both sides of the political spectrum. For Billa Flint, there was always a scheme or a project of some sort in the future, and he meant to make some money out of it one way or another.

After the rebellion, Belleville was made part of Hastings County, and the new sheriff of Hastings County was John Dunbar Moodie, the husband of renowned writer Susanna Moodie. Mr. Moodie had garnered his position due to persistent campaigning with the lieutenant governor and other officials, mostly conducted by his wife. He had proven himself to be no farmer and a good position like this was a great relief.

The Moodie family moved to Belleville from the Otonabee River region, near Peterborough, in late 1839. Sheriff Moodie would perform his duties adequately but would be under constant pressure from the local Tory forces, who saw his friendship with the Reform Party leader, Robert Baldwin, as a direct threat to their interests. Mrs. Moodie would go on to make herself a beloved presence in Belleville. Her sister, Catherine Parr Trail, was also a prolific writer. The sisters produced many publications that would educate thousands of readers, including potential settlers still in the old country, about the challenges and the joys of pioneering in the back woods in Upper Canada.

The hour of rest passed quickly, and the travellers reluctantly returned to the sleigh. Many hands were shaken and greetings expressed, but finally the sleigh with a fresh team, sparkling livery, and a new flickering torch, pulled away from Mansion House and proceeded down the Kingston Road. The governor general and Captain Le Marchant were in good spirits, having much enjoyed their sojourn in Belleville. Mr. Weller was gratified that his old friend, Mr. Munro, had come through for him at this critical moment. He would make a point of thanking him personally after this enterprise was completed.

21

Shannonville, Deseronto, and Napanee

THE TRAVELLERS SOON MOVED FROM THURLOW INTO TYENDINAGA TOWNSHIP. After two relatively short stages, William Weller found it easy to let the horses go a little longer in this stage. The next village on the road was Shannonville, but he did not want to stop there, so in the village he followed the York Road in a southeasterly direction. This would lead to the village of Culbertson's Wharf, later to be known as Deseronto. The modern driver will see that Number 2 Highway goes straight through Shannonville, but it's not hard to see that a significant road branches off to the southeast. This south branch is called the York Road and in 1840 was part of the Kingston Road.

The travellers followed this road across relatively flat land to a point on the shoreline at the eastern extent of the Bay of Quinte. In 1784, a group of twenty Mohawk families had settled here under their leader, Captain Deserontyon (aka Deseronto),[1] taking advantage of grants from the Crown to found what we know of today as the Tyendinaga Mohawk Territory. The first church built by these settlers was St. George's, which was completed in 1794 and would have been in use when the governor general rode by in 1840. Just three years later, it would be replaced by Christ Church.

A grandson of Deseronto, John Culbertson, was granted title to the land of the town site in 1837 and built a mill, starting the settlement that was called Culbertson's Wharf. A major development occurred in 1848 when part of the land was acquired by Amos S. Rathbun and a larger saw mill was built. By 1850, the village was known as Mill Point, which is the name we see on the *Beldon County Atlas Map*, dated 1878.[2] The village was incorporated in 1871, and in 1881, it took the name Deseronto, in honour of the Mohawk chief who brought the first settlers there.

Darkness had fallen in the last hour and William Weller watched closely in the light of the torch, as the miles slipped away under the sleigh runners. He knew the roads were likely to be in rough shape along here because he had driven over them many times before. While the ground was relatively flat, there were some difficult low areas that presented a challenge. His helpers had been out patching a few of these and waved to him as the sleigh sped by. In a couple of places, the driver had been forced to slow down a bit, where the dirt road began to disappear into a marsh. The horses were experienced with these conditions, persistently slogging to the other side, leaving these ugly patches of road behind.

William Weller took up his horn once more as the sleigh approached the village of Culbertson's Wharf. A fresh team was ready at the tavern where arrangements had been made, and the change was quick, sending the travellers on their way.

Soon after leaving Culbertson's Wharf, the travellers moved out of Tyendinaga Township and into Richmond Township. This also took them out of Hastings County and into Lennox County, still part of Midland District. The Kingston Road skirted the north shore of the Napanee River on its way to the town of Napanee. William Weller urged the team to a solid gallop and hoped to make good time in another section of relatively flat country. It was evening now, and most of the local traffic had disappeared, leaving the road clear for the governor general.

The sleigh passed through the heavily wooded countryside, marking the occasional ray of light from the window of a cabin. The terrain along the north shore of the Napanee River was mostly flat with some marshy spots to navigate but nothing that caused much delay. William Weller was anticipating the next stop, which would be well past the town of Napanee, but he was more concerned with how they would manoeuvre through the town.

The modern driver cruises peacefully along Number 2 Highway toward Napanee and encounters the Napanee sign several miles from the centre of town. In 1840, the lonely road ran in the same place, but Napanee was much smaller, clustered around the mills at the bridge. A few shops and homes could be seen on both sides of the Napanee River, but it was obvious that this was a mill town.

In the very early years of settlement, the Napanee River was recognized as a great source for water power. It was larger than most streams in the area and provided falls and rapids that were opportunities for water power development. In preparation for settlers coming to Canada after the War of Independence, the government had built a grist mill at Cataraqui, at the east end of Lake Ontario. This had been a long-standing trading and military post and would be named Kingston in 1788.

By 1786, the need for a mill farther west was satisfied when a mill was built at the falls of the Napanee River.[3] Initially the place was called Apanee Falls, but it later evolved into Napanee. The grist mill was located on the south side of the Napanee River because the ground on that side was less uneven than on the north bank. Both of these grist mills, at Kingston and Napanee, had been built with government funds, while Major Robert Clark, an experienced millwright, was responsible for construction and operation. They were much appreciated by the settlers, who had to carry their corn and grain from their homes, often a great distance away. There were no fees for using the mill, which was also much appreciated at a time when currency was scarce and people were struggling to survive.

In 1792, Richard Cartwright[4] purchased both mills. Cartwright was an aggressive Kingston businessman who had managed to corner the market for flour, and the two mills were very profitable for him for a number of years. He was in the right place at the right time to take advantage of the growing population of Upper Canada and the resulting demand for flour and other goods.

Richard Cartwright also built a saw mill and a grist mill on the north side of the Napanee River in Richmond Township. In the early days, the small village that grew up around the mills on the north side would be called Napanee, and the village on the south side, along the river near the older mill, was called Clarkville, after Robert Clark, who had built the mill there.

When William Weller approached Napanee in February of 1840, he would not have seen many buildings until he was close to the mills. The area to the west was swampy and uneven, but later in that same year, plans would be carried out to extend the village in that direction. Also in 1840, Napanee would see the construction of a canal along the south side of the falls, which would help to control the flow of water to the mills below the falls.

Mr. Weller's main concern at Napanee was the condition of the floating bridge across the river. This had been an ongoing problem over the years, and he had given explicit instructions to his contacts in Napanee to make sure that the old structure was sound and free of obstacles when he came through with the governor general. As he approached the bridge, a fellow was there to wave the sleigh across, and the driver gave a sigh of relief. He was glad to be across the old bridge and noticed with a grin that materials were already being piled nearby for the new and much improved covered bridge to be built once the spring came.

The new bridge would be solid and reliable, requiring little maintenance. Its unique latticework sides would make it a conversation piece and a favourite landmark. It became legendary as one of the best and most long-lasting bridges in Ontario, performing its duties until being removed in 1909, after sixty-nine years of excellent service. After their favourite old bridge was disassembled, town folks would note proudly that most of the planks were sound enough to be used in other construction projects, even after all these years of constant use. They don't build 'em like that anymore![5]

22

Morven and Odessa

AFTER CROSSING THE NAPANEE RIVER, THE TRAVELLERS WERE IN NORTH Fredericksburgh Township, still part of Lennox County. The Kingston Road would make a beeline across the northeastern corner of the township, on its way to the village of Morven, which was at the border with Ernestown Township. William Weller was happy to be across the river and moving ever closer to Kingston, making good progress in their trip. However, there was a challenge as well as an oddity to deal with in the meantime.

The challenge was a long, steep hill that confronted them only a few hundred yards from the river. This was Roblin Hill, so-called because David Roblin, from Prince Edward County, had decided to build a house on top of this rocky prominence. The location afforded a wonderful view of the river valley, but folks were wondering how the family would find water up on this stony ground.

Today we may be accustomed to the sight of rock walls where road construction over the last century has minimized the grade by blasting out tons of rock. However, the kind of rock cut that we see as Number 2 Highway climbs away from Napanee would have been a rare sight for travellers in 1840. The Kingston Road would climb over the top of Roblin Hill, and the horses and driver would have to cope with it. Mr. Weller knew this piece of road very well and simply set the team to the task with persistence and lots of encouragement. Patience was important in places like this because the pace would be reduced to some extent. You just had to get on with it.

The oddity they encountered was the surface of the road. Beginning on the south side of the Napanee River, a new gravel road presented itself to the travelling public. In February of 1840, the governor general and his travelling companions would encounter only one piece of gravel road along the whole length of the trip from Toronto to Montreal. Actually, they called it a macadamized road in those days. There were a few very small experimental examples of this new method for building a road, but they were often in bad shape or actually under construction. None approached the extent or quality of the macadamized road from Napanee to Kingston.

This new piece of road had been completed just a few months previous to the governor general's sleigh ride, and it was still the talk of the countryside. It was one of the largest road-building projects in the province, and it was promoted and championed by none other than John Solomon Cartwright, the youngest son (along with his twin brother Robert David Cartwright) of the old entrepreneur, Richard Cartwright of Kingston.

John Solomon Cartwright[1] had inherited the family fortune and would enhance it in many ways. He became a lawyer and practiced for a time in the law firm of John Beverly Robinson in Toronto. Then he pursued his own law firm in Kingston, which was very successful for many years. In 1832, he became a director with the new Commercial Bank of the Midland District and was immediately chosen as president. As expected, he entered politics in 1834, and after one defeat was elected in opposition to the reformer Marshall Spring Bidwell in 1836. John S. Cartwright would serve in the Assembly for the rest of his life.

Cartwright was involved in many developments in real estate in Kingston, Napanee, and elsewhere, along with generous donations of land and money for churches and schools. It was in the context of Parliamentary committees that John Solomon Cartwright was able to apply his influence to gain approval for this very expensive road-building project in the Midland District. The government set aside $120,000 for the project, which it expected would be repaid through the implementation of toll booths at five mile intervals along the new road.[2]

Many important businessmen in Kingston and Napanee had been asking for a better road between these two major centres. The mills at Napanee were closely connected to the commercial activity in Kingston, and there was lots of traffic in teamster wagons full of flour, lumber, and many other goods, along this critical artery. It was not a unique situation in Upper Canada, but the presence of a man the stature of John Solomon Cartwright, who was willing to expend political capital, made the prospect a reality.

Construction had begun in 1837 and was completed in 1839. Mr. Cartwright encountered some trouble in the Legislature as the original budget for the project proved to be grossly underestimated. Another $12,000 was granted by the government to cover the full cost of completing the road. The politicians in Toronto would ask why this piece of road was so expensive, far more than any other. The answer was that this was a macadamized road, and it was, in this unique case, built according to standards.

Today we would call it a gravel road. In fact, as they became more popular in the next couple of decades, every locality would have at least one gravel road, and often several, in the community. For many years, a gravel road was novel enough for residents to use the word in the familiar name they called the road. In the author's home of Brighton Township, there was The Brighton and Seymour Gravel Road, which would develop into Number 30 Highway, running from Brighton to Campbellford and then to Havelock. Most folks just called it The Gravel.

The word macadamized comes from the inventor of this method of road building, John Loudon McAdam.[3] He was a Scottish civil engineer who made it his life's work to improve road building; he also hoped to make the building of roads less expensive. Roads had been made of stone since Roman times, but in most cases the process was very labour intensive and therefore expensive. As traffic on the roads grew in the later 1700s and early 1800s, there was great pressure to increase the quality of the roads and to reduce the cost of building the increasing number of miles of roads the public demanded.

McAdam developed a method that would step away from the traditional need for a solid stone foundation and developed a method that used small stones on a surface made up of a mixture of crushed rock and soil. The idea was that the small stones would work their way into the surface through contact with vehicles and hooves. His method also included a much more specific design for the foundation of the road, ensuring strength and durability.

In Canada, macadamized roads were slow to catch on, because of their cost and because there was no central authority responsible for road building. John McAdam had written complete instructions, not only about how to build the road, but also how to maintain it. One of his primary recommendations was to have a central organization responsible for road building and to fund the organization adequately. Unfortunately, in Canada in the 1830s, this was just not possible. Local municipalities and prosperous individuals would try to improve the roads, but they seldom found enough money to do a complete job. The first experiment with macadamized roads north of York, in the 1820s, experienced serious problems because the contractors had limited funds and scrimped on the vital components of the roadbed.

And don't even mention maintenance! McAdam made it very clear that a macadamized road would need constant maintenance of a certain type in order to keep the road in good shape. Few local governments in Canada could justify this kind of ongoing cost, and as a result, many of the earlier roads, even if well done in the initial construction, would be in very bad shape in a few years because they were not maintained properly. In the end, it all came down to money.

The governor general reclined in the sleigh and thought of the futility he had witnessed in Upper Canada in this regard. This wonderful road he was riding on had been possible only because a powerful member of the Family Compact had championed it, forcing the large expense through the Legislature. It was clear who would benefit the most from this one large expense – the wealthy merchants and businessmen of Kingston.

He knew that Kingston was a Tory stronghold. He had already engaged in conflict with Mr. Cartwright over the issue of the union of the provinces. Mr. Cartwright had countered his original proposal by adding amendments to ensure that the capital of the Province of Canada would always be in Canada West and that the only language allowed in government would be English. Mr. Thomson had been able to fend off the conservative forces on the first issue but had given way on the second. You had to pick your battles carefully.

As he hunkered down into the warmth of the sleigh and watched the torch light flicker on the side of the road, he grinned with satisfaction. This road was a perfect example of why he would force the creation of a Board of Works, which would be responsible for the planning and construction of roads across the province. It must be managed on a larger scale by qualified engineers, and it must be funded adequately. He believed that every community, not just the wealthy merchants in Kingston, deserved to have a road like this, and the Board of Works should make that happen in the future.

William Weller was familiar with the character of the new road and was looking forward to making better time on the smooth, even surface. On the other hand, he was concerned about damage to the hooves of his horses, due to contact with small pieces of stone. At the very least, it caused horseshoes to wear out much faster than on dirt roads.

In anticipation of this situation, William Weller had shortened the next two stages. He was always conscious of the fifteen-mile guideline and had largely kept to that standard. Even then, there was no rule about making a stage shorter in order to ensure safety and comfort for the horses. He was always very aware of the health of the team and would take steps to ensure their welfare if he felt the need.

The sleigh topped Roblin Hill and moved out onto the flat plain. The Kingston Road stretched arrow-straight in a southeasterly direction, across wooded lands with farmhouses here and there. The driver encouraged his team to take advantage of the solid, smooth road surface, and they picked up the pace accordingly. They were near the end of the stage, but still had lots of energy. William Weller enjoyed these moments, speeding along a good road, letting a good team of horses run hard, with a paying customer in the coach. That is what the stagecoach business was all about.

Four miles from Napanee, William Weller pulled out his horn and gave several loud blasts, in order to alert the folks at the Fralick tavern. At the same time, the sleigh passed the four-mile marker that stood on the north side of the road a short distance west of the Fralick tavern. Today, the same marker sits off the road beside a cornfield, displaying "N IV" on the Napanee side and "K XLX" on the Kingston side. They were four miles from Napanee and fifty miles from Kingston.

The Fralick tavern[4] was one of the most popular stagecoach inns on this section of the Kingston Road. John Fralick,[5] a member of a well-known United Empire Loyalist family, had acquired the land here in 1809 and soon built a simple frame building on the north side of the road. It was constructed in two parts; the larger west side was the main hotel and the smaller part on the east side was the bar room. On the south side of the road were the stables. These buildings are still standing today, although the hotel and bar were converted to a private residence many years ago. Even then, a quick glance from the road is all it takes to realize that this is an historic site. The barn across the road is a bit careworn, but you would be too if you were that old.

22.1 Four Mile Marker. Just west of Morven stands one of the few remaining mile markers of the Napanee and Kingston Gravel Road. Legend has it that markers were installed so that travellers chased off the road by bandits would know where they were when they returned to the road.

This establishment occupied a very strategic location right on the main road and at the intersection with Townline Road, which separated North Fredericksburgh and Ernestown Townships. It was known for excellent hospitality and rousing social life at a time when whisky was cheap and the growing prosperity of the travelling public left a few coins for entertainment.

William Weller pulled the sleigh over to the right side of the road where the fresh team waited. People stood on both sides of the road, over to the left in front of the tavern and on the right beside the stable. There was much clapping and shouting, and it was hard to tell whether it was for William Weller or the governor general.

John Fralick was over seventy at this time, but he insisted on leaving his rocking chair in the front room of the tavern to step outside and greet his guests.

22.2 Fralick Tavern. The popular Fralick tavern stood a few yards east of the four-mile marker on the north side of the Napanee-Kingston Gravel Road. Even today, original features are evident in the clapboard and simple bargeboard along with a pillared veranda.

The governor general drew the window covering for a moment as the old gentleman bowed respectfully. Mr. Fralick was a dedicated reform supporter, and he appreciated the work that Thomson was doing to change the government. Finally, here was a governor general who would do something for the regular folks in this land and not just for the wealthy. Governor General Thomson nodded and then sat back with some satisfaction. It was easy to smile when you were in friendly company.

The reality was that the governor general was at a solid reform establishment when he stopped at the Fralick Tavern. The distinction was well known in the community. Like-minded citizens tended to gather in certain taverns to discuss their political opinions over beer and whisky. Everyone was welcome at the Fralick Inn, of course, and sometimes travellers would be unaware of the context. At election time, however, the partisan divisions were tangible and this place buzzed with excitement.

Elections in general were rowdy affairs in those days, before badly needed reforms were carried out. Money flowed from candidates, and their supporters would make sure that the maximum number of local farmers and mechanics made it to the local tavern, which was often an official polling place. Of course, it was expected they would cast their public vote for the fellow who was paying the tab.

Arrangements were also made to disrupt speeches or to impede the nominations of rival candidates. Elaborate plans were carried out to perform coordinated attacks at the right time and place. Of course, whisky was a powerful tool, used both as lubricant before the event and as welcome payment for a job well done after it was over.

Barrels of whisky were supplied to polling places, and the result was often loud arguments that deteriorated into brawls. Otherwise quiet and sensible men would engage with gusto in these donnybrooks and come home with black eyes to prove they had done their part towards the governance of the country. Elections often stretched out over three or four days, which provided the tavern keeper with a perfect opportunity to maximize his revenue. Certainly, he would have to deduct the cost of damage to his property, but all of this was an accepted part of doing business.

The fresh team was in place quickly and the driver wasted no time pulling back onto the Kingston Road. The new gravel road stretched out flat and straight in front of them, faintly illuminated by the torch light. Mr. Weller was anxious to make good time on the way to Kingston because he knew that the worst of the roads were ahead of them. The weather, too, could be unpredictable. The thaw continued although he was seeing more of the winter snow still present along the road as they moved east. They might have a blizzard at any time, so they had to move along when they could. As the old folks used to say, make hay when the sun shines.

A few miles along the road, Governor General Thomson asked Captain Le Marchant, "Is this where the famous political meeting took place in 1834? The one Mr. Weller told you about?"

The aide-de-camp thought for a moment and said, "Yes, I believe it is. He said it was half way between the taverns of Mr. Fralick and Mr. Gordanier, so I assume that means somewhere in this vicinity."[6]

The two men discussed the story that Mr. Weller had told Captain Le Marchant one day at the General Stage Office in Toronto. The event was a nomination meeting for the upcoming election, which was to be held on Saturday, April 12th, 1834. Mr. Weller had not been at the meeting but had arranged for some stages to be available in the area. Many men wished to attend from all around, even from Kingston and Belleville. It had been a good day for the stage drivers in the area.

The novelty of this meeting never ceased to solicit laughter from an audience, and Mr. Weller was practised in telling the tale. The event was held in a farmer's field on the Kingston Road, exactly half way between the two taverns. This had been decided by the opposing parties as a practical compromise to avoid the inevitable disturbances that would occur if the meeting were held at one or the other of the two establishments. Besides, nobody wanted to give the other guy any advantage.

The Fralick tavern at Morven was a reform haunt, and John Gordanier's tavern, a few miles east at Violet Road, was a Tory stronghold.[7] There had been hot conflict between the two tavern owners for many years, very much based on their opposing political points of view, but also due to the additional tug of family connections. John Fralick had married Lydia Gordanier back in 1796, which linked him directly to his rival tavern owner. John Fralick and John Gordanier were brothers-in-law.

The meeting in 1834 was well attended, the newspaper reporter estimating the crowd at between 800 and 1,000 people, mostly men with some boys as well. There were many well-heeled gentlemen: office-holders or businessmen from Kingston, Napanee, and Belleville, who were clearly Tory supporters. They were there to make sure that their man, John Solomon Cartwright, went home with the nomination. Also in attendance were many plain gentlemen, apparently farmers, mechanics, teamsters, and blacksmiths, who had come to support their man, Marshall Spring Bidwell.

The proceedings were conducted in an orderly manner with Mr. McPherson in the chair and Mr. Detlor as secretary. Everyone had their say, from the wealthiest lawyer and mill owner down to the meekest farmer just in from the field. The result of the vote was much to the satisfaction of the reform gentlemen. Mr. Bidwell would be the nominee and Mr. Cartwright would have to wait until 1836, when Tory sentiment ran high and more resources could be brought to bear. But for now, the reformers had their victory. After the meeting, the assemblage split up, each party retiring to their respective inn to satisfy their thirst after such hard work.

The passengers kept an eye out, and when they passed Violet Road, they could see the lamplight outside of Gordanier's Inn, a lively place even at this time of the evening. Mr. Weller waved to some gentlemen that were standing outside in the yard, and they returned his greeting. Then the travellers continued up the Kingston Road. The gentlemen at Gordanier's Tavern would spread the story about seeing the governor general race by with fire spewing from the rear of the sleigh.[8] The real story was that the iron strips Mr. Weller had added to the sleigh runners interacted with the bare gravel road to cause sparks to fly up behind the vehicle. This odd phenomenon would be reported in the newspapers, and then repeated in terms that would support the speaker's political bent.

Here was another long, straight, and mostly flat section of road that William Weller wanted to see behind him quickly. As much as this new gravel road was easier to drive on, the old horseman grumbled to himself about the damage all these little stones were doing to the horses and sleigh runners. He worried that the horses would suffer, and that was not tolerated in William Weller's stage business. There wasn't much he could do about the fact that this new road existed, and he expected to see more of them as time went by, but he resolved to meet with Mr. Munson in

Cobourg to see if there was a method for dealing with this new problem. It seemed there was one problem after another coming up in front of him. Oh well, it was just part of the business.

As he drove along in the dark, Mr. Weller would not have seen the twelve-mile marker at the side of the road just west of the village of Mill Creek. However, we can see it today, a little west of Odessa, on the north side of Number 2 Highway. There is a well-tended garden featuring this anchor to the past. It is a low, grey stone, hewn on four sides and engraved with the distances from Kingston, designated with a K, and Napanee, designated with an N.

The Napanee-Kingston gravel road was a toll road. William Weller knew that his vehicle was exempt because he carried the governor general, but did the toll booth operator know as well? Drivers complained constantly about the behaviour of toll booth operators, and there were often confrontations when disagreements turned nasty. It could be a lucrative business enterprise to hold the commission for a toll booth in front of your house or at the corner of your barn, but the cut you could take from the tolls hardly made the abuse worthwhile.

A short distance along the road, a cluster of lights at the side of the road identified the small village of Mill Creek. At this time there were a few wooden buildings scattered around John Link's grist mill on the creek. A new covered bridge had been built over Mill Creek so that travellers on the Kingston Road had convenient passage through the village.

One building that William Weller may have glimpsed in the torch light, as the sleigh sped through Mill Creek, was the store of Parker Smith Timmerman[9]. This was a handsome, new stone building on the southeast corner of the Kingston Road (Main Street) and Factory Street, a little east of the bridge. Parker S. Timmerman was an enterprising young businessman who had run a general store for a time, before building a new structure to house an expanded operation. He would later build an almost identical building on the west side of the same corner. Both of these historic stone buildings still stand on either side of Factory Street in Odessa, important parts of the built heritage of the community.

Not long after the governor general sped by his store, Parker S. Timmerman took over as postmaster for Mill Creek, using space in his new store for the post office. He would also rename the village Odessa in 1855 in recognition of the success of the British in the Crimean War, which he was following closely from news reports. He would be engaged in the development of Odessa in many ways over the following decades.

22.3 Timmerman Store. Today there are two very old and almost identical stone buildings on either side of Factory Street in Odessa. The building on the east side (left in picture) is now 155 Main Street and was built by Parker Smith Timmerman before 1840 to host his general store and the local post office. The building on the west side of Factory Street, now a bank, was built using the same design a few years later.

There is a small but important story connected with Parker Smith Timmerman and his work as the postmaster at Mill Creek.[10] He became frustrated by the extensive time required to search through the large mail bag every time a mail stage stopped at his post office. At any time of the day or night, the post master was expected to stop what he was doing and search through all the mail in the bag to find those items destined for his post office.

Young Mr. Timmerman was impatient with this sort of inefficiency and resolved to do something about it. He suggested to post office authorities that mail addressed to different regions or towns could be carried in separate bags. This meant that items were sorted when they came into the mail stream. In effect, the mail stage could carry several small bags, each dedicated to a region or town, rather than one large bag. This suggestion came at a time when the volume of mail had grown dramatically and the complexity of addressing the mail had increased. The managers of the system saw this idea in a positive light, and it was implemented.

The modern reader might grin at this, but we should remember that complex systems, such as the post office, evolved over the last couple of centuries with practices coming from Europe and also evolved based on the practical needs on the ground in Canada. Procedures for common services we take for granted were in their infancy when William Weller drove the sleigh past Mr. Timmerman's store. Small, incremental steps such as this were happening every day, in all walks of life. In his own way, Mr. Weller was contributing to that kind of growth and change by the way he managed his stage lines.

But one might wonder how Mr. Weller reacted when his mail stage drivers were told to carry half a dozen small bags instead of one large one. A change like this would have practical effects on how his drivers carried the bags, where they stored them, how they handled them at each stop and what measures they took to protect them from theft and damage. Taking a longer view, we can see that this may have been the beginning of the later move toward dedicated mail wagons as well as strict regulations about who could carry mail and how it would be handled.

23
Kingston

THE SLEIGH MOVED EASILY ALONG THE KINGSTON ROAD IN A SOUTHEASTERLY direction, taking advantage of smooth terrain and a good road surface. The temperature had edged down below freezing as the evening progressed. Both driver and passengers were pulling their coats more tightly around their shoulders to keep warm. The horses ran mechanically as the miles passed under their feet, each step bringing them closer to the next stage stop.

Soon the travellers moved from Ernestown Township into Kingston Township, part of Frontenac County. The next small village down the road was called Slab City, because of the large slabs of wood used for building houses, which were produced at a local sawmill. Later this place would be called Westbrook.

It was time for another change of horses, so William Weller picked up his horn and gave a few blasts as they approached Slab City. It was very dark, but Mr. Weller could see lamplight in front of the tavern. As he drove up, he saw that a fresh team was standing ready. A quick change was made, and in less than five minutes, the sleigh was on the road again. The town of Kingston lay ahead.

William Weller was very familiar with the long-standing problem with the Kingston Road in this area. Collins Creek came north from Collins Bay and branched southeast of Slab City, sending one branch west and the other on to the northeast. The west branch proceeded directly west just below Slab City and then turned north across the road a mile or so west of the village. There were some low and wet spots to the west, but they were minor compared to the large boggy area to the east of the village. For many years, this area was known as one of the worst sections of the Kingston Road, especially in spring and fall.

Here was a place where William Weller welcomed the new macadamized road, in spite of his trepidations about wear and tear on the horses. The Napanee and Kingston Road Society had spent the money necessary to build a solid roadbed to support the new road across the wetlands. It could flood at times in the spring but the surface of the road was high enough now that travel was not impeded, as it would have been in previous years. This was progress!

Today, your GPS will say that Princess Street starts at the big Kingston sign between Odessa and Westbrook. However, William Weller saw no such sign and knew of no such street name as he approached Kingston. As far as he was concerned, he was still on the Kingston Road, and he would follow it down Store Street, all the way into the middle of the town. Store Street had been named well before the War of 1812, suggesting the presence of a large government store at the end of the road, near the wharf. Store Street was changed to Princess Street late in 1840 in honour of Queen Victoria, who had come to the throne on the death of her father, William IV, in 1837. Little did they know at the time that Victoria was destined to become Britain's longest serving monarch, only to be exceeded by Elizabeth II, in 2015.

The next cluster of buildings the travellers would pass was the village of Waterloo. This prosperous little community of farmers and tradesmen had recently built a new brick Methodist Church, replacing the original wooden structure that had been built in the 1790s. The church and much of the village was north of the Kingston Road, along Loughboro Road, which is now Sydenham Road.

Within a decade, the village of Waterloo would be chosen as the location for a large new public cemetery for the city of Kingston, very much in response to the fear of disease from burials in many locations around the city. The Cataraqui Cemetery Company was formed in 1850, representing a very new approach to urban cemeteries that would be utilized around the country. The cemetery was located on seventy acres in Waterloo village, and it would be organized as a corporation administered by a Board of Trustees.

Soon after, the name of the village would be changed to Cataraqui, partly to reflect the cemetery but also because of a conflict in the postal system with the duplicate town name of Waterloo, which was located west of Toronto. The Cataraqui Cemetery would be managed based on emerging standards and techniques, and would become the lovely garden cemetery that draws visitors as a tourist destination today. Many early settlers and local personalities have found resting places in the pleasant wooded grounds, including Canada's first prime minister, Sir John A. Macdonald.[1]

At Waterloo, the Kingston Road swung to the right, continuing in a southeasterly direction, towards the town of Kingston. William Weller was very familiar with the hills and valleys in this area, but was confident that the team would have no trouble. The new macadamized road was truly a benefit in places like this, in contrast to the previous dirt road, which could be very difficult to navigate up and down these hills. There were several miles to cover on the way into Kingston, where they would have their next change of horses. The evening was getting late by this time, and the temperature was below freezing, but the travellers were making good time.

The countryside this far from Kingston was still very rural, mostly woods and the occasional farmhouse. Two important intersections would appear on the Kingston Road in short order. The first was Portsmouth Road, which came north from the village of Portsmouth, on the shoreline just west of Kingston. United Empire Loyalists settled there in 1784, and the construction of the Kingston Penitentiary in 1833 spurred the growth of a village in support.

The second intersection was Bath Road, which was a very early road that connected Kingston to the town of Bath to the west. It was on the first concession line and had functioned as the route into Kingston from the west, long before the Kingston Road came down from the northwest to meet it after the War of 1812. Today, it is also known as Highway 33, or Loyalist Parkway.

This was a major intersection on the new macadamized Kingston Road, so a toll booth was present. William Weller had experienced no problem with toll booths along the Napanee to Kingston section, until now. The toll booth keepers knew that government officials were exempt from tolls, and the queen's coat-of-arms on the door of the coach was enough to make it very clear if the attendant was unaware of the situation. Besides that, Weller's messengers had been all along the line in the previous few days, making sure everyone knew to simply let the governor general through.

However, the toll booth at Bath Road was constructed with a gate that needed to be manually lifted and lowered to let travellers pass. A large wooden box acted as a counter-weight on the short end of the gate, and it was heavy enough to require one large man pushing down on it to lift the gate, or maybe two teenagers working together. As Mr. Weller approached the toll booth, he saw that the gate was down, so he sounded the horn to alert the toll booth keeper. When the sleigh came to within a few dozen yards, he could see that the gate was still closed.

He blew on his horn once more, this time long and hard. As the sleigh came up to the closed toll gate, a young fellow came scurrying out of the building with his hand out, waiting to be paid, as was his normal habit. Mr. Weller yelled very loudly, "It is the governor general, sir! Let us pass!"

The young man stood stock-still, drowsy from his snoozing and uncertain what to do. His father, who was the owner of the toll booth commission, had taught his two sons to persist with travellers because many folks would try to avoid paying. Mr. Weller yelled again, and this time pointed to the coat-of-arms on the side of the coach.

Finally, the young man caught on and scrambled to the toll gate. He struggled to put enough weight on it to lift the gate. His brother was already in bed, and by himself, he was not quite heavy enough to tip the scales. Mr. Weller could see that this was not going to work, so he jumped from the sleigh, ran to the toll gate and pressed down on the counter-weight beside the boy. The gate swung up, and Mr. Weller jumped back onto the sleigh, took the reins and moved the sleigh under the open gate. Not looking back, he encouraged the team to resume their pace.

The young man at the toll booth stood there feeling like an idiot. No less than the governor general had been delayed going through their toll booth. He feared he would be in trouble. As he returned to the house, he saw his brother in his drawers at the front door. "Sorry, Jimmy, I forgot to tell you the governor general was coming through tonight." The brothers spelled each other off on the toll gate during the day, and the message had not been passed on to the brother who would be on duty later in the evening. The boy at the door snickered and said, "Oh, well, if Pa finds out, he can thrash both of us."

William Weller was not concerned about the boys at the toll booth but was intent on wasting no more time on the run into Kingston. Once they were south of Bath Road, they were on Store Street, which would go straight into the centre of Kingston to the Lambton Hotel. They would do a quick change of horses there and then take the Cataraqui Bridge across the Cataraqui River to continue the trek toward Montreal.

There were only a few buildings along the Kingston Road below Bath Road, and the travellers continued in darkness except for their own torch light. Soon they came to a primary intersection, where Division Street crossed Store Street. This was a main road, which led into Kingston from the northern concessions. Not far past Division Street, Store Street bent slightly to the east to complete its last run into Kingston.

The town of Kingston, which the travellers approached, was still the largest urban centre in Upper Canada. It had been incorporated only two years before in 1838. During the 1830s, Kingston had experienced significant growth due to the completion of the Rideau Canal in 1832, which had its southern terminus at the mouth of the Cataraqui River. Traffic in lumber and wheat came through the town, and many settlers departed from Kingston for the upper concessions. The population of Upper Canada doubled during the 1830s, and Kingston was very much part of that growth.

This strategic location at the east end of Lake Ontario had been recognized by the French fur traders who came out from New France in the seventeenth century. Fort Frontenac was built in 1673 on the north shore, at the mouth of the Cataraqui River, and a cluster of log buildings around the fort was called Cataraqui. It served as a fur trading post and military base until it was captured by the British and then destroyed in 1758.

At the end of the American Revolutionary War, United Empire Loyalists fled to Upper Canada. The location of Cataraqui was recognized once more as being very important, and reports indicated that the land beyond was well suited for settlement. A British Naval base had been established during the war on Carleton Island in the St. Lawrence River, but that island was ceded to the Americans at the end of the war, so the navy had to move. The mouth of the Cataraqui River was seen as a perfect place for a harbour and naval base, so Fort Frontenac was restored and a dockyard and garrison established.

During the war, a group of loyalists had come to Carleton Island, along with the military. Then, in 1783, when Carleton Island was ceded to the Americans, some of them moved over to Cataraqui. These included Molly Brant, sister of Joseph Brant, leader of the Six Nations, as well as Richard Cartwright, who would become a prominent businessman and politician. Michael Grass brought another group of loyalists to the area in 1784. Around the year 1788, the village of Cataraqui, which had been commonly known as the King's Town by soldiers and settlers alike, was shortened down to Kingston, and the name stuck.

Inside the sleigh, the governor general considered the town of Kingston as he drew near. He saw it as a Tory stronghold where his reform agenda encountered serious opposition. There were some very powerful people here, such as John Solomon Cartwright, and the governor general never felt very welcome. His reputation as a reforming force preceded him, and while there were reform-minded folks in Kingston, it was the members of the Family Compact that seemed to be most vocal. Reclining comfortably in the sleigh on this chilly night, Mr. Thomson was happy to be passing through.

Very early in the settlement of Kingston and area, the presence of excellent limestone was discovered in the area, and many limestone buildings would be built over the following decades, creating the moniker, "The Limestone City". Some of the earliest military buildings were of limestone, along with commercial buildings and homes. After the Rideau Canal was complete in 1832, an influx of unemployed stonemasons took advantage of the growing demand for fine homes in Kingston.

At Clergy Street, William Weller saw St. Andrew's Presbyterian Church, which had been built only a few years before. It is considered the first stone church in Kingston. At a meeting in this church, less than a year before, a young lawyer named

John A. Macdonald had seconded a motion that led to the founding of Queen's University. Macdonald had opened his own law office in Kingston in 1835, and four years later moved both office and home to the more fashionable Queen Street. He was an up-and-comer in Kingston and would make his mark on his adopted homeland by driving towards Confederation and becoming the first prime minister of Canada in 1867.

After passing Clergy Street, William Weller took up his horn once more and gave several blasts to alert the folks at the Lambton Hotel of their imminent arrival. The sleigh passed Montreal Street, and then on the right, the Lambton Hotel sign could be seen in the light of two lamps in front of the building. They crossed Rear Street, which would later take the name Bagot Street, honouring another governor general. Then they came to a large yard that led to the front of the hotel. A fresh team stood ready in the yard with several people standing around in anticipation.[2]

As the sleigh pulled into the yard and stopped, there was much shouting, clapping, and waving of hats. William Weller was well known at this establishment, and the presence of the governor general would always draw a crowd. One of the gentlemen standing near the team shouted a greeting to Mr. Weller, and the driver stood and bowed elegantly in return. This was Mr. Osterhout, the proprietor of the Lambton Hotel. The two men had done business for several years and were good friends. Mr. Osterhout ran a tight ship at the Lambton, ensuring that the travelling public enjoyed prompt and efficient service in the stables and dining room. Mr. Weller appreciated this sort of business associate, and there had been little choice as to the establishment for this stop.

The Lambton was one of the most popular hotels in Kingston at that time, sharing the business with the British-American Hotel and the Royal Exchange.[3] Only two years before, it had taken the name Lambton from the governor general who had preceded the passenger in Mr. Weller's sleigh. The naming of the hotel honoured John George Lambton, 1st Earl of Durham,[4] whom we know today as Lord Durham. It was a popular marketing method of the time to use the name of the most important public figure of the time. It's no surprise that the names of governors general appear all across our maps today.

Lord Durham had come to Canada just after the Mackenzie Rebellion and was charged with reporting to the government in London about the conditions that had led to the rebellion. What were these Canadians so distressed about that they would go to the unacceptable length of an armed uprising? English gentlemen simply could not understand it.

Durham was a well-known reformer with rather radical tendencies, and when he issued his Durham Report[5] in January 1839, it recommended the union of Upper and Lower Canada and many other changes that would kick the governance of the colonies into the modern age. Governor General Thomson, his successor, was then sent to Canada to implement these changes.

The naming of the Lambton House may indicate another reason why William Weller counted Mr. Osterhout as a friend as well as an associate. Lord Durham had raised the hackles of the Family Compact by his penchant for reform, and we might expect that naming one's hotel in his honour would be seen as a partisan act, especially in the strong Tory town of Kingston.

The change of teams was performed in the usual time, and the stop was uneventful except for the substitute of the governor general's flask for the water jug, which was very welcome for the hard-working driver. A good nip of port certainly hit the spot! With that, the travellers were once more on their way down Store Street.

The sleigh was now moving through the busy downtown of the largest town in Upper Canada. Even at this hour, there were a few pedestrians and men on horseback, possibly on their way home from the tavern. Buildings lined the streets here, and it was very dark except for the occasional lamp at a hotel or tavern. Wellington Street came up quickly, and just across on the left side, William Weller could see a three-storey stone house amongst the older wooden buildings. This building can be seen today at 85 Princess Street, having survived all these years.

A few buildings farther along on the same side, there was a large, two-storey stone building with distinctive gables. Built in 1820 as a coffee house to support the stagecoach traffic between York and Montreal, this building has hosted many different businesses as well as a library and grammar school. Today, it continues that tradition at 75-77 Princess Street and is one of the key stops on the history walking tours.[6]

Across the street there is another very old structure, at 68 Princess Street. We might be fooled by the date "1893" high up in the unique central gable, but underneath this relatively modern façade is the traditional stone of the original 1820s house, which William Weller would have seen as he sped by in 1840.

Very soon, the sleigh neared King Street, where the driver was going to turn left. King Street had been the primary east-west street in downtown Kingston for many years, providing the through route from Portsmouth to the crossing over the Cataraqui River. The modern driver can follow the signs for Number 2 Highway all the way down Princess Street, to Ontario Street, turn left, and follow along to the Cataraqui Bridge. However, in 1840, Ontario Street was called Front Street. It was not a main artery, but used to service the wharfs, hotels, and commercial establishments near the shoreline.

23.1 Coffee House. Today, the structure at 75-77 Princess Street is Vandervoort's General Store.

As William Weller turned left onto King Street, he was passing along the edge of an area that would change dramatically in the next few years. The market was located along the west side of Store Street and north of Front Street, just off to his right. In 1842, a spectacular new courthouse and jail would be built on this site, facing the shoreline with a dramatic façade and commanding tower.

As the sleigh skidded along the plank road on King Street, the governor general may have been contemplating the political opposition he would have to cope with in this town, but he had no crystal ball. Within the next year, while the union of Upper and Lower Canada was being finalized, there was much heated argument over where the capital of this new Province of Canada would be located. It was a contentious partisan issue. The French wanted the capital in Canada East, and the English wanted it in Canada West. Compromise was hard to find.

Finally, Governor General Thomson was able to suggest a solution that nobody liked, but was grudgingly supported by both sides. It was called the "ambulatory method", which means that the capital would be located in one district for four years and then would go to the other side for four years. There were actually two issues combined in this fight: one was the use of the French language in the Legislature and the other was the location of the capital. Thomson was able to win the struggle to make French a part of the procedures in the Legislature, but he had to construct a virtual road down the middle of intransigence for the other issue – thus the ambulatory method.

Kingston was selected as an acceptable location for the capital in the first four years. The governor general was initially not very happy about this, but he cut his losses and made a deal that would allow the process to move forward. On July 11, 1841, he wrote to London on the topic: "I have every reason to be satisfied with having selected this place (Kingston) as the new capital. There is no situation in the province so well adapted for the seat of Government from its central position; and certainly, we are as near England as we should be anywhere else in the whole of Canada. My last letters reached me in fifteen days, from London! So much for steam and railways."[7]

The merchants and leading town folk of the town were ecstatic! Finally, their town would have its due recognition. Several decades earlier, Kingston had been overlooked in the selection of the capital of Upper Canada, when Lieutenant Governor John Graves Simcoe chose to build a new town at York and make it the capital. The attitude amongst the powerful at the time, like merchant Richard Cartwright, had been indignation at the folly of building an entire new town, when a perfectly good one existed with a military base and excellent transportation facilities. Kingston was already acting as the supply depot for military activities on and around Lake Ontario, as well as providing help for settlers coming to the area. This slight had never been forgotten.

Now Kingston would boom as the capital of the Province of Canada. Government would move in and need large and very fine buildings, streets would be upgraded, and the town would grow by leaps and bounds. The population of Kingston would grow dramatically in the next few years. Imagine the profits the developers and merchants would realize as this played out over the decades in the future. Of course, there was little talk of the ambulatory method whereby the capital would move in four years. How could they? That would be the ultimate folly! The capital would stay in Kingston, and that was that.

As a result, a large multi-use building was planned and constructed on the lot where the old market had been, east of Store Street and south of King Street. It would include government offices, courthouse and jail, marketplace, post office, customs office, and more. Front Street was much improved and renamed Ontario Street. Optimism permeated the community from 1840 to 1844 as many fine stone houses were built, a good number of them to the west of the new complex in the area of the hospital and university. Much of Kingston's built heritage stems from this rush of development around 1842.

Then, in 1844, the wheels fell off. The capital was moved to Montreal, much to the chagrin of the merchants and others in Kingston who had made major investments and had started to make many improvements across the region, banking on the capital being in Kingston. Many loans were over-extended, and finally, defaulted. Buildings sat empty for years afterward, including large parts of the wonderful complex on Ontario Street.

The travellers moved quickly down King Street on a relatively new plank road similar to King Street in Toronto. Soon they crossed Barrack Street and came to the new development called Place D'Armes, immediately north of the Tete Du Pont Barracks. This area was under construction at this time but would result in a wide boulevard with businesses on east and west sides.

Most of the barracks buildings that existed in 1840 had been built in the 1820s, as the military presence increased due to the threat of American incursion. Today, this location is the home to the Fort Frontenac National Historic Site,[8] where visitors can take a glimpse back into the earliest days of Canadian history. Archeological work has uncovered original stone walls from the time of La Salle in the 1600s.

William Weller was intent on leaving the town behind and making better time in the unpopulated areas to the east of Kingston. Their trip through the town had been surprisingly uneventful, and the driver hoped his good luck would continue as they crossed the Cataraqui Bridge. He had crossed this bridge many times before but always felt uneasy until he was all the way across.

23.2 The Cataraqui Bridge was built in 1829 to replace a ferry service between Kingston and Point Frederick. This watercolour by Ella Isabell Fraser shows the toll booth and the long, low shape of the bridge and the draw bridge.

The causeway and bridge that crossed the Cataraqui River was built by the Cataraqui Bridge Company and officially called "The Cataraqui Bridge", although most folks called it the "Penny Bridge" when it opened in June of 1829.[9] It was a toll bridge which cost a penny for pedestrians. The long, low, squat structure was 1,800 feet long and 25 feet wide, with a rough plank road on top, supported by timber cribs and pilings. Near the middle, there was a building that housed the toll booth, and there was also a drawbridge that allowed boat traffic through.

The Rideau Canal opened in 1832, with its southern terminus at the head of Cataraqui Bay. Boat traffic dramatically increased between the lumber town of Ottawa and the business centre of Kingston, so it was a growing challenge to keep vehicle and pedestrian traffic moving on the bridge and also allow boats to cross between the upper Cataraqui River basin and the St. Lawrence River.

Since the first years of settlement, there had been a ferry across the river at this location, operated by James Knapp. The ferry was described as an old scow that was guided by a rope connected at either shore and propelled by soldiers from the barracks. Local lore suggests that Mr. Knapp's last ferry lies forgotten under the waves of the Cataraqui River.

The Cataraqui Bridge required constant maintenance. There were routine tender requests in the newspapers around the time the governor general drove across, asking for contractors to replace timber with stone, drive more pilings, and repair planking on the road. Management of the toll booth was contracted out as well, with the hope that a private business could take a cut of the tolls to make it worthwhile. The fact that the toll operators changed so constantly might suggest that it was not a particularly profitable enterprise.[10]

Mr. Weller slowed the team to a walk and eased them onto the west end of the bridge. The planking was very worn and much weathered, cracked, and broken in some places. The ravages of another harsh Canadian winter were awaiting routine spring repairs. Many plank roads were known to be rough, but the stretch across the Cataraqui Bridge was particularly bad. You had to go slow and take care.

It was almost midnight when William Weller sounded his horn on approaching the toll booth. The attendant had been snoozing inside the building, but came out on hearing the horn. He recognized Mr. Weller right away and hurried to raise the gate. He waved the governor general across with a slight bow, probably meant more for Mr. Weller than his passenger. Toward the east end of the bridge, the drawbridge was crossed, and soon the team set foot on the soil of Pittsburgh Township. The city of Kingston was behind them.

On the map of Pittsburgh Township in the *Beldon County Atlas* (1878),[11] the Kingston Road is shown to go directly east from the Cataraqui Bridge and touch the head of Navy Bay, before swinging sharply north and meeting the concession line at Barriefield. The entire section below Barriefield is labelled as "Military Reserve". The modern driver sees a slightly different arrangement as Number 2 goes northeast from the bridge and does not go near the head of Navy Bay.

The village of Barriefield was started as early as 1814, when homes were needed for the increasing number of military officers manning the Naval Dock Yards on Point Frederick and Fort Henry at Point Henry. These sites were enhanced again during the Mackenzie Rebellion, as the location at the confluence of the St. Lawrence, Lake Ontario, and the Rideau Canal was seen as critical for the defence of Upper Canada.

Many of the original buildings from the 1820s have been preserved in Barriefield to leave a wonderful collection of heritage sites that are protected by the Barriefield Heritage Conservation District Plan,[12] recently updated in 2016. A visit to Barriefield provides a fascinating glimpse of a common streetscape in the mid-1800s.

William Weller was happy to say goodbye to Kingston and the macadamized section of the Kingston Road. Yes, he agreed that the gravel surface was helpful in some ways, but he was glad to be back on good old dirt, a sentiment he expected his horses would share. He let the team find a good pace, and the travellers set out on the relatively flat and straight road that skirted the uneven shoreline of the St. Lawrence River east of Kingston.

24

Gananoque

NOW THAT THE TRAVELLERS WERE EAST OF KINGSTON, THEY WERE NO LONGER ON the Kingston Road. From Kingston to Montreal, the main road along the shoreline was generally known as the King's Highway, although this name was applied less persistently than was the case west of Kingston. Closer to Montreal, it was often called the Montreal Road. No matter what you called it, the road from Kingston to Montreal would present greater challenges, a fact that was very well known to the driver.

There were very few settlements in the twenty miles between Kingston and Gananoque, but it was a bit too long for a stage run. The driver knew of a small place called Pitts Ferry, about half way to Gananoque and had made arrangements with the proprietor of the local blacksmith shop to service them tonight.

But first, they had to navigate a difficult causeway across an inlet of the St. Lawrence River. The modern driver will identify this spot very easily, just west of Abbey Dawn Road and leading across to the Treasure Island Marina. Number 2 Highway is high and dry today, after more than a century of building up the causeway, but we might expect that in 1840, no such structure existed. There may have been a floating bridge such as the one at Napanee.

Whatever the structure, William Weller had tackled this crossing many times before and knew how to handle it in all types of weather and road conditions. Before starting across, he stopped and asked his passengers to join him on the bench, just in case the sleigh encountered problems on the way across. Then he eased the team across, talking to the horses with his calm tone and keeping a persistent presence on the reins. There was still ice up to the bridge on both sides, but the structure swayed and undulated, creaked and groaned, as they passed over, leaving the governor general hanging on to the bench with white knuckles on both hands. He had great confidence in Mr. Weller, but just for a few moments, he began to entertain some doubts about this bridge.

Then the ordeal was over, and the horses stomped onto the solid ground on the other side. The passengers took up their normal position in the coach, much relieved to be rid of this dangerous point in the trip.

The travellers had moved out of good agricultural land in the last few miles and began to encounter more rocky hills and swamps. For many miles to come, the King's Highway would follow up and down over hills and around the edge of swamps, responding to the natural terrain. On a map, the road looks relatively straight but that's not what Mr. Weller would see on the ground. He always planned to spend extra time dealing with this section. There were dirt sections here and corduroy sections there, all in more or less passable condition. He knew that the best roads he would see on this trip had passed under the sleigh long ago.

The night was pitch black, and the temperature had dipped below freezing. The driver squinted into the darkness ahead of the horses, trying to determine the condition of the road ahead. In a few cases, he stopped the sleigh and walked ahead a few paces with the torch, to make sure that the corduroy in a certain spot was adequate or to check the integrity of a small bridge. His associates had done a good job of removing obstacles, even out in this more remote part of the route. The sleigh kept moving.

Mr. Weller could always tell he was drawing near Pitts Ferry because the ground flattened a bit and more cleared fields with farm houses appeared. At Pitts Ferry, he turned south onto the road that led to the ferry across to Howe Island. There were several farms on Howe Island and lumbering was under way, so there was a small ferry port and wharf along the north shore of Bateau Channel.

Howe Island is a large island in the St. Lawrence, hugging the north shore with the narrow Bateau Channel on its north side and the larger St. Lawrence River on the south. William Casey had been the first settler here, stationed as a guard during the War of 1812.[1] The forests on the island were early targets of the timber and lumber trade, and its location made harvesting and delivering product easier than going inland, so these acres were cleared early.

In 1840, down at the ferry port, there was a blacksmith shop, which could double as a stage stop in a pinch. Mr. Weller pulled out his horn as he approached and hoped against hope he would see some activity. As he came to the front of the ramshackle wooden building, a teenage boy was struggling to lead a team into place. He was all alone and carried a very inadequate torch, but was able to make the horses ready, with harnesses more or less in place, as the sleigh came out of the darkness and stopped.

Mr. Weller was off the sleigh in a second and assisted the young fellow in changing the teams. This would not be a quick five-minute stop, but the job was accomplished, and Mr. Weller could not be too critical. Some of the more remote locations were persistent problems for stagecoach proprietors, not just for special requests like this one, but for general daily stage runs. There were few experienced people in the area, and you had to make do with the service you could find.

Pitts Ferry would have a post office in later years, and the modern traveller can see the same service with a bank of postal boxes along the road just below Number 2. Today, the road down to the ferry is a bit farther east, and this old road, called Channelview Road, goes down to some lovely modern homes. The current ferry crossing is at the end of Howe Island Ferry Road, which as it heads north of Number 2 is the Joyceville Road.

The team galloped along the King's Highway east from Pitts Ferry, enjoying the flat terrain for a time. Then, there was another challenge at a bridge over an inlet of the St. Lawrence. The bridge was rickety, but solid enough to help the travellers on their way with no problem. A few miles along, the travellers left Frontenac County and entered Leeds County, without benefit of the roadside signs we enjoy today.

The small hamlet of Willowbank slipped past in the darkness as the driver kept his attention on the road and the team. His passengers snoozed as best they could in the warm furs of the coach. They would not notice the old Willowbank Cemetery on their left as they came to the village, a resting place for the original settlers and builders of this village as well as the town of Gananoque, soon to appear to the east.

Today, an historical plaque at Willowbank Cemetery celebrates first settlers Johan Gottlieb Loede and his wife Mary Lang Klein who met at Fort Haldimand on Carleton Island in the summer of 1783, before the British forces moved to Kingston the next year.[2] The young Hessian soldier would take the Anglicized name "Lloyd", and the young couple would settle at Willowbank, on the north shore of the St. Lawrence, at a place dominated by large willow trees hanging over the banks of a creek.

A memorial for Col. Joel Stone[3] is also here, even though his early home was to the east in Gananoque. As a young merchant in Connecticut with obvious loyalist sentiments, Stone had his property confiscated and was forced to flee to New York, where he volunteered with the British forces. He was imprisoned by the patriots but managed to escape, returning to the merchandizing business in New York. Then he spent some time in England, petitioning for compensation for his losses before returning to Canada.

By the early 1790s, Stone was established at the mouth of the Gananoque River, engaged in trade between Montreal and York. He acquired real estate on the mainland and on Howe Island and developed mills and other commercial enterprises, including the first ferry across the river. Stone was a persistent petition writer and managed to obtain several positions in local government, such as justice of the peace, customs collector, and roads commissioner. Every little settlement had its own mover and shaker and Joel Stone served in that role for Gananoque.

On entering Gananoque from the west, the modern traveller on Number 2 Highway is instructed by a large overhead sign that he or she is entering the "Canadian Gateway to the Thousand Islands." William Weller would not have seen a sign like this but might not have been surprised to know that this beautiful region would become one of the most popular Canadian tourist destinations. He would also miss the many motels and resorts that line the road into town for the modern driver.

In 1840, Gananoque was a growing centre of trade and commerce located at the mouth of the Gananoque River. There were saw and grist mills up the river and wharfs and a substantial port at the St. Lawrence. Around the wooden bridge across a narrower part of the river, the beginnings of industrial Gananoque had been established. It would have a painful downturn for a time but then would develop, in the next decades, into what came to be known as "The Birmingham of Canada,"[4] with its extensive skilled labour force and many factories producing bolts, rivets, and shovels as well as carriages and the many replacement parts required to maintain fleets of stagecoaches and teamster wagons.

The team galloped along the main road, now called King Street West, in the darkness of the wee hours of the morning. On the right side, William Weller would see Main Street, which led down to the lakeshore and the wharf area. Soon after Main Street, the road turned left to cross the wooden bridge. Torches had been lit on each end of the bridge by one of Mr. Weller's helpers. The young man stood shivering in the cold, waiting for his famous friend to drive by.

Just across the bridge, now on King Street East, the driver pulled out his horn and gave the normal warning blasts. On the south side of the road, a fresh team stood ready at a tavern. The change was done quickly, and the sleigh was off again. On his left, Mr. Weller may have seen a lantern at the stables beside the finest house in Gananoque. This large, two-storey brick house had been built in 1831 by the wealthy John McDonald,[5] who ran a very large grist-mill complex on the river in Gananoque. His milling business benefited greatly from a colonial privilege granted in the 1830s for wheat and flour produced in Upper Canada. This complex of factories and mills was, in 1840, one of the largest and most modern industrial sites in all the Canadian colonies. In 1911, the McDonald family deeded the house and property to the town of Gananoque, and today the building is utilized as the Gananoque Town Hall.

24.1 McDonald House, Gananoque, today Gananoque Town Hall

William Weller encouraged the fresh team to run at a good pace as they left Gananoque behind. At this point, the King's Highway moved in a northeasterly direction, away from the St. Lawrence River, avoiding the inlets and running on high, dry ground. It was pitch black with only the flickering of the torch to light the way. No traffic was on the road at this hour, and the surface of the road had hardened to a degree due to the lower night temperatures. The road in this area was relatively good, and the travellers took advantage of it to move swiftly along.

The first settlement along the King's Highway east of Gananoque was Legge, so named for Joseph Legge, who had married a sister of Charles McDonald, early developer of mills at Gananoque and older brother of John McDonald. Joseph Legge had moved from Gananoque in 1827 to take up residence two miles east, where County Road 34 meets Number 2 Highway. His son, Charles Legge, would be a prolific civil engineer, engaged in canal and railway building.

The next stage would be a quiet one for the three travellers. The governor general and Captain Le Marchant were trying to sleep as much as they could under the warm buffalo robes, in between bumps and swerves of the sleigh. The driver pulled his coat tight around his shoulders against the chill, damp night and squinted into the blackness ahead. They still had a long way to go.

The small settlement of Wilstead passed by quickly, and then Keyes Corner appeared, so named because of the early settlers Asahel and Sarah Keyes. The house on the northwest corner of Keyes Road and Highway 2 is associated with the Keyes family. This area north of the St. Lawrence River had been settled a little later than townships to the east and west, due to the rocky nature of the terrain near the river. As a result, in 1840, when the governor general drove through, there were fewer farms than they were accustomed to seeing on the road.

Driving on into the night, the sleigh sped past Ebenezer and then approached the settlement at Lansdowne, the intersection of the King's Highway and Reynolds Road. On the north side of the road, just before Reynolds Road, hidden by darkness and trees, was the substantial stone house of Alexander McNeil and his wife Abigail, who was a daughter of Asahal and Sarah Keyes. Mr. Weller may not have seen the lovely stone house, but today we can see it, proud in its survival all these years. This thriving settlement had grown up at the intersection around the McKelvey Inn, with the addition of a log school by 1826. Then, when the railway was built north of the road in the 1850s, the town moved to be near the railway station.[6]

The road had been relatively good so far, but William Weller knew that the next section before the next stage stop at Springfield would not continue that trend. The terrain east of Lansdowne and through Waterton became more uneven, with many more wet spots where corduroy had been put down. The night was cold, and frost was still in the ground, so most of the corduroy was fairly solid, with only a few sections that caused the team to slow down to avoid broken logs and wet holes.

As he approached the tiny community of Springfield, much later to be called Escott, William Weller sounded his horn once more. As he drove up to the inn at the corner of Rockport Road, a team was waiting. The change was performed quickly, and they were on the road again.

The road was in fairly good shape east of Springfield, and the driver was thankful for that. On the other hand, the wee hours of the morning brought biting winds that threatened to carry away his hat. It was not long before the sleigh passed the unmarked boundary between Escott and Yonge Townships. The travellers had been passing through Leeds County since Willowbank, west of Gananoque, and were now entering the eastern part of that county. Three townships along the river, Lansdowne, Escott, and Yonge, would later be divided north and south to be labelled Front and Rear, but in 1840, it was still just Yonge Township.

The largest settlement in Yonge Township was the village of Mallorytown. The modern driver can learn about one of the unique historical charms of this village, just east of Guild Road on the north side of Highway 2, where there is an historical plaque commemorating a short-lived but ambitious enterprise. Near here was the site of the first glassworks factory in Canada.

The founder of Mallorytown was Nathaniel Mallory,[7] who came to this location from Connecticut, via Vermont, one of many United Empire Loyalists escaping persecution after the War of Independence. In 1784, he landed on the north shore of the St. Lawrence at Mallorytown Landing and later came inland to find good land for farming. The village of Mallorytown grew up over the years as a result.

A grandson of Nathaniel Mallory, Amasa Whitney Mallory, decided to start a glassworks at Mallorytown in 1839. It was an extremely difficult undertaking at the time, and in the end only operated for about eleven months. In February of 1840, when William Weller sped by with the governor general, the glassworks had been in operation for a few months and would continue for only another few before closing later in 1840.

However, in those few months of production, the Mallorytown Glass Works[8] gained a reputation for excellent workmanship and unique design. A distinctive aquamarine colour common to glassware produced here is believed to have been due to unique local materials. Even today, there are a few pieces of Mallorytown glassware in existence, mostly in museums like the ROM and the Arthur Child Museum in Gananoque.

The fresh team found their rhythm and pressed on into the darkness. The cluster of frame buildings along the road at Mallorytown was soon behind them, and both driver and team were intent on only one thing – moving ahead at a good pace. The next village along the road was Yonge Mills, which at that time was a thriving mill town situated at Jones Creek, the source of ample water power for the mills. Here is another example of the disruption in communities caused by the construction of the railways. In the 1850s, the railway went north of the original village, and many businesses moved to be near the railway station.

William Weller was aware of the potential difficulties of the next few miles, all the way to their next stop in Brockville. The King's Highway swung more easterly after they passed Yonge Mills and progressed closer to the St. Lawrence River on the way to the major trade and commerce centre at Brockville. At the same time, the terrain became more challenging as rocky hillocks alternated with swamps.

One of the first trouble spots was the bridge over Lyn Creek. Mr. Weller had sent instructions to his friends in this area to make sure the bridge was in good shape, but he worried, none-the-less. As the sleigh approached Lyn Creek in the darkness, the glow of a torch appeared ahead, and Mr. Weller was gratified to see two young fellows, each carrying a torch, standing at each end of the rickety bridge and waving him through. He slowed the team to a walk and waved to his friends as the sleigh passed over the bridge. One more challenge met.

Not far along, Sherwood Springs Road passed by quickly in the darkness. Soon, the King's Highway swung to the left and took up its normal orientation, following more closely the northeasterly direction of the mighty St. Lawrence River. In the darkness, William Weller could not see the wide, cold waters of the St. Lawrence off to the right, but he could sense its presence in the dampness of the chill air.

25

Brockville and Maitland

IT WAS WELL AFTER THREE IN THE MORNING WHEN THE TRAVELLERS APPROACHED Brockville. Arrangements had been made for a quick change of horses at Lusher's Hotel, which was located on the south side of Main Street, just east of the market. Eri Lusher had been providing good service to the travelling public since establishing himself at this strategic location in 1830, so it was the obvious place to stop. Many years later, the establishment at this location, 21 King Street East, was called the Albion Hotel.[1] It enjoyed the reputation as the oldest hotel business in Brockville when the building was demolished recently to make way for a modern retirement facility.

The property that hosted Lusher's Hotel was owned by Hon. Charles Jones. The Jones family owned a lot of land around Brockville. However, the earliest settler of the land where Brockville stands was William Buell,[2] who was granted five hundred acres for his service with the British during the War of Independence. He established a home and farm at the small bay, which took his name, and he sold town lots as the community grew.

Among his neighbours were Charles and Jonas Jones, sons of Ephraim Jones,[3] a United Empire Loyalist who had provided assistance to General Gage during the war. Both sons would become prominent landowners and businessmen and would be heavily involved in judicial and political activities in Brockville and Upper Canada in the following decades. As the years passed, conflict and competition grew between the Family Compact group headed by the Jones family and the reform-minded folks like William Buell.

In the 1830s, William Buell, Jr.,[4] the settler's son, would own the *Brockville Recorder*, the most influential reform newspaper in the area. During the Rebellion, Buell disowned Mackenzie and showed his loyalty to the crown by participating in the militia. After the Rebellion, however, he resumed his support for reform, through his newspaper.

Originally, the village was called Elizabethtown, after the township. There was much discussion about a proper name, and for a time, some people called it Williamstown after the first settler, Mr. Buell. Of course, the Jones family did not agree with that, and the conflict was not resolved until 1812 when everyone was able to agree on the name Brockville in honour of the commander of the British forces in Upper Canada. Tragically, General Brock was killed at Queenston Heights a few months later, lending a certain reverence to the choice.

Governor General Thomson had roused himself as the sleigh approached Brockville, and he and Captain Le Marchant were discussing some of the people and stories they had heard in the last few months about the politics in Brockville and Leeds County. In the 1830s, Brockville experienced some of the most contentious political fights in the province, as the Family Compact and Reformers vied for power and positions. The Jones and Buell families were prominent and well known in the halls of Parliament in Toronto, but others from Brockville could be thought of in the same breath.

One of the figures that Governor General Thomson recalled first was Levius Peters Sherwood,[5] a judge and very powerful politician living in Brockville. Sherwood demonstrated the practice of the time where wealthy and powerful men gained positions in both the judiciary and the government, as well as carrying on various business and real estate activities. On the one hand, Sherwood did much to build up education and church institutions, and on the other, made himself a target for those who would change the system.

This was just the kind of practice that the governor general's legislation in Toronto and Montreal was designed to curb. As far as Mr. Thomson was concerned, the heyday of the Family Compact was at an end. No longer would judges be able to hold political office and be able to further their business interests through influencing government policy. That's not to say that all these gentlemen were corrupt. Most were moral and upstanding men. But the potential for conflict of interest was so strong that it was hard for anyone to avoid being pulled in. Contrary to this, the trending idea was that the courts and the Parliament should be separate. It would take a while, but this concept would take hold and become one of the cornerstones of Canadian democracy.

As the sleigh entered the town, the driver sounded the horn to warn the fellows at Lusher's Hotel to get ready. At this hour of the morning, there was little traffic on the streets, even in the downtown, where the new flagstone sidewalks would be crowded with people in a few hours. Schooners, steamers, and barges were at the wharfs down at the shoreline, and the occasional teamster wagon could be seen rolling down to the bay.

On the left, they passed the homes of Charles Jones and Ephraim Dunham. On the right was Paul Glasford's store at the corner of Home Street. Glancing toward the river, William Weller could see that lamps were already casting shadows at Billy Flint's wharf at the end of St. Andrew Street, where workmen were unloading goods from a schooner, mostly merchandise destined for Mr. Flint's general store.

Known in Brockville as Billy Flint,[6] he was the father of Billa Flint, who had moved to Belleville in 1829 to make his own way in the merchandizing business. The senior Flint was well known as a very astute businessman, but he could also be nasty and brutish. Many reports in the archives for the Brockville courts demonstrate the angry and violent behaviour that made his son, Billa Flint, anxious to make his own way in Belleville. Regardless of his history, Billy Flint was a fixture on the waterfront of Brockville.

25.1 Brockville Court House

At the next street, if Mr. Weller could have seen through the dark night, a wide boulevard led north of the King's Highway up to the Brockville courthouse and jail. The first courthouse had been built on land provided by William Buell in 1810 and then expanded and renovated in the early 1820s. As the travellers passed through Brockville, plans were being formulated to replace it with a larger and more modern structure, which would be in place in 1842.[7]

After another blast from the horn, the driver drew the sweating team into the yard in front of the Lusher Hotel and watched closely as the stable boys changed the horses. A flask was offered and a good swig of rum fortified Mr. Weller against the morning chill. With a tip of the hat, the travellers were back on the King's Highway. To his right, down past Water Street, Mr. Weller saw more lanterns at the wharfs of H. & S. Jones. Just ahead, on the south side of the King's Highway, was the establishment of Charles and William Dyer.

William Weller knew that the King's Highway between Brockville and Prescott and on to Johnstown was in good shape. The merchants and traders of these busy riverfront towns made sure resources were used to keep the road passable. It was partly a sense of the public good, but also the very clear reality that business prospered where goods and people could travel easily between towns, especially to wharfs where steamers and schooners would carry farmers' produce and factory products to market. Good roads meant good business.

The King's Highway would run smooth and straight along the north shore of the St. Lawrence River for some time, and the driver was intent on taking advantage of the best roads he might see between here and Montreal. He encouraged the team up to a gallop, and the sleigh moved smoothly along in the dark and cold. The passengers settled down for another snooze.

The next village along the King's Highway was Maitland, a bustling commercial centre with wharfs at the shore of the river and a long history to boast about. The shoreline juts into the river at this location, and the French called it Point au Baril, finding it convenient as part of their trading system between Quebec and Detroit in the middle of the 1700s. Fortifications were built here in 1759, but the British took possession the next year as part of their victory on the Plains of Abraham at Quebec.

United Empire Loyalists came to the area in 1784, and by the 1820s, the name was changed to Maitland, after the lieutenant governor of the time. When William Weller drove by in 1840, the most notable structure in Maitland was the Longley Tower, which stood imposingly on the shoreline in the middle of the village. This tower was built as a windmill in 1828 by George Longley, with the intent of generating power for mills. However, the power he could generate was not adequate, and he soon installed a steam engine, which proved to be a much more efficient and reliable source of power. The old tower became a distillery and over the years played several other roles before being designated as a heritage site in 1923. Today it is a fascinating historic site, easily available on Number 2 Highway. Don't be surprised if you see some renovation activity on the site, since the property has recently changed hands and the new owner is intent on honouring the history of the place, while giving it a modern purpose. Good news![8]

Two miles east of Maitland, William Weller may have noticed the large stone house that stood up a slight rise, north of the road. This was Homewood, the residence of Dunham Jones, son of Solomon Jones. The elder Jones settled in Augusta Township as a United Empire Loyalist in 1785 and around 1800 built this substantial home. For many years, he was the only doctor between Cornwall and Kingston, so rooms in the lower floor were used as a surgery and doctor's office.

The property remained in the hands of the Jones family until it was sold to Du Pont in 1951. The threat of demolition in the 1970s alarmed the community, and a successful campaign led by the Grenville Historical Society resulted in donation of the property to the Ontario Heritage Foundation in 1974. Much archeological excavation work has been done around the property to identify outbuildings. The site is now operated as Homewood Museum[9] by the Ontario Heritage Trust.

Several miles along the road, the travellers galloped by the Blue Church Cemetery and the accompanying Blue Church. The church was one of the oldest structures in the area, built in 1809 and used until St. James was built in Maitland in 1829. In 1840, the poor old Blue Church was in bad shape, suffering from a recent fire and many years of neglect. In a few months, it would be taken down, and then in 1845, it was replaced by another Blue Church,[10] which is the one we can see today at the corner of Number 2 and the Blue Church Road.

26

Prescott, Johnstown, Edwardsburgh

THE KING'S HIGHWAY STRETCHED OUT IN FRONT OF THE SLEIGH, FLAT AND RELA-tively straight for the next few miles into the town of Prescott. In many places, if not for the rhythmic pounding of the horses' hooves, William Weller might have heard the lapping of the waves of the St. Lawrence just off to his right. At this hour of the day, in dull, cold February weather, the river was only a deep blackness off to the south.

As he approached the town of Prescott, William Weller found many thoughts racing through his mind. As he concentrated on driving, he knew he was entering a very familiar place, almost like a second home. Certainly not as much as his current home in Cobourg, but he felt a certain affinity for the place where he got his start in his chosen business. Fifteen years ago, in 1825, Weller had moved his young and growing family from Canton, not far south of Ogdensburg, New York, to Prescott, just across the St. Lawrence. He moved to Prescott to pursue his involvement in the stagecoach business. It is unclear how long William himself lived in Prescott because he was probably travelling a lot, but we know that two of his children were born there. The boy, Albert Freeman Weller, died at only two years of age, but his daughter, Caroline, born in Prescott in December 1825, was a sweet fifteen-year-old and the darling of his life.

His time in Prescott was very productive. A big break came when he entered into partnership with Hiram Norton, a very active businessman, who already operated stagecoach lines. Norton had been born in Vermont and then moved to New York

State, just like William Weller. The two men were also the same age. As young men in the 1820s, living just south of the St. Lawrence River, a career in transportation was an obvious choice.

It was the time of canal fever in the U.S. and Canada. The Erie Canal had been completed in 1825, opening up an efficient route for passage of settlers to the west and produce to the east, focussing the traffic on New York and Boston. The Welland Canal opened in 1829 to bring the increasing produce of the west to the markets of the east, supposedly through the Canadian port of Montreal. The Rideau Canal would open in 1832, conceived largely as a military route, but it would become an important commercial asset because it helped mitigate the effect of the rapids on the St. Lawrence. All of this resulted in direct competition between the Canadian ports of Montreal and Quebec and the American ports of Boston and New York, all vying for both American and Canadian business. It was an exciting time to be young, energetic, and looking to make your mark.

However, Hiram Norton would not be in Prescott when William Weller drove through in 1840. Norton had also been active in politics through the 1830s, being elected as a representative for Grenville County from 1831 to 1838. As a strong voice for reform, he engaged in the struggles that led up to the Rebellion, adding to the feeling by some that Leeds and Grenville were hotbeds for rebel sympathizers. After Norton was re-elected in 1836, he and several other reform members did not take their seats in Toronto due to obvious and persistent threats of physical violence. Completely aside from that, after the rebellion was over, Hiram Norton was forced to resign as a member of the Board of Commissioners for the Cornwall Canal, due to a serious conflict of interest.[1] All things considered, he decided to move his home and business interests to Illinois, where he would build a considerable fortune.

The town of Prescott that the travellers would gallop through in 1840 was a very busy and thriving commercial centre. Prescott was the western terminus for what was called the Forwarding Trade. The rapids in the St. Lawrence River from Cornwall to just below Prescott presented an almost insurmountable obstacle to the movement of people and goods. Rafts of timber could be floated down the river from Upper Canada to the timber merchants in Montreal, but travelling west, up the river, was a very different matter.

Early settlers to Upper Canada often told tales of their experiences travelling this route. Lady Simcoe accompanied her husband, Lieutenant Governor John Graves Simcoe, on their first trip to Upper Canada in 1792, and she wrote in her diary, "The batteau men kept as close to the shore as possible, and by dint of exertion and labour they pole and tow the boat up against the current."[2] By 1830, the roads and coaches were much better, but the rapids remained an obstacle for Susanna Moodie and her family as they made the trip from Montreal, first in a coach to Lachine, then on a steam ship to Cornwall. From Cornwall to Prescott, the party of nine were crammed into a narrow coach covered with canvas, shivering in the chill September night. At Prescott, they boarded the new steam ship, *William IV*, for a pleasant run to Cobourg.[3] Susanna Moodie's famous book *Roughing It In The Bush* provides a personal and practical version of this trip, which was an experience shared by tens of thousands of settlers.

The forwarding trade was the system of warehouses, boats, barges, wagons, coaches, horses, and men organized under several different companies, all vying for the business of moving goods and travellers. Wagons and bateau would be unloaded after coming up from Montreal, with the goods stored temporarily in warehouses at the wharfs on the shore at Prescott. The passengers would find beds at hotels in the town. Soon, the goods and the people would be loaded onto steamboats and schooners to sail down the wide St. Lawrence to Kingston, Cobourg, York, and other points west. It was a hectic, loud, and constantly churning business that employed hundreds of men and made money for the smart operator.

Today, the Forwarder's Museum sits on Water Street in Prescott, a testament to the business that built this town. The building itself was constructed around 1810 by William Gilkison,[4] who began the first organized forwarding business at Prescott. Gilkison was a Scottish naval officer who had sailed a schooner owned by John Jacob Astor for the North West Company, running on Lake Erie between Fort Erie and Detroit. He married Isabella Grant, daughter of the

26.1 Forwarding Museum, Prescott

wealthy and powerful Commodore Alexander Grant of Detroit and worked for a time for his father-in-law.

In 1810, William Gilkison came to Prescott to engage in the forwarding trade. He was only in Prescott for two years before General Isaac Brock asked him to take a naval command during the War of 1812. As a result, he was at Crysler's Farm to receive the surrender of the American forces on November 11, 1813.

The town of Prescott was founded by Major Edward Jessup, who had raised a contingent of forces in support of the Royalist cause.[5] The name "Jessup's Rangers" is well established in the history of the War of Independence. After the war was over, his men were allotted land in the townships of Edwardsburgh, Augusta, and Elizabethtown. Jessup supervised the settlement of his associates on land in these townships in 1784, and then, in 1788, brought his family to settle in Augusta Township. In 1810, he converted a portion of his land to lay out a town, which he named Prescott, after General Robert Prescott, governor of Canada from 1796 to 1799. The original town was located within the limits of West Street and East Street, which can be seen in Prescott today.

William Weller maintained a crisp gallop along King Street through Prescott. The town had been incorporated as a Police District in 1832, and the population in 1840 was around seventeen hundred with numerous fine stone buildings. The activities of the last few years had drawn attention to the east side of town where Fort Wellington stood. In fact, the Fort Wellington that William Weller drove past in February of 1840 was brand new, having been rebuilt in 1839 in response to the perceived threat of American invasion.

The modern visitor can walk around in Fort Wellington[6] and see what the life of a soldier might have been like in the 1840s. A walk up to the parapet is rewarded with a commanding view of the St. Lawrence River, exactly the same view as the pair of cannon pointed out over the river. The Fenian excitements of 1864 and 1865 would raise alarms all across the border defences between Canada and the United States, but these cannon would not be fired in anger.

A few miles up the shoreline from Prescott, William Weller would have noted the presence, near the shore to his right, of the windmill where, less than a year and half before, the Battle of the Windmill had taken place. The people of Prescott and area were still much excited about this event, and stories of military exploits were still the currency of the day.

After the Mackenzie Rebellion was quashed in Toronto in late 1837, many rebels, including Mackenzie, escaped to the United States and continued to agitate for an invasion of Canada from south of the St. Lawrence River. The Patriot Hunter Lodges grew rapidly at this time, taking in all sorts of men who were spoiling for a fight. They believed that if they simply made a gesture of military invasion, the poor, downtrodden Canadians would rise up against their despotic leaders and welcome the Americans as saviours. Hmmm... Sound familiar?

The windmill east of Prescott became the centre of this effort after a poorly led attempt to land on the west side of Prescott had been rebuffed and their ship floated down the river to Windmill Point. The leader of the remaining combatants saw the tall, stone windmill as an ideal place to protect his men and give them time to plan for an attack on the town. Canadian forces soon gathered around the windmill, both local militia and British regulars. There were several days of sharp fighting in which many casualties were incurred on both sides. The British brought up some big guns and eventually the assault on the windmill resulted in the surrender of the invaders. The windmill is still there, in the Battle of the Windmill National Historic Site, just off Number 2 Highway east of Prescott.[7]

William Weller encouraged the team to press on along the King's Highway. They were approaching Johnstown where they would change horses, but first they must navigate the bridge at Johnstown Creek. The waterway and wetland that had once been called Old Breeches River presented an obstacle for travellers and a succession of bridges had been built to solve the problem. Mr. Weller had requested that his contacts in the area make sure the bridge was secure so the governor general could pass by with no trouble. True to form, a torch was sighted at the bridge, and a young man waved the sleigh across. The driver slowed down to ensure the horses would not be too nervous crossing the bridge, and they passed by easily.

Not far ahead, the driver sounded his horn and slowed down as he approached the cluster of buildings that made up the village of Johnstown. This place has a connection to Johnstown, New York, as the two towns were named after the same man, Sir William Johnson.[8] He had been an agent for the British among the natives of the area during the years leading up to the War of Independence. Back in 1759, he had been second in command to General Amherst, who led British forces in defeating the French at various locations, including Fort Levis, on Chimney Island, just south of Johnstown, Ontario, in the St. Lawrence River.

Sir John Johnson,[9] a son of Sir William Johnson, became the superintendent of the Six Nations Indians. After the War of Independence was over, Johnson acquired many land grants in Upper Canada, including property at the location where a mill was established at the Old Breeches River, later to be called Johnstown Creek. When they were searching for a name for the new village, Johnstown seemed obvious.

The sleigh was brought to a stop in front of a small inn at the intersection of the King's Highway and the Spencerville Road in Johnstown. The change of horses was performed quickly, and the travellers were on their way.

William Weller was beginning to feel that his enterprise might be successful. Each minute that went by, he began to feel it in a more real and direct sense. Sure, he had signed the contract because he felt the means of accomplishing the terms were in his hands. But, you just never knew if things would work as planned. There were so many towns, so many bridges, so many miles of road. But it was starting to seem possible, if they could only keep up this pace.

The King's Highway followed close to the shore of the St. Lawrence River between Johnstown and the next village of Edwardsburgh. As he approached this bustling little village, Mr. Weller hoped he could avoid the traffic along Dundas Street that would likely be increasing as the night inched into morning. There were several mills and numerous businesses along Dundas Street, which was the King's Highway as it bent down into Munro Point.

Edwardsburgh was founded by Hugh Munro, Sr., who obtained two hundred acres at this location. His son, Hugh, Jr., inherited the property and became a primary citizen of the town. A grist mill was built about 1796, and more mills were added over the years, mostly located in the eastern side of the village. Munro would also build a small raceway along the side of the river to provide water power to the mills. He was very active in military affairs as well, reaching the rank of colonel of the Grenville Militia.[10] He saw action during the War of 1812 as well as during the Mackenzie Rebellion.

The story of Edwardsburgh may be a bit confusing in terms of both the main road and the town's name. After some study of the history of the place, it is clear that today's straight-as-an-arrow Number 2 Highway through the village of Cardinal is not what William Weller would have seen in 1840. The landscape would change dramatically in 1846, when the Galop Canal was built from the village of Iroquois, right through the middle of the village of Edwardsburgh. The old King's Highway was moved to the north side of the new canal, leaving the old route on Dundas Street as a local, dead-end street. As for the name changes, the village of Edwardsburgh had gained a post office in 1837, making that name official. Then, in 1864, the village was known as Elgin. Finally, in 1880, it was incorporated as the village of Cardinal.[11]

William Weller guided the team as the road swung down into Edwardsburgh, along Dundas Street. There were wagons and horses and men on the street, getting an early start at the day's work in the mills. The sleigh was able to move quickly along, and once through the busy mill district near the east end of town, came back to the shoreline and the open road to the east.

27

Iroquois and Williamsburg

A FEW MILES ALONG THE KING'S HIGHWAY, THE TRAVELLERS CROSSED INTO DUNDAS County and Matilda Township. The road continued to hug the shoreline along the river, and in some places, water lapped at the edge of the road. The terrain was even, and the road was straight so the sleigh made good time. Daylight was on its way, but the cold, damp night gave way grudgingly. It was still chilly up on the bench, and the driver looked forward to the middle of the day when it might warm up a bit.

The village of Iroquois was located on the north shore of the St. Lawrence, extending southward along the east side of an angled protrusion called Iroquois Point. The St. Lawrence flowed almost north and south along the bottom part of Iroquois Point, turning abruptly east at the face of the town. This strategic location had been used by native groups for many years and thus the name: Iroquois.

William Weller knew that there was a very good inn along the King's Highway east of Iroquois, so he was intent on moving quickly through the village. As in Edwardsburgh, wagons, horses, and men were on the roads, especially around the mills, beginning the work of the day. The road angled northeast across Iroquois Point and entered the main business district, turning easterly again along the shoreline.

As in Edwardsburgh, the experience of today's traveller will be much different at Iroquois. William Weller and the governor general went through the town only a couple of years before the Galop Canal[1] was built along the north shoreline from Iroquois to Edwardsburgh, designed to bypass the dreaded Galop Rapids. The canal cut on an angle from the shoreline in front of the village, extending southwesterly to the shoreline west of Iroquois Point, thus converting the peninsula into an island. At the same time, the King's Highway would be moved north of the canal.

This all would change over the years as the canals grew in size and complexity to meet the needs of the time. Finally, in the 1950s, the St. Lawrence Seaway project resulted in the complete dislocation of the town of Iroquois. The houses that were south of the old canal, as well as the buildings of the main downtown, were moved north to higher ground. The King's Highway moved as well. Part of the old town is now parkland and a golf course. The new seaway locks were built right across the middle of old Point Iroquois, and much land was flooded to bring the water up to required levels.

The sleigh kept moving along the King's Highway, through Iroquois and then into the countryside east of town. The road was close to the shore with some stretches of corduroy over the wetlands. Soon they crossed Doran Creek on a causeway that had a lift bridge towards the east side. The modern driver might check Dr. Miller Road (off Golf Club Road) to see where Mr. Weller travelled in 1840. Today we can see remains of the old causeway in Doran Creek, just south of the current bridge on Number 2 Highway.

William Weller was relieved to see that the bridge was in place at Doran Creek. Another of his helpers stood at the west end of the bridge, waving him through. The driver was glad to be through Iroquois and on open road again. However, he knew that the rest of the day would be filled with crossings of the many creeks and inlets along the north shore of the St. Lawrence.

If the travellers had stopped to visit with local residents near Doran Creek, they might have heard the stories of the large American force that had landed on the eastern bank of Doran Creek during the War of 1812. The Americans later moved up the shoreline until being confronted by British regulars and some determined militia, resulting in the Battle of Crysler Farm.

Not far east of Doran Creek, there was another large inlet where a causeway had been constructed near the mouth of the inlet, again with a lift bridge near the east side. The road moved south to the shoreline, and the travellers followed it across the long causeway and over the bridge, relieved to be across another obstacle. The modern driver needs to look at Lakeshore Drive, which follows the shoreline east of Iroquois. Check out the small pieces of the old road that still exist, including Grisdale Road and Dr. Stevens Drive.

The next stretch of road would be snug to the shoreline along solid terrain, flat and fairly straight – a place to make good time. The driver gave the team a bit more head and let them run comfortably along. Occasional vehicles and people on horseback were on the road now, as the sky became lighter but threatened rain at the same time.

Several miles at a good pace brought them to John Flagg Bay where a solid bridge traversed John Flagg Creek. John Flagg had acquired land just east of the creek in 1818, and operated a wheel-wright shop, then became the proprietor of a general store. This was a busy intersection, and it was no surprise to see wagons and horses and men on the road, heading for the mills along the creek, some of them coming from the northern concessions of Matilda Township. William Weller followed a wagon loaded with flour across the bridge and had to slow down until someone near the other end waved the teamster over, to let the governor general pass.

Mr. Weller may have noticed, as he crossed the bridge, the large and stately home north of the bridge, on the west side of the creek. This exceptional building had been built by Captain John Munro,[2] who acquired large tracts of land in Matilda Township because of his extensive work as a soldier and administrator for the British from the Seven Years War to the War of Independence. He had been forced to leave major property holdings near Albany, New York and Shaftsbury, Vermont and was rewarded accordingly with large grants of land in Upper Canada. Munro built grist and saw mills along the St. Lawrence River in Matilda Township during the 1790s and contributed much to the early development of the town of Iroquois and the surrounding area.

The immediate destination for Mr. Weller was the Findley House, a mile east of John Flagg Bay. This establishment had been the most popular stage stop along the King's Highway between Iroquois and Williamsburg since the 1790s. It had been called the "Blue House" due to a unique paint job, and for a long time it was operated by Allen Patterson, a former North West Company fur trader, who had married a daughter of Captain John Munro. The property had been handed down through relatives of Mr. Patterson and was now operated by the Findleys, thus called Findley House.

The Blue House[3] had been located very strategically on the lakeshore at the head of the Rapid de Plat, a very nasty set of rapids in the channel between Ogden's Island and the north shore. Flotillas of bateau would hug the shoreline, with muscular young men poling and pulling the craft against the surge of the rapids. When they reached the western end of the rapids, the Blue House provided rest and sustenance that was very welcome. Along with the river men, the Blue House accommodated the elite of Upper Canada, including the occasional royal visitor, making the trip to York.

Mr. Weller sounded his horn as he approached Findley House and was gratified to see a cluster of men and boys standing around a fresh team in front of the popular meeting place. It was around seven in the morning, so darkness was giving way grudgingly, and the lanterns in front of the building sent a glow across the assemblage. A water jug was passed to the driver and passengers, the change of horses was done quickly, and the travellers were on their way to cheers and waving hats.

The King's Highway hugged the shoreline for the next few miles, and now Mr. Weller could see the river and hear the roar of the rapids as he encouraged the team along the flat and relatively smooth road. With the daylight, he took stock of their position. They had been lucky to avoid any serious delays due to bad bridges or obstructions on the road. His passengers were quiet, doing their best to practice patience. At this point, the driver would have been very happy to know that his aching bones and sore posterior would endure this ordeal for only twelve more hours.

The sleigh soon came to the village of Mariatown, which signalled that they had crossed from Matilda into Williamsburg Township. At Mariatown Bay, the road crossed a bridge and swung northeast, away from the shoreline, with the village to the south of the road. Mariatown had been one of the earliest settlements along "The Front", as it was called when Richard Duncan acquired lots thirty-six and thirty-seven of Williamsburg Township. He named the town after his daughter, Maria. However, its influence along this stretch of shoreline would be reduced after the Williamsburg Canal was built a few years after Mr. Weller travelled through.

Not far along the road, there was a very long causeway and bridge across Stata's Bay, and William Weller made note of the building nearby, which had been one of the better stage stops on this stretch of the King's Highway for many years. Then they entered the village of West Williamsburg. At this time it was a small community, begun around 1813, but it would experience considerable growth during the construction of the Williamsburg Canal, which was completed in 1847.

In 1851, the village of West Williamsburg was renamed Morrisburg in honour of Sir James Morris,[4] a resident of Brockville. Morris was a member of the Legislature for Leeds County and was a persistent advocate for the building of canals along the north shore of the St. Lawrence River. He had been involved in the first meetings in Brockville on the topic of canals, and in 1838, he became a commissioner to administer funds raised by debentures for the building of the canals. The canals would be built during the 1840s and would result in a surge of growth and prominence for Morrisburg in the region.

Lakeshore Drive, along the shoreline in today's Morrisburg, traces the route of William Weller and the King's Highway in 1840. The main street of Morrisburg disappeared toward the east end of town, with the development of the St. Lawrence Seaway in the 1950s, and the land along the shore was converted into a golf course and waterfront park.

The travellers in 1840 followed the King's Highway straight through West Williamsburg and continued along the lakeshore east of town. The next potential obstacle was at Nash Creek where a long causeway and a bridge crossed the mouth of the creek. A young fellow was on the bridge, waving his hat, when he saw the sleigh approach. He jumped up and down and shouted as they drove by, yelling good luck to Mr. Weller. It was an exciting day for a young farm boy who dreamed of travelled across the country in one of Mr. Weller's stagecoaches.

Nash Creek was another point of interest for local veterans of the War of 1812. In early November 1813, American Brigadier General Jacob Brown led his large force east along the King's Highway toward a showdown with British and Canadian forces at Crysler's Farm. On seeing the American's approach, seventeen-year-old John W. Loucks,[5] a Provincial Light Dragoon, employed as a scout at this important crossing, immediately burned the bridge at Nash Creek in order to slow them down. He then raced east to notify the settlers along the way. Not satisfied with this, he hid his horse, climbed a tree, and watched as the American forces marched by. When the coast was clear, he headed west to notify the trailing British forces of the American strength and makeup. Not a bad day's work for a young scout.

The Battle of Crysler's Farm[6] took place on November 11, 1813 and was a critical point in Canadian history. Victory here prevented a large American force from continuing with the St. Lawrence Campaign. The Americans had planned to take Montreal, thus dividing Upper Canada from Lower Canada. The British Regulars and Upper Canada Militia, who fought hard to stop the Americans, were outnumbered and outgunned, but they used good military tactics, aggressiveness, and coordination to upset the larger force. Eventually, the Americans were forced to withdraw from the field and the country.

The *Beldon County Atlas Map* (1878) for Williamsburg Township[7] shows the location of the "Crysler's Farm Battle Ground" along the shore in lots nine to twelve of the first concession. When William Weller drove along the King's Highway, past Crysler's farm in 1840, he would have seen a few houses and barns as well as fields and forest. Much later, in 1895, a large monument was erected on the north side of the road, and in 1920, the

27.1 Battle of Crysler's Farm Monument

area was designated as a National Historic Site. However, the area was submerged in 1958 with the flooding of the St. Lawrence Seaway. The monument from 1895 was moved to Upper Canada Village and can be seen there today, commanding the river, just west of the village.

The modern driver can motor along Number 2 Highway and pass the actual site of the Crysler's Farm battlefield without knowing it is under water some distance south in the St. Lawrence River. William Weller would have kept to the King's Highway, passing the farms of the Fetterlys and Casselmans, who had been much impacted by the presence of large military forces in their fields and along the road.

The travellers would then pass Cook's Tavern, a popular hotel and stage stop near the spot where part of the American forces came ashore just before the Battle of Crysler's Farm. Michael Cook had built a tavern on the main road well before the war and would have been distressed to see it destroyed, as it was taken over by American soldiers and eventually burned down. He petitioned the British government for compensation after the war and won a settlement, which allowed him to build a substantial, two-storey brick building and continue the tradition of the well-known Cook's Tavern[8]. This second Cook's Tavern has survived and sits proudly in Upper Canada Village. It was moved to this site along with other buildings in preparation for the flooding that resulted from the building of the St. Lawrence Seaway.

The sleigh sped along the King's Highway, happy for the daylight, such as it was. There would be no sunshine to warm the governor general on his way to Montreal, but the driver was grateful for this, because a thaw in the roadbed could delay their progress. He was cold and wet there on the bench, with aching shoulders and hands, but he knew that the cold was his friend for the next few hours.

28

Ten Lost Villages

NOT FAR ALONG THE ROAD, THE TRAVELLERS MOVED OUT OF DUNDAS COUNTY AND into Stormont County, from Williamsburg Township into Osnabruck Township. The next village along the King's Highway was Charlesville, which was founded in the 1780s by a group of disbanded soldiers from the King's Royal Regiment. In 1840, it was a small village with a tavern and post office along with a few merchants taking advantage of their location on the King's Highway and the north shore of the St. Lawrence River. The name Aultsville would be applied to the village in the 1860s in honour of Samuel Ault, a member of the first Parliament of Canada in 1867, who was a resident of the community.

Much later, in the 1950s, Aultsville and nine other villages along the north shore of the St. Lawrence would become the Ten Lost Villages,[1] so-called because they were flooded in preparation for the opening of the St. Lawrence Seaway. This huge international project was designed to eliminate the Long Sault Rapids and produce much-needed hydro-electricity. In the process, the water level was raised, flooding land along the shores of the river. The residents and buildings of Aultsville were moved to the new village of Ingleside, a short distance east and on higher ground away from the river.

Today, Ault Island remains as a result of the flooding, just east of Upper Canada Village. Of course, along with the inundation of the ten villages, old Number 2 Highway, or the King's Highway, as William Weller knew it, was flooded as well.

Along this part of the north shore, the current Number 2 is some distance north of the original road.

Farran's Point was the next village along the shoreline and the next stage stop for the travellers. This was one of the most substantial communities along the north shore of the St. Lawrence. There were grist and saw mills, along with all the normal merchants and tradesmen of a thriving community of the day. The village took its name from Jacob Farrand, who acquired land at this location in the 1780s. He had served with the British throughout the conflict, ending the war as a lieutenant in Captain John Munro's company.

The prospects for the village would improve in 1847 with the building of a small canal and lock, and then the railway helped again in the 1850s. However, Farran's Point became the second (west to east) of the Ten Lost Villages flooded before the St. Lawrence Seaway opened in 1958. The homes and businesses of Farran's Point were moved, along with those of Aultsville, to the village of Ingleside on Number 2 Highway, which is immediately north of the old village of Farran's Point, now under shallow water in the river.

William Weller sounded his horn as he approached Farran's Point and then made his way along Main Street, pulling over and stopping where the fresh team was ready. The normal greetings were exchanged, along with the water jug, and the travellers were on their way. Down Main Street, the driver tried to avoid the busy morning traffic of wagons, horses, and people. Finally, the village bustle was behind them, and the sleigh sped along the shoreline, crossing wobbly bridges and stepping through broken corduroy, always moving east. A few miles along the road they passed the village of Woodlands and then Santa Cruz. Both would disappear and become Lost Villages (sometimes called Lost Hamlets), with the flooding of the seaway in 1958.

Very soon, the sleigh came to the bridge over Hoople Creek, a significant waterway that emptied into the St. Lawrence River, just west of Dickinson's Landing. The creek was named after Granny Hoople, a legendary figure in the area. Granny was actually Mary Whitmore, who had been abducted from her home in Pennsylvania after her parents and two siblings were killed by Delaware Indians. She lived among the Indians for seven years before escaping. She married Henry Hoople in 1788, and they settled on the second concession of Osnabruck Township, on the creek that would take their name. For many years Granny Hoople took the role of community doctor, practicing the medicine she had learned while captive in a native village.

The sleigh crossed Hoople Creek on a solid bridge and moved along the King's Highway through Dickinson's Landing. This was one of the most prosperous villages between Montreal and Kingston with many merchants, mills, and some factories. Its position at the west end of the Long Sault Rapids had made it a strategic location for transferring goods and people to boats after the necessary land trip between Cornwall and Dickinson's Landing to avoid the dangerous waters of the river. The French explorer, La Salle, had set up a trading post here in 1669, and it was well established as an important location when United Empire Loyalists came to the area in the 1780s.

The town was named after the Dickinson brothers, Barnabus and Horace, who began a stagecoach business immediately after the War of 1812. They obtained the first contracts from the British Post Office to carry the Royal Mail between Montreal and Kingston,[3] replacing the uncertain and slow method of men on foot or horse-back. The Dickinson brothers were from New York State, just south of Ogdensburg. Their father, General Lemuel Dickinson, had served the patriot cause in the War of Independence, and Horace had been on guard at the arsenal in Russell, New York, when Ogdensburg was raided by the British during the war of 1812.

But after the war was over, many people in northern New York State were anxious to return to profitable trading with their neighbours in Canada. In that era before canals, the St. Lawrence River was the primary trade route, and many businessmen cared less whether political power emanated from Washington or London – they just wanted to do business. The Dickinson brothers, Barnabus and Horace, were young and ambitious fellows who saw opportunity in the transportation business along the St. Lawrence, and they took action.

After they managed to obtain the mail contract in Montreal, Horace Dickinson initially set up an office in Prescott, across from Ogdensburg, New York, to manage the stagecoach line. Later, he moved to Montreal to organize and grow the business. His brother Barnabus located in the new village at the head of the Long Sault Rapids that would take his name: Dickinson Landing. They set up the nuts and bolts of the stage business, hiring drivers and making deals with farmers and tavern keepers along the way. They needed lots of stage stops and horses to keep their stage line running.

William Weller was well aware of the Dickinson brothers and may have worked with them as a young man in New York State, since they came from the same general area south of Ogdensburg. Certainly, they were in business by the later 1820s, when advertisements for their stage line showed that Weller was the agent in York, Hiram Norton in Kingston, and Horace Dickinson in Montreal.[4] The Dickinsons became active in many other businesses as well, including building and operating steam ships. Horace Dickinson died suddenly in Montreal during the devastating cholera epidemic of 1832, but his brother Barnabus was still very active in the family business in 1840.

As the sleigh made its way through the busy morning streets of Dickinson's Landing and toward the east end of the village, the driver could see that his information was correct. His contacts had told him that he might encounter delays due to construction of the new canal. There were piles of lumber and other supplies along the waterfront that suggested something was in the works. However, the project was on hold at this time, and the King's Highway was not obstructed.

Sod had been turned in 1834 to build a nine-foot-deep canal along the north shore of the river to bypass the treacherous Long Sault Rapids. A commission had been set up to manage the project, promoted very persistently by James Morris of Brockville. In the years from 1832 to 1837, much work had been done, and the canal was considered about eighty percent finished. In some places, tons of rock had been dumped into the river to build up an embankment, and in other places, a ditch was dug along the shoreline.

Then, in 1837, the Mackenzie Rebellion caused most major projects to be delayed or stopped. Money was simply not available. Thousands of workmen were sent home and communities along the shore were hit hard. However, not long after William Weller took Governor General Thomson along the King's Highway in 1840, the new Board of Works and its funding mechanisms took effect, and the work resumed. The Cornwall Canal[5] would be completed in 1842, stretching from Cornwall to the east end of the waterfront of Dickinson's Landing.

The modern driver will not see Dickinson's Landing or the route William Weller took in this area in 1840. Dickinson's Landing was the fifth (west to east) of the Lost Villages that were flooded when the seaway was built in 1958. The buildings of Dickinson's Landing were moved to the new village of Ingleside, and the closest we can come to seeing it today is Dickinson Island, one of eleven islands connected by the Long Sault Parkway. Near the middle of the Parkway, we can see Hoople Island, and then across a causeway to the east is Dickinson Island. If we look south while crossing this causeway, it is easy to imagine the scene William Weller saw in February 1840 as he crossed the bridge over Hoople Creek, heading into Dickinson's Landing.

The village of Wales was another of the Ten Lost Villages, recalled today in at least three places. There is a Wales Drive in Ingleside and another Wales Drive also called Highway 12, north from Number 2, just east of Hoople Bay. There is also Wales Island in the St. Lawrence River between the modern shoreline and the islands supporting the Long Sault Parkway. Wales did not exist in 1840 but was created as a result of a Grand Trunk Railway station located on Hoople Creek, north of Dickinson's Landing. It was initially called Dickinson's Landing Station, but in 1860, it was renamed Wales in honour of the visiting Prince of Wales, who took a steamboat ride down the rapids, thus generating the respect of the locals.

A few miles to the east of Dickinson's Landing, the travellers moved out of Stormont and into Cornwall Township. Very soon, the road swung to the northeast to skirt around Sheik's Island and the north channel of the river.[5] The St. Lawrence had been divided into three channels at the Long Sault Rapids, with Sheik's Island to the north, on the Canadian side, and Barnhart's Island to the south, in the U.S.A.

The village of Moulinette was located on the north channel, the first town inside Cornwall Township. This section of the King's Highway had been moved north due to the canal and was now well inland, straight and well constructed. Then, just after a bridge over a creek, there was an intersection. If the traveller continued straight rather than turning here, he would drive out into the middle concessions of Cornwall Township, well back from the river. This was the eastern extremity of the King's Road, which ran well north of the river, all the way into Lower Canada, coming back down to the St. Lawrence at St. Zotique.

The King's Road had been surveyed in 1792 on the orders of Lieutenant Governor John Graves Simcoe, who envisaged a safe, functional road all the way from Montreal, across the newly-created provinces of Lower Canada and Upper Canada, meeting up with roads he was already having built in the southwest. In his mind, it would ultimately go through the new capital he planned on the Thames River and then to Detroit. He had big plans but was pre-empted by his superiors, who insisted that the new capital would be at York.

While there was a broader scheme, at least in Simcoe's mind, the eastern section of the road was locally inspired. The early settlers of Stormont and Glengarry complained that they had no route to Montreal, other than along the St. Lawrence River.[6] Roads along the shore were very bad, and in some places, non-existent in those early years. Simcoe ordered that this eastern section be surveyed, and over time it became an important artery between eastern Upper Canada and Lower Canada. The name King's Road would stick to this road. Originally surveyed all the way to Kingston, the western parts migrated down to the King's Highway, and eventually this intersection just west of Moulinette became its western terminus.

Early in the planning process for this trip, Mr. Weller had considered the King's Road as a possible route, but in the end decided to stick to the shoreline. There were definitely pros and cons. The King's Road was certainly built on much higher ground across its entire length and was straighter, flatter, and smoother. Of course, this would seem to mean they could make better time. However, it was also nine miles longer and that represented close to an entire stage, which the driver was not willing to concede, considering the time constraints of his contract.

Any other time of the year, he might have gone by the King's Road. The roads along the shoreline became impassable, or at least very difficult, in the spring and also in the fall. Winter was the best time to travel along the shoreline route because the ground was frozen. Bridges were much improved now, even compared with two or three years ago, and his contacts would do their best to fix any problems or let him know ahead of time if there were bad spots.

William Weller was very familiar with running Royal Mail stages along the shoreline of the St. Lawrence all the way from Cornwall to Montreal, and many people along the route knew him and would be ready to help. He felt comfortable picking the shorter route, knowing that the road would still be decent and he would have support in case of trouble.

At the intersection west of Moulinette, the sleigh turned right and drove into the town. Moulinette was busy with people, wagons, and horses. Grist and saw mills had been built farther away from the canal in anticipation of the flooding, but the woollen mills were still operating over on Sheik's Island, anticipating the time when they would have to be moved. The situation was very uncertain at this time in Moulinette.

The disruption that the Cornwall Canal had caused in Moulinette and the other villages immediately to the east resulted in loss of income and much extra cost for many people. On the other hand, hundreds of workers were hired to work on the canal, and many local businesses benefitted from the surge in activity. Stores and hotels and blacksmiths did very well, but if your land was in the path of the canal you might not be very happy.

Moulinette was located on land granted to Sir John Johnson in 1784 and later came into the hands of Adam Dixson, who constructed a dam from the north shore across to Sheik's Island, with the idea of producing water power. He built mills on the island near the end of the dam, and this became the most prosperous establishment in the area. Moulinette had acquired a post office by 1832 and was a small but busy community when the canal set it reeling. Later, in the 1850s, the newly established town to the north of the canal would prosper when a railway station was established there.

William Weller may have been impressed with the scope and scale of the undertaking of the canal, but likely cringed at the waste and disruption that was being endured by the people, because the project was on hold. All they had at this moment was an ugly ditch. Until it was completed and flooded with water, the promise of the canal would be a dream, something to hope for in the future.

In 1958, Moulinette became another of the Ten Lost Villages. Some of the homes and businesses were moved to the new villages of Ingleside and Long Sault. Christ Church, originally built in 1836 on land donated by Adam Dixson, was secularized in 1957 and moved to Upper Canada Village. Many gravestones from Christ Church Cemetery and others of the Lost Villages were preserved and mounted on brick walls at the Pioneer Memorial, also in Upper Canada Village. Today, there is a Moulinette Island at the east end of the Long Sault Parkway.

The sleigh travelled out of Moulinette and swung southeast to meet the edge of the new canal, coming to the brand-new community of New Mille Roches. The small village of Mille Roche, situated across the river from the east end of Sheik's Island, was even more disrupted than Moulinette in these years of the building of the Cornwall Canal. The route of the canal went east of the village, effectively isolating it from the mainland.

The solution was to move the village north a little, and to the east side of the canal. For some time afterward, the new village would be called New Mille Roche, and the old village would be called, sensibly, Old Mille Roche. This disruption caused much financial stress for the people of Mille Roche. For years afterward, many people would petition the government for restitution, with only meagre results.

William Weller followed the road through New Mille Roche, then along the east side of the canal, missing the old village completely. Not far along, they came to the small hamlet of Maple Grove, which had also been divided by the canal. This was the last of the Ten Lost Villages.

The St. Lawrence Seaway had two major objectives.[7] First, it was meant to provide much easier water transportation between the Great Lakes and the rest of the world, bypassing the rapids and the various smaller canals, which, each in their own time and place, had improved the situation based on current technology and resources. Second, both the United States and Canada wanted to use the power of the river to generate large amounts of electricity, which was in great demand by their growing populations.

Our travellers in 1840 would never have imagined the size and complexity of the Moses-Saunders Power Dam,[8] which created Lake St. Lawrence as it flooded the land on both sides of the river in 1958. The technology of the two power generation plants, one on each side of the border, amazes modern visitors. Located just west of Cornwall, the R.H. Saunders Power Generating Station offers displays and tours for visitors and is well worth a look.

We can say that the main objectives of the Seaway were met, but at a significant cost. Thousands of people were uprooted and their lives changed forever. Environmental damage is still being studied, including pollution from industrial installations that located in the area because of the availability of power.

Also, the Mohawks of Akwesasne took a terrible loss as a result of the flooding. Thousands of acres of reserve lands as well as traditional lands, were flooded without consultation with the people who would be most affected. Settlements have been reached for compensation and environmental stewardship, but it can only be hoped that lessons learned from the St. Lawrence Seaway project will help us do better in the future.

29

Cornwall

THE TRAVELLERS NOW APPROACHED CORNWALL, THE LARGEST TOWN THEY HAD encountered since Kingston. Cornwall was the administrative centre for the Eastern District, which was called Lunenburg during the first decade of settlement. The first settlers came in 1784; officers and families from the First Battalion of the King's Royal Regiment, as well as some of the 84th Royal Highland Regiment, led by Sir John Johnson.

For a short time, the town was called New Johnstown, in honour of their leader, but would soon be named Cornwall, in honour of the Duke of Cornwall, who commanded the British military in the Canadian colonies during the 1790s. The town's position at the eastern entrance to the Long Sault Rapids gave it great importance from a military point of view, and later it was critical in the forwarding trade. The movement of people and goods between Montreal and Kingston increased dramatically during the early decades of settlement.

As William Weller approached the western side of Cornwall, he followed the road away from the shoreline, into the town on Second Street West. He initially followed the main road by turning right, but then turned left off the King's Highway onto First Street West. He might have kept to the main road, which went farther south to Water Street, but in this case, he was intent on making the next stop at his favourite place in town, Chesley's Inn, which was over at First Street West and Augusta Street. He had stopped there many times in the last decade and knew that

John Chesley always provided excellent service. Certainly, he could expect nothing less in this very special case. After all, he was driving the governor general!

The modern driver may recall passing under the looming International Bridge at the west edge of Cornwall, and maybe following the route over the bridge to visit the United States. Today, the situation in this area is much different. In 2015 and 2016, the old bridge was removed and a new, low-level bridge, now takes the road to the U.S.A. across the old canal to the Three Nations Crossing.

As soon as the sleigh hit First Street West, William Weller took up his horn and gave the normal warning. He blew it again when the sleigh reached Augusta Street. It was obvious that the folks at Chesley's Inn[1] were waiting for him, as there was a crowd milling about in front of the building as he drove into the yard. The people made room for him beside the fresh team that was stationed in the yard, ready to go.

29.1 Chesley's Inn, Cornwall

Chesley's Inn was a handsome two-storey frame building with clapboard exterior,[2] which had been built by John Chesley's father, Allsaint Chesley, in 1814. Three

Chesley brothers had fought for the patriots during the War of Independence, but only Allsaint brought his family north to Cornwall in 1800 in order to engage in trade. This caused a serious rift in the family, especially when Allsaint did a lot of business providing the British forces with supplies. Of course, it did not help when his sons fought for Canada during the War of 1812. It was not uncommon that these terrible conflicts tore families apart, pitting brother against brother and father against son.

John Chesley had carried on his father's hotel business, and through the years built a solid reputation for this excellent establishment. Well-known writer Charles Fothergill visited Chesley's Inn in 1817, and Catherine Parr Trail commented about the place on her trip into Upper Canada. Legend suggests that Charles Dickens slept here one night on his tour of the Americas, a few months after Mr. Weller came through in 1840.

Over the decades, this building has changed a lot. Sheriff Daniel E. McIntyre purchased the property from the Chesley family in the 1860s and converted it into a fine home with brick exterior in the Georgian style, where he and his family lived for many years. Today, Chesley's Inn is still there, at 40 First Street West, revitalized as a comfortable bed-and-breakfast, offering the modern traveller a pleasant experience in an historic setting.

John Chesley was in the yard when the sleigh carrying the governor general arrived. He waved his hat and yelled hello to Mr. Weller along with the others. He quickly approached the driver as the team was being changed, offering a vigorous handshake, a flask of rum, and good wishes. Mr. Weller took a good swig from the flask and then handed it into the coach so that his passengers could indulge as well. The change of horses was quick in spite of all the people in the yard, and very soon the sleigh was back on First Street West, heading east again.

This time, there was another sleigh following along. John Chesley and his friend John Lonney had made arrangements with Mr. Weller to supply the horses for the next stage of the trip, and they sent a couple of their men along on the trip to Lancaster. A newspaper report about this appears in the *Cornwall Observer,* saying that "…it is but justice to them to state that they accomplished that distance, sixteen miles, in one hour and ten minutes…"[3]

The pair of sleighs rushed past the post office on the north side of First Street West and then made a quick right turn onto Pitt Street, the main north-south road of the town. On their immediate right was the imposing Eastern District courthouse and jail and just a few yards along, they came to Water Street. A left turn put the travellers back onto the King's Highway.

The town of Cornwall had experienced a major spurt of growth in the several years starting in 1834, when construction of the Cornwall canal began. Many tradesmen and labourers had come to the area, looking to take advantage of the many jobs involved in digging the ditch, building up the embankment, and preparing the locks. Property values in the middle of Cornwall had risen quickly, and several lots near the canal had already been developed. The impact of all this activity was felt in the stores and blacksmith shops as well as on the nearby farms. Teamster wagons loaded with food and lumber were on the roads constantly, and the young farm boys in the area had no trouble finding a good-paying job for a change.

But then it all collapsed. In the spring and summer of 1838,[4] the financial problems came to a head. Up to this time, £430,000 had been allocated to improvements along the St. Lawrence River and £350,000 had already been spent. It was estimated that £50,000 would be needed to complete the project. However, the finances of Upper Canada were in such terrible shape that no more money could be found. The commissioners, including Hiram Norton, William Weller's one-time partner, managed to find £29,000 through the sale of debentures, but this would only allow them to wind down the work and pay off immediate debts. The work ground to a halt.

By the time the governor general came through Cornwall in 1840, the effect of the stoppage of work had created a virtual recession. All of that wonderful optimism of the middle years of the 1830s had given way to anger and fear. What was going to happen? Surely the government must complete such an important project, but when? It was the primary topic on the minds of the people in these parts.

Unknown to them, the gentleman inside the sleigh had come to Canada with a big cheque in his pocket. The government in London was willing to provide more than one million pounds to Upper Canada in order to pay off the huge debt that had been accumulated, largely through major infrastructure projects like the Welland Canal. They also advocated rolling Upper Canada's debt into the new Province of Canada, which made the legislators of Upper Canada very pleased but was not too popular in Lower Canada.

Eventually, these new funds and the changes in government would allow projects like the Cornwall canal to continue. Mr. Thomson would not be drawn into the question of how many votes for his reforms of the government had been garnered by this large pot of money, although basic human nature suggests that it must have been a powerful incentive.

But the inhabitants of Cornwall had a much more immediate problem. The canal had been built across the face of the waterfront, starting at the east end and going all the way across the town. It blocked off much of the convenient access that people had enjoyed to the southern shoreline and to Cornwall Island, across the channel to the south of town. The plans for the canal included a culvert under the channel as well as a ferry, but the town folk saw this as a penny-pinching approach that would put them at a disadvantage.

A hew and cry went up from the town and government officials had to deal with a barrage of petitions asking that a proper bridge be built over the canal and the channel.[5] There was little sympathy from the officials, who asserted that the culvert and ferry were enough, so nothing came of it. Eventually, after the canal finally opened in 1842, the real effect of the canal became evident. Following more petitions and much acrimony, the officials relented and agreed to build a bridge.

The sleigh was now on Water Street East, skirting the north side of the half-completed canal. Many buildings had already been removed to make way for the canal, and others would move when the canal was enhanced in later decades to accommodate larger boats. An industrial area was taking shape at the eastern end of the town, below Water Street East and near the eastern outlet of the canal into the St. Lawrence River.

Today, a stroll in the beautiful Lamoureux Park[6] at the waterfront in Cornwall only hints at the industrial dynamics and commercial enterprise that took place on these few acres during the active life of the Cornwall Canal. A picture from 1950 shows the canal right beside Water Street, and the large Stormont Mill straddling the plateau between the canal and the shoreline. Today, part of the wall of the canal is evident, along with historical plaques and memorials. At the east end of the park, the eastern entrance of the canal runs by the marina and abruptly stops, replaced by pleasant lawns and paths. This place has been repurposed.

William Weller was glad to be out of Cornwall and charging east by the middle of the afternoon of the second day of their trip. If this continued, he might just meet the terms of the contract and enjoy the payday he anticipated. He sat on the bench, urging the horses along and marvelling at their luck so far. There had been no major interruptions and no breakdowns or disasters to deal with. This might just work!

During his musings, Mr. Weller caught a glimpse of Fort Augustus, on rising land to the north of the road. Originally a windmill, the round fieldstone structure had been converted into a fort in 1838, during the panic about possible invasion from the United States. It was soon abandoned and deteriorated over time, as the suburbs of Cornwall surrounded it. Finally, the Township of Cornwall demolished it in 1944. Today the Windmill Fort is commemorated by an historical plaque on the side of Windmill Apartments, at the corner of Easton and Felix Streets, just one block north of Number 2 Highway.

The travellers continued on the King's Highway, more accurately called the Montreal Road from Cornwall to Montreal. They quickly passed through the village of Lorneville, and soon the road ran snug to the shore of the river, gratefully with no ugly brown ditch in sight. They were back to a route that the modern driver would recognize as well, away from the effects of the flooding of the St. Lawrence Seaway and back to the old road along the river.

Several miles along the Montreal Road, Mr. Weller might have noticed the commanding mansion called Inverarden House, up a slight rise to the north of the road. This luxurious estate looked out over the St. Lawrence River, demonstrating very clearly the wealth and prominence of John McDonald, its creator. Often called John McDonald of Garth[7] to reflect his origins in Scotland, the young McDonald had come to Canada in 1791 to pursue a career with the North West Company, serving in the west at trading posts such as Moose Lake, Manitoba, Fort George, Alberta, and Fort Augustus, later called Fort Edmonton. In 1813, he participated in the assault on Fort Astoria in Oregon Territory and then was back in Canada in 1814 to mediate between the Nor'Westers at Red River and the Selkirk colonists.

Later in 1814, he retired from the fur trade and two years later, purchased property to the west of Gray's Creek, which was just inside the western boundary of Glengarry County. Cornwall was the largest town nearby, a dozen miles to the west. McDonald's autobiography must be taken with large dollops of salt at many points, but it does describe the life of a daring and aggressive young man who participated in many large events of the day.

The home he built overlooking the St. Lawrence River, just west of Gray's Creek, was spectacular at the time and even today retains its power and dignity as a unique and important part of the built history of Stormont County. The site was recognized as a National Historical Site[8] in 1968, due to its historic and architectural significance. It was the perfect home for a wealthy adventurer wishing to relax from his travels and adventures.

30
Glengarry

THERE WAS NO RELAXING FOR WILLIAM WELLER. HE KNEW THE NEXT PART OF THE trip would be challenging, but he took heart as the sleigh approached the bridge over Gray's Creek. They were about to enter Glengarry County, the most easterly county in Upper Canada, and the gateway to Lower Canada and their destination in Montreal.

Crossing into Charlottenburgh Township, the travellers crossed Gray's Creek, the first of many significant creeks that flow into the St. Lawrence River in Glengarry County. Gray's Creek was named for the Gray family, which had settled east of Cornwall after the end of the War of Independence. James Gray had been a major in the 1st Battalion of Sir John Johnson's King's Royal Regiment and received land after the war as a result. However, his son, Robert Isaac Dey Gray[1] would be much better known.

The younger Gray had gone to Quebec with his family where he studied law. In 1795, Lieutenant Governor John Graves Simcoe appointed him Solicitor General of Upper Canada. Then, in 1804, he was a passenger on the ill-fated ship, H.M.S. *Speedy,* which sunk off Presqu'ile Point near Brighton, with the loss of all souls on board. Of the twenty-two people lost that day, the solicitor general of Upper Canada, Robert Isaac Dey Gray, was included. Legend has it that Gray wrote a will before embarking on the dangerous trip and in the will arranged for the freeing and subsequent care of several slaves that he owned.

Today, forty-three acres in this area are protected in the Gray's Creek Conservation Area,[2] which falls under the management of the Raisin Region Conservation Authority. The trails, landscape, and wildlife provide many opportunities for enjoyment by the public.

Both Charlottenburgh and Lancaster were known as "Royal Townships", named for members of the royal family at the time. The earliest settlement of United Empire Loyalists in this area was encouraged by Sir John Johnson, who selected a site well inland on the River aux Raisin. He would name the settlement Williamstown, after his father, Sir William Johnson. The River aux Raisin had been an important water highway for traders and natives, and the settlers used it to establish settlements away from the marshes that were common along the shoreline of the St. Lawrence. This turned out to be an excellent site for a settlement.

Sir John Johnson brought with him many soldiers who had served with him during the war, and a significant proportion of them were Highland Scotsmen. He built himself a substantial home at Williamstown in 1785, and this building, called The Manor House, is now a National Historic Site[3] and the home of the Glengarry Archives. Currently, the building is undergoing major renovations.

In 1787, Reverend John Bethune[4] came to Glengary (it was spelled with one r in the early days) and purchased a house in Williamstown that had been built by Peter Ferguson. Bethune built a large addition to the house in 1804 where he lived with this family until his death in 1815. He had been chaplain to the 1st Battalion of the Royal Highland Regiment and had set up the first Presbyterian church of Canada in Montreal immediately after the war was over. His oldest son, Angus Bethune, was a wintering partner with the North West Company and travelled over the Rocky Mountains with explorer, David Thompson.

After John Bethune died at Williamstown in 1815, his house was taken over by David Thompson[5] and still stands today as the Bethune-Thomson House, owned by Ontario Heritage Trust. The children of Rev. John Bethune would become members of Upper Canada's elite, including: James Gray Bethune, a businessman of Cobourg; John Bethune, principal of McGill University and dean of Montreal; and Alexander Bethune, bishop of York.

The Montreal Road hugged the shoreline inside Charlottenburgh Township and soon the sleigh approached the old home of Lieutenant Colonel John Macdonnell, today called Glengarry House, near the town of Glen Walter. Macdonnell had served with the Royal Highland Engineers, then Butler's Rangers, and received grants of land in Charlottenburgh after the war. He represented Glengarry in the Legislative Assembly and would be named the first speaker of that body in 1792. Today, Glengarry House is only a ruin, represented by stone walls hidden behind trees to the south of the road. There is a cairn and plaque at Stonehouse Point Road commemorating this significant National Historic Site.[6]

None of this was of much concern for William Weller as he guided the team along the Montreal Road at the shoreline of the St. Lawrence River. Initially, the road was relatively good as it skirted the shoreline and dipped inland to avoid marshy areas. While the terrain was relatively flat, this area was much less populated than territory to the west, so there were not many villages.

After a time, the road swung northeast to follow an increasingly uneven shoreline along the wider part of the St. Lawrence River, called Lake St. Francis. Then, they started to see more stretches of corduroy on the road. The travellers had experienced corduroy roads, but none to equal this. As the sleigh headed toward the next stop at Lancaster (now called South Lancaster), it would have to deal with many long sections of corduroy. Along the shoreline in this area, the waters of Lake St. Francis extend far into the land, creating large marshy areas, punctuated by several large creeks that drain into the river.

For the first dozen miles or so, the progress was good. Then, looking ahead, William Weller saw several men on the road. One of the men was walking toward the sleigh, waving his hat and yelling for them to stop. The sleigh came to a halt, and the man came forward to speak to the driver. He explained that there was a very bad section of corduroy ahead and that his crew of men would be several hours repairing it.

The story was that several teamster wagons, loaded with lumber, had come this way the day before, leaving many broken and displaced logs. Mr. Weller's contacts in Cornwall had inspected the road and immediately called some local saw mill workers to do a quick repair. They were making good progress but the damage extended several hundred yards, so they would not be finished until later in the day.

Mr. Weller considered the situation for a moment and then asked the man, "Can you spare two men for a few minutes? Have them clear any obstacles on the south side of the road, and I will drive down the side of the road, avoiding the damaged corduroy as much as possible. I have the governor general on board, and we must make haste to Montreal. We cannot wait."

The man turned back to his crew, picked two men with shovels and crowbars, and they began to clear the logs and stones away on the south side of the road.

At this moment, Captain Le Marchant opened the door of the coach and asked, "Mr. Weller, do you wish us to walk?"

Mr. Weller considered his offer for a moment and then replied, "No, Captain, it will be safer and more convenient for the Guvner if you maintain your position. I will let you know if we need to clear the coach."

The leader of the work crew then took the team in hand, speaking to the horses calmly and guiding them off to the side of the road. The horses protested at this irregularity, but with encouragement from the driver, they proceeded to pick their way along the rough and muddy side of the road. The sleigh itself had no problem passing over rough patches because of the wide runners and the metal re-enforcement attached to them, but Mr. Weller was concerned for the safety of the horses. In this wet and low area, a small pothole could develop quickly into a deep and dangerous pit, where a horse might break a leg very easily.

At one point, a large log presented itself, and Mr. Weller suggested that, instead of taking time to dig it out, they should manoeuvre the sleigh back onto the corduroy, while the crew might fix the worst of the pieces of corduroy in this immediate location to allow the team to pass safely. This done, the sleigh proceeded along the side of the road again. After a while, the men and horses got the hang of it, and the sleigh passed safely along.

For the modern traveller along Number 2 Highway, the town of Summerstown leads to Charlottenburgh Park, which provides a large campground with trails and picnic area. Farther along, at Fraser Road, No. 2 skirts the Cooper Marsh Conservation Area,[7] a cherished wetland that is part of the larger Charlottenburgh Marsh. The modern highway is high and dry, smooth and comfortable, and it might be hard to imagine the travails of the 1840 traveller. Mr. Weller knew that it was part of the package when he decided to take the shoreline route rather than the King's Road to the north. Now, it was a matter of limiting the delay as much as possible.

Eventually, the sleigh was through the worst of the broken corduroy and could come back onto the road. The leader of the crew came over to speak to Mr. Weller and was greeted by a small leather pouch tossed down from the driver. Coins in the pouch jingled as the man caught the pouch in one hand. "Pass this among the men," said Mr. Weller, then he took to the reins and started the team along the road, leaving the man standing with his hat in one hand and the pouch in the other.

Yes, the man thought to himself, *that William Weller was a fine feller, just like he had heard many times from others.* Now he had his own proof.

William Weller gave a sigh of relief at being delivered of this dangerous obstacle in a reasonable amount of time. There had been a considerable delay and that was unfortunate, but they were still very much within their time, as long as nothing happened to delay them further.

There was more corduroy to deal with as the sleigh made its way northeast along the north reaches of Charlottenburgh Marsh. Finally, the road swung more easterly and within a short time, the travellers came to the bridge over the River aux Raisin. Long before United Empire Loyalists settled in Glengarry, French traders used the river to access the interior, where they would trade with native peoples who supplied the furs that were in demand in Europe. The river acquired its name due to the wild grapes that grew along its banks. If you were heading up this way, you could say you were going "aux raisin." Today, this extensive river system is managed by the Raisin River Conservation Authority.[8] Unlike in early settlement times, traffic on the river is largely recreational.

The modern driver can glance to the south while crossing the bridge over the River Raisin and see a wooded island a little way off shore. When William Weller drove the governor general across the wooden bridge that was across the river at that time, little did he know that plans were being made by the Highland Militia of Glengarry to build a cairn on the island to commemorate the services of Sir John Colborne, who had been the lieutenant governor of Upper Canada from 1828 to 1836. Colborne had also been the commander of British forces in the Canadian colonies at the time of the Mackenzie Rebellion. During the summers of 1840, 1841, and 1842, a large conical cairn was built on the island. In 1905 it was repaired and a plaque[9] was added. In 2009, the island was included in native land claims, and since then, access to Cairn Island has been restricted.

William Weller was glad to see that the bridge over the river had been repaired recently, after winter damage, and he was able to cross quickly. The village of Lancaster was located just to the east of the river. It had acquired this name in 1787 but was sometimes called Riviere Raisin, or Kirktown, or Lower Village. The *Beldon County Atlas map* for Lancaster Township[10] shows that, in 1878, the village was called "Kirk Town or Lower Village". When the Grand Trunk Railway came through here in 1855, a station was established about a mile north of the original village, and it became New Lancaster, or later just Lancaster, with the old village taking the name South Lancaster.

After crossing the bridge over the Raisin River, the travellers also crossed the border between Charlottenburgh and Lancaster Townships. William Weller continued straight along the Montreal Road and pulled out his horn to alert the innkeeper and stable boys at the next stage stop. At the corner of King Street, he swung over to the side of the road, where the fresh team was waiting, and a quick exchange was done, sending the travellers on their journey.

The modern driver might be a bit confused here. Today, when driving east toward South Lancaster, we are inclined to follow Number 2 around a long curve to the north and miss the town altogether. If we continue along, we cross over the 401, then head east on Number 2, as the two roads run shoulder-to-shoulder until almost the Quebec border.

Look a little closer. If you keep going straight after coming off the bridge, you will leave Number 2 Highway and find yourself on the Old Montreal Road. William Weller would not have called it the "Old" Montreal Road because in 1840 it was "the" Montreal Road. Follow this modest street east, and you will cross Cairn View Road, which recognizes the importance of Cairn Island. Farther along are King Street and Calvin Street. Notice how many older houses there are on this street, positioned right at the road, which was common in the early days.

A little east of Lancaster, the Montreal Road swung south and then east again, crossing another bridge at the next creek and then on along the shoreline. At some point in time, the Montreal Road was moved north, to the First Concession Line at Lancaster, avoiding the creeks and marshes at the shoreline. The map for Lancaster Township in the *Beldon County Atlas* (1878) shows the Old Montreal Road going east of Kirk Town, but stopping abruptly in lot 35. This tells us that the main route was moved north of Lancaster sometime before the 1870s. The South Service Road may be closer to the old road in terms of roads we can drive on today.

William Weller was persistently concerned with making good time. Daylight hours allowed him to urge the team to a bit more speed, and luckily, most of the road was still frozen and no major breaks in the corduroy were encountered. The sleigh was now on the straight line of the concession road, avoiding marshy areas such as Mud Pond and Point Mouillée. At Sutherland Creek, another bridge was crossed and then again at Gunn and Woods Creeks. Soon after, the travellers passed from Upper Canada into Lower Canada, which meant they were even closer to their destination in Montreal.

31
Lower Canada

THE ONLY INDICATION THAT THE TRAVELLERS HAD ENTERED LOWER CANADA WAS the small village of Rivière-Beaudette, scattered along the shoreline of Pointe Beaudette, a sizable protrusion into the St. Lawrence River. French traders had stopped here and found a burned-down shack, which contained a metal cot known as a "baudet", and the name stuck. The Montreal Road proceeded east from here, well back of the shoreline.

Today, the name of the road changes at the Quebec border. From Stormont/ Glengarry County Road 2, it becomes Quebec Route 338. Until the 1970s, it was called Route 2, and was seen as an extension of the interprovincial Route 2, which stretched from Windsor, Ontario to Halifax, Nova Scotia. Route 338 will, to a large degree, identify William Weller's journey from the Rivière-Beaudette to Vaudreuil-Dorion, where it meets Autoroute 20.

A long stretch of straight road lay out in front of the travellers, as William Weller once more contemplated his situation. It was well into the afternoon. The objective was to be in Montreal before nine o'clock that evening. The contract stipulated thirty-eight hours, and some quick figuring took the trip from Toronto, at seven in the morning on Monday the seventeenth, to nine in the evening on Tuesday the eighteenth, altogether thirty-eight hours. They must arrive at the Exchange Coffee House in Montreal before nine o'clock. The objective was clear.

How they were going to achieve the objective was a little less clear. As William Weller drove the team through the tiny settlement of Saint-Zotique, the sleigh passed quickly by the intersection where the King's Road came down to meet the Montreal Road. At this point, the choice between the two options was moot.

Mr. Weller figured that they were just over forty miles from Montreal. He was going to stop and change horses in Coteau Landing in a short time, and he was planning on three more stops after that. Even if the roads were in good shape, which they generally were as you got closer to Montreal, there were major obstacles in the form of the St. Lawrence River with its islands and ferries and ice roads and so much more. The list was daunting when he thought of them all in succession.

The travellers were entering a landscape that was much different from any they had driven through in the last day. Since they had passed through Lancaster, Lake Saint Francis, a vast darkness off to their right, offered a safe and convenient water highway for the traffic of people and goods going from Coteau Landing to points west. Along here, stagecoach operators took a loss because there was limited population along the shoreline and demand for their services fluctuated wildly with the seasons.

Then, near Coteau Landing, Lake Saint Francis narrowed back into a river channel, and the waters churned over dangerous rapids between there and Cascades. The next opening in the river was Lake Saint Louis. It was one of the worst sections of rapids in the St. Lawrence River, and was a major obstacle to traffic between Upper and Lower Canada.

Far back in time, Coteau Landing had been an important gathering point for the indigenous peoples of the region, and French traders used it in the early days of European settlement. Its position at the eastern end of Lake Saint Francis ensured a busy commercial village in the days of bateaux, Durham boats, and steamboats on the lake. Much later, in 1899, Coteau Landing became the southern terminus of the Soulanges Canal,[1] a modern facility with locks powered by electricity from a power-generating station. Today, the canal is closed, and a pleasant cycling path follows the canal, which lies on the west side of the Chemin du Fleuve.

The Montreal Road hugged the shoreline as the sleigh approached Coteau Landing. The driver pulled out his horn and gave the normal blast to alert the innkeeper and stable boys. Mr. Weller had made arrangements, through his messengers, to take advantage of a local stage stop in a popular inn on the Montreal Road in the village. In the middle of the afternoon, there was a crowd gathered at the inn, waiting to catch a glimpse of the famous Stagecoach King. Maybe some hoped to see the governor general, if that was really who the passenger might be. Folks were sceptical of that. Why would the governor general travel this way? Why not wait for the comfort of steamboat travel in a few weeks, when navigation opened on the lakes and rivers?

The governor general huddled in the coach, happy to avoid any contact with the citizens of Lower Canada, until he could get to Montreal and was able to directly address the legislators and power brokers of that province. The folks at an inn at Coteau Landing were not likely to be sympathetic to his methods or objectives, so better to avoid potential discomfort. He knew what he had to do and how he would do it. *Just get me to Montreal, Mr. Weller, and we shall see how things go.*

The change of horses was accomplished with the normal efficiency, and the sleigh regained the Montreal Road, as it continued along the shoreline, which soon swung north. The modern driver will be thwarted in following the same route. Rue Principale follows the shoreline through Coteau Landing, but ends at the east side of the village, where the Soulanges Canal produces a "Fin" sign. In 1840, the Montreal Road went straight through here to hug the shoreline. Keep to Mr. Weller's route by taking the Chemin du Fleuve off Route 338 as it heads north, with the canal on the left and attractive private homes as well as public parks on the right.

As William Weller drove the team along the shoreline from Coteau Landing, he may have recalled the widely reported accident that had occurred here in January of 1836, which involved a Montreal mail stage.[2] The stage was on its way to Kingston and had stopped at the post office at Coteau Landing to exchange mail. The driver had taken the mail bag into the building and left the six passengers waiting in the stage. For some unknown reason, the horses started on their journey by themselves, heading directly out onto the ice, which was just behind the post office.

The passengers were oblivious to their danger until the ice broke and water started rushing into the coach. They had to break the curtains to make an escape from their potential coffin. Luckily, all six managed to find a solid piece of ice large enough to support them until help arrived. Unfortunately, the Coteau-du-Lac Rapids claimed the horses, the coach, and all the baggage. In the end, there was, miraculously, no loss of life, but some bankers in Montreal were much agitated at the loss of £4,000 in unregistered bank notes.

The rapids roared in his ears as the sleigh quickly approached Coteau-du-Lac, the next village on the Montreal Road. This location had been recognized as a critical military position during the early years of the War of Independence. There were significant delays in transporting troops and supplies from Montreal to Newark (Niagara-on-the-Lake) and Detroit, and the worst place was the rapids near Coteau-du-Lac. The solution was to build a canal from the mouth of the Rivière Délisle across a small peninsula. This would allow bateaux to edge along the western shoreline of the river and then enter the canal to avoid the worst of the rapids.

Constructed between 1779 and 1781, the original canal seems puny by modern standards, at only 100 metres long and 2.5 metres wide, but it provided an important service. Then, during the War of 1812-1814, it was widened considerably to accommodate the larger Durham boats. After the war was over, the emphasis changed from military transport to commercial and passenger travel. Waves of settlers had to be shipped to Upper Canada, with all their baggage, and the trade in merchandise to support the growing populations to the west required massive shipments of goods. The construction of the Carillon Canal, on the Ottawa River, the Chambly Canal on the Richelieu, and the opening of the Rideau Canal in 1832 would syphon away a lot of traffic from Coteau-du-Lac, as the northern route became popular for a time.

During the Mackenzie Rebellion of 1837-1838, the threat of American attack led to the construction of fortifications and barracks near the old canal. Most of the soldiers were gone by the time William Weller drove by in February of 1840, but he would have seen the octagonal block house and barracks buildings as he drove by. However, the writing was on the wall. Later in 1840, the town would lose its customs office and then, in 1845, the opening of the Beauharnois Canal on the south side of the St. Lawrence would reduce traffic at Coteau-du-Lac, and the fortunes of the town suffered. In recent years, the original canal site and the fort have been designated as a National Historic Site,[3] where visitors can see ruins, as well as fascinating illustrations of the bustling and dangerous times of the past.

Conversation inside the coach of the sleigh turned to the current political situation, as Captain Le Marchant mentioned to Mr. Thomson that one of the gentlemen he was considering as a possible political ally, lived in Coteau-du-Lac. Mr. Thomson began to ruminate over Mr. John Simpson, who had lived in this town since 1822 when he was appointed overseer of his majesty's locks, which was an important job at this critical place on the river. This man seemed to have an unusual resume, which made players on both extremes of the political spectrum distrustful of his real ambitions.

John Simpson[4] had come to Quebec as a failed farmer and merchant from England. He managed to gain the favour of Lord Dalhousie, who was governor of Canada in 1819. Subsequent good work resulted in his election to the Assembly of Lower Canada and his appointment to several positions, including the one at Coteau-du-Lac. Leading up to the Mackenzie Rebellion, he began to be associated with reform, but when rebellion broke out, he quickly organized the militia at Coteau-du-Lac and prevented the town, canal, and fort from falling into the hands of the Patriotes. Sir John Colborne praised him for his zeal. Then, Jean-Joseph Girouard, one of the Patriote leaders, surrendered himself to Simpson at Coteau-du-Lac. John Simpson recommended leniency to Lord Durham, a position that gained him praise from the more moderate voices and condemnation from the conservatives, who wanted harsh sentences for all rebels.

Governor General Thomson was already thinking about how he would pass the legislation in Lower Canada to make all the changes that his bosses in London expected. One approach was to make sure to pick candidates for the next election very carefully. John Simpson was on the list. In 1841, Simpson would run in Vaudreuil County, and the governor general would pull out all the stops to make sure he won. Blatant favouritism was exercised in moving the polling station far away from possible opposition voters. There was violence at the polls, which most folks attributed to ruffians hired by a mysterious but powerful hand. Simpson would win, and Governor General Thomson would get his legislation passed, but the tactics of this election would be used in later years to explain how not to run a fair and legitimate election.[5]

On the bench, the driver was contemplating the dramatic changes that were happening in this region – things that directly impacted his stage business. Even though he operated mostly between Toronto and Kingston, he often had contracts with operators along the route between Cornwall and Montreal. His objective was to extend the geographical reach of his own stage lines for the transportation of both passengers and the Royal Mail.

It was a constant challenge to keep these deals current and functioning. Steamboats appeared on the lakes and rivers, often operated by the same men who owned the stagecoach lines. Horace Dickinson had competed with several other businessmen in this region during the 1820s, vying for licenses to run passenger lines and working to obtain contracts to carry the Royal Mail. Gradually, steamboats were beginning to show their worth, often reducing the demand for stage travel, at least in the summer. The business of stagecoaches and Royal Mail contracts had become much more complicated in the 1830s.[7] Old agreements merged into new ones, and larger companies gobbled up smaller ones. The players and the technology changed constantly, and it was difficult to stay in business, let alone make a profit.

Not far north of Coteau-du-Lac, the travellers crossed the Rivière Rouge and sped along the Montreal Road, which for the modern driver is the Chemin du Fleuve (River Road). The river is tame today, but that is not what our travellers saw and heard. The roar of the rapids would have been a constant backdrop for the persistent pounding of the horses' hooves on the road.

The sleigh sped along the Montreal Road at a gallop, hugging the lakeshore. The next village along the shore was Les Cèdres, originally called The Cedars, because of large cedar trees growing near the portage that was commonly used by the French traders and soldiers travelling between Montreal and Cornwall. The team clattered across the bridge over the river near Les Cèdres, and Mr. Weller did not hesitate as the small cluster of buildings fell behind. This was a critical point in the trip. Miles had to be eaten up quickly.

They were approaching the small settlement of Cascades Point where the sleigh would turn north to follow the shoreline of the western branch of the Ottawa River. Now called Pointe des Cascades, this peninsula provided a critical portage at the bottom of one of the worst rapids on the St. Lawrence River, which opens up into Lake St. Louis just east of the point.

The village would grow in the 1890s, when it became the eastern terminus of the Soulanges Canal, but in 1840, the taverns, inns, and stores supported the bateaux men who struggled to pole and pull their craft along the shoreline. Warehouses stored goods to be portaged, and often the road provided a safe and solid, if very rough, alternative to travellers who were terrified by the violence of the rapids.

The path that William Weller took through Point des Cascades may be unclear to the modern traveller, since a lot has changed since 1840. The Soulanges Canal divides the village, and today's Chemin du Fleuve, which was William Weller's Montreal Road, follows the shoreline south of the canal and terminates at the end of the point. However, before going to the end, you need to turn left at Rue Centrale, which will take you over the canal. Route 338 can then be accessed using the Rue Aqueduc, just north of the canal, or the small Avenue des Cascades a little farther along Rue Centrale. Boulevard de Soulanges carries Route 338 through Pointe des Cascades and along the shoreline of the Ottawa River, more or less the path that our travellers would have taken in 1840.

32

On the Ice to Lachine

THE IMMEDIATE OBJECTIVE FOR THE TRAVELLERS WAS TO GAIN THE NORTH SHORE at Saint-Anne-de-Bellevue, from which it would be easy to enter the ice road to Lachine. First, they had to cross the West Ottawa Channel, to the big island called Île-Perrot. Mr. Weller planned to change horses at the entrance to the short ice road that crossed to Île-Perrot. As he approached the inn where arrangements had been made to change horses, he blew his horn to alert the innkeeper and stable boys. When the sleigh pulled into the yard in front of the inn, a man recognized the driver and came over to offer a flask, while a quick change of the team was under way. Mr. Weller asked the man if the ice was in good shape, and the response was emphatically positive. There should be no trouble on the ice today.

William Weller guided the fresh team down the slope at the shore, and out onto the ice. The horses in this area were accustomed to running on ice roads, so they made short work of the leg to Île-Perrot, churning up the dirt at the shoreline to reach the road across the island. It was not long before the sleigh was back on the ice, this time crossing the east channel of the Ottawa River.

An image that William Weller could not fathom in 1840 is commonplace for the modern traveller. The Techereau Bridge[1] spans the Ottawa River from Vaudreuil-Dorion to Pincourt on the northwest side of Île-Perrot. Then, the Galipeault Bridge[2] spans the distance from the north shore of Île-Perrot, across the eastern channel of the Ottawa River to the town of Sainte-Anne-de-Bellevue. Both bridges carry four lanes of Autoroute 20, which is a primary artery west of Montreal.

At St. Anne-de-Bellevue, William Weller took to the Lakeshore Road for only a few miles, and then steered the team back down to the ice. Along the north shore, there would be several ice roads, maintained by different local concerns, extending the road across the approximately twelve miles to Lachine. The population along this shoreline was made up mostly of farmers, with some merchants in the villages. The traffic was a mix of local folks visiting their family and friends along the shoreline, as well as many long distance travellers either coming from or heading to Montreal.

Once on the ice road along the north shore, the sleigh made a beeline for the east, ratcheting up the speed to a persistent gallop. These horses were very accustomed to running on the ice and revelled in the sheer joy of constant motion. William Weller could sense his team's mood, and gave them freedom to run. He was sore and tired and ready for a soft bed, but this was fun, such as it was, for a stagecoach driver.

In those days, the ice roads were critical for basic communication during the long, cold winters. Ice roads had been established for many years at Quebec and Montreal to cross the St. Lawrence River, allowing people and goods to move across the river and linking populated areas. It was no simple job to establish and maintain an ice road. First, they had to wait until around the first week of January for the ice to freeze thick enough to form a solid foundation. Then, crews of men would go out on the ice and lay out a route. Over time, the route of the ice road might have to be changed based on shifting and breaking ice. After all, it was not permanent pavement they were dealing with.

32.1 Ice roads were a way of life in Lower Canada. This watercolour by Philip Bainbrigge depicts a well-organized ice road from Montreal to La Prairie around the time of Mr. Weller's trip to Montreal.

Trees were stuck in the snow at intervals as direction indicators, so travellers would not lose their way, especially during snowstorms. On some more well-established routes, there were small ice houses drawn out onto the ice and placed strategically to provide shelter and refreshment at mid-points, in support of travellers and maintenance crews. Contracts for the maintenance of ice roads were often let to local companies who could find men to do the work. For many farmers it was a way to earn some extra income in the winter months.

Today we might look back and shudder at the thought of driving horses and sleighs across a large sheet of ice. In fact, our experience with winter cold is slightly different than it was for people in the middle of the 1800s. Research has shown that the mean temperature in winter was several degrees colder in the northeastern part of the North American continent between the years 1740 and 1850.[3] The weather was warmer both before and after that period. Winters were colder and lasted longer in those days.

In practical terms, this suggests that William Weller was accustomed to seeing the St. Lawrence River frozen solid for several months of the year, making ice roads very safe. In the minds of those living along the river, ice roads were a common and expected part of daily life in the winter. The freezing usually took effect in the first week of January, and breakup was a major event everyone looked forward to in the middle of April. Of course, the timing of these events varied from year to year, based on immediate weather conditions.

During this long run to Lachine, William Weller once more analyzed his situation. He was not sure of the exact time and was not going to risk handling his pocket watch while in motion. The darkening, overcast sky suggested it was late afternoon, inching into evening. He felt that if nothing bad happened on the ice, they could reach Lachine before six o'clock. Then, the last stage from Lachine into the Exchange Coffee House in Montreal would be only about nine miles. That would put them at their destination around seven o'clock, and well within the limit set out in the contract of thirty-eight hours. He was pleased with this analysis, but was not counting his chickens just yet. It really meant that if problems arose, he had lots of time to work through them and still arrive within the prescribed time. Keep your fingers crossed!

However, with a bit of time to think about it, for the first time William Weller started to feel excited about the imminent success of his project. He knew it had been a risk, engaging with the most powerful man in the colonies in a race to Montreal under contractual obligations. On paper, the time of thirty-eight hours had seemed so short. But, he was a risk-taker at heart, certain of his abilities to make an enterprise succeed, but not so fool-hardy as to expect it to happen without strenuous effort and lots of good planning. Luck seemed to come along as a guest in his business ventures, and good fortune was certainly sharing the bench on the sleigh as a silent partner.

People often told William Weller that he was a lucky so-and-so, always with a grin and a clink of glasses. Well, in business you make your own luck. He thought about the people at the General Stage Office in the Coffin Block in Toronto. They had scrambled night and day to prepare for the trip, writing letters and sending messengers down the road in the days preceding departure. These letters and messengers set in motion a chain of events that resulted in roads being patched, bridges secured, wet spots inspected, and corduroy logs put back in place. Toll booths had been handled, for the most part, to allow quick passage. Most importantly, they also resulted in fresh teams of horses, standing ready at the side of the road when the governor general's sleigh arrived. This happened twenty-four times, no delays, no interruptions. The occasional flask for the driver was icing on the cake.

The extent of this team of helpers was well beyond people he knew or had ever met. When the Stagecoach King needed help, lots of folks were willing to step up and do what they could, from the farm boy working at the stable at a stage stop, to the innkeeper impatiently booming out commands to his employees to get the fresh team ready. Everyone listened for the horn and knew they must be ready to kick into action when it sounded. Here on the ice heading for Lachine, William Weller pulled his coat snug around his neck against the damp cold and just for a moment shook his head and smiled to himself, marvelling at the wonder of it all.

The ice road followed the shoreline, more or less, and land was often in sight off to the north. Signs had been stuck in the snow along the road to indicate villages that were nearby. They would pass the places we know today as Baie-D'Urfé, Beaconsfield, and Pointe-Claire. Then, the shoreline was out of sight, as the ice road crossed Baie-de-Valois. The shore appeared again at Dorval. For a time, they could see land on both left and right, as the sleigh sped by Dorval Island.

An hour on the ice brought the travellers to within sight of the end of the ice road at Lachine. The sleigh left the ice and climbed onto the shore to the west of Upper Lachine. The driver guided the sleigh onto the road that ran along the north side of the Lachine Canal. Mr. Weller blew his horn to alert the innkeeper just down the Montreal Road, where he had arranged for a stage stop. Today, this street is called Boulevard Saint-Joseph. The sleigh stopped in front of the inn, and the horses were changed quickly, sending the travellers on their last stage of the trip. The next stop would be the Exchange Coffee House in Montreal – their final destination.

Lachine was founded in 1667, by Robert Cavalier de la Salle, who owned the seigneurie west of Montreal. La Chine was the French term for China, which La Salle had been confident was just to the west and would make them all rich beyond their wildest dreams, if they could only get there. China turned out to be nowhere in sight, but this important portage became a critical link in military and commercial travel west of Montreal. There is a plaque in the park along the Lachine Canal, honouring La Salle as the founder of Lachine in 1667 and the builder of Fort Frontenac in 1675.

Lachine was a busy place all year round because it was the most important portage at the upper end of the Sault-Saint-Louis (Lachine Rapids), which prevented navigation of the St. Lawrence River above Montreal. In the winter, it was busy because it was the eastern terminus of the ice road across the north shore of Lake Saint-Louis. As early as the 1660s, the French had recognized the need for a canal from Ville-Marie, later named Montreal, to the upper reaches of the rapids. A project was undertaken with much difficulty and was making progress, until the attack on Lachine by Mohawk warriors in 1689, which left eighty residents dead and put a stop to all work on the canal.[4]

The need for a canal from Montreal to Lachine became critical after the War of 1812, when the merchants of Montreal realized that the audacious plan to build a canal from the Hudson River to Buffalo and Lake Erie in New York State threatened to undermine the dominance of Montreal as the centre of the trading network for the Great Lakes region. The merchants felt they could not compete effectively without significant improvements in the navigation of the St. Lawrence River between Montreal and Kingston. However, government officials were reluctant to commit such huge sums of money. The start of work on the Erie Canal in 1817 finally provided some real impetus, and after several years of planning, work began on the Lachine Canal in 1821.

It was also in 1821, that the two competing fur-trading companies merged to form a great monopoly: the Hudson's Bay Company. George Simpson became the new superintendent of the company and York Factory was made the head office in the northwest. After this, the bulk of furs were sent to England through Hudson's Bay and not down the Ottawa River through Lachine to Montreal. In spite of this, Montreal merchants were anxious to provide better transportation for the bulkier and heavier trade goods that were now the focus of their business. Instead of furs, they were transporting timber, lumber, and wheat, as well as thousands of settlers and their baggage. The business was changing, and they needed the Lachine Canal to support their profits.[5]

When the Lachine Canal opened in 1825, it stretched nine miles (fourteen kilometres) from Montreal harbour to Lachine, at the point where the Upper Lachine Turnpike met the lakeshore. The canal then proceeded along the front of the town at the shoreline for a short distance, until it emptied into Lake Saint-Louis at the west end of town. There were seven locks that could handle bateaux, Durham boats, and other small craft that were the lifeblood of river navigation.[6] Loads of all kinds of products could be brought to Lachine, across Lake Saint-Louis, and passed up the canal to Montreal, expending much less work, time, and cost than before. It became a vital part of the transportation system of the St. Lawrence River.

32.2 The Lachine Canal was a vital link in a nation-wide transportation system, but today, a pleasant park separates the canal from the river. All along the Lachine Canal National Historic Site, there is more traffic on the bike paths than in the water.

William Weller sped along the road beside the canal at Lachine with a fresh team of horses. He was not surprised when he had to contend with the traffic of wagons, horses, and people, around the busiest enterprise in town: Dawes Brewery. Thomas Dawes had come to Montreal in 1808 and was soon involved in the brewing business. Shortly after the Lachine Canal was opened in 1825, he built a brewery on the Montreal Road in Lachine, and it would be one of the primary businesses in the town well into the 1950s. Several generations of Dawes men would operate the business until, in the 1860s, it was the second largest beer producer in Quebec. Dow was the largest, and Molson's was third. Eventually, mergers would make it part of National Breweries Limited.

Well known as Dawes Black Horse Brewery, the Black Horse name and logo were used to make this product one of the most popular beers in Quebec. Today, the old Dawes brewery building still looms over the street, refreshed and re-purposed as L'Entrepol[7], a popular and busy arts and performance centre. A large sign near the street advertises the exhibition of a collection of artifacts from the history of Dawes and Black Horse beer, complete with the familiar big black horse. The old Dawes brewery buildings are some of the most fascinating pieces of the built heritage in Lachine.

In 1840, the Lachine Canal was feeling its age. Plans were afoot to enhance the size and function of the canal, which meant building new locks, so that much larger craft could be accommodated. The improvements, along with the completion of the Cornwall Canal and several other canal systems along the dangerous parts of the St. Lawrence, would dramatically affect the nature of travel in Canada. All of these developments would help to some degree, but the problems of the river would not be fully solved until the 1950s, when the St. Lawrence Seaway addressed the old problems in a modern way, resulting in much more dramatic changes.

Not far down the canal, William Weller would have seen the Hudson's Bay warehouse, on the south side of the canal. This stone building was built in 1803 by the North West Company, a competitor of the HBC, and the organization that utilized Lachine as its primary eastern station, where the bulk of its furs had passed through on the way to Montreal. After the merger of the two companies, the warehouse was acquired by HBC. Over the years, this building was used in different ways, including as a residence and storage facility for the Sisters of Sainte-Anne, who owned it from 1861 to 1977. A fire destroyed the interior of the building, but Parks Canada restored it to its original state, and today, the public can enjoy the Fur Trade at Lachine National Historic Site,[8] providing fascinating displays and artifacts related to the fur trade in Canada.

More noticeable for travellers on the road would have been the home of George Simpson, the superintendent of the Hudson's Bay Company. This stately manor was across the road from the HBC warehouse, on the current site of the Saint-Anne Collégial International. In 1826, George Simpson[9] became governor of both Northern and Southern Departments of the HBC and moved his headquarters to Lachine in order to be closer to Montreal. Management of HBC was becoming increasingly an international activity because of conflicts with American and Russian interests in the far west. Simpson was a constant traveller, and Lachine was a more central location from which to work. On one of his trips to England in the next year after Mr. Weller passed by, George Simpson would be knighted and become Sir George Simpson.

The canal was frozen over when the governor general's sleigh ran quickly along its edge on this day in February of 1840. Mr. Weller was not concerned about the congestion of boats in the basins or the prospects for the traders after navigation opened in the spring. Today, all he wanted was a clear road to Montreal.

Near the east end of Lachine, the Upper Lachine Turnpike turned up from the lakeshore and headed north-east, well to the north of the canal. This road, variously called the Turnpike Road, Upper Lachine Road, and Upper Lachine Turnpike, had developed from earliest settlement times, so was in place long before the canal was built. It was the most direct land route from Montreal to Lachine. The Upper Lachine Turnpike did not go straight to Montreal, by any means, initially made up of various pieces of local roads, which followed creeks or valleys for convenience. With the increasing traffic of the 1820s and 1830s, it saw much improvement, with the intent of making it better for the long-distance traveller and for heavily loaded teamster wagons.

33

The Governor General Is Here!

ON TODAY'S MAPS, THE ROUTE THAT WILLIAM WELLER TOOK IN 1840 CAN BE FOL-lowed to Montreal, although it is a challenge. In Lachine, Boulevard Saint-Joseph goes east, through an industrial area, and then at the interchange for highways 20, 4, and 138, it changes to Rue Saint-Jacques. Over the years, the old route has been submerged in freeways and suburbs in the western approaches to Montreal. Rue Saint-Jacques is disrupted at the Turcot Interchange, where highways 20, 720, and 15 meet west of downtown Montreal. Drivers will need patience and a good GPS in order to follow the old turnpike route east of there on Rue Saint-Jacques. Then, in today's Saint-Henri, the old turnpike route jumps onto Rue Notre-Dame and follows this long street all the way to downtown Montreal.

William Weller was happy to be through the congestion of Lachine and anxious to cover the remaining nine miles of the trip as quickly as possible. The turnpike was well travelled, which meant that the road surface could deteriorate in the late winter, but it also meant that they were close enough to the big city of Montreal that the Montreal Turnpike Trust made its impact felt. The Trust was responsible for all main roads coming into Montreal, and this one to Lachine was near the top of its priority list.

As a stage driver, Mr. Weller struggled with bad roads constantly. He often com-plained to the authorities, but seldom saw much evidence of an effective system of road construction and maintenance. However, his entreaties did not land on deaf ears when he explained to the governor general that a larger, centralized organization was needed to better manage the development of roads, bridges, and canals across all the Canadian provinces. Mr. Thomson agreed wholeheartedly with this.

To some degree, Mr. Weller was repeating the same ideas that John McAdam had included, more than two decades ago, with his instructions about how to make a good gravel road. William Weller would give the idea a Canadian context, which was useful to Mr. Thomson. As part of the governor general's reforms, the Board of Works would take the role of central co-ordinator and funder for many projects that were badly needed.

The Montreal Turnpike Trust was a local example of advanced road management. It was supported by the city government and local merchants with the intent that money be allocated and spent to improve access to the city. One could always complain about a particular wet hole or broken surface, but in general, the roads around Montreal were well kept.

Well kept, but they were still mostly conventional dirt roads.[1] There was much agitation all around the country about the construction of plank or macadamized roads. The rebellion had put most projects of this type on the back burner, but by 1840, old projects were being revived and new ones planned. The Montreal Turnpike Trust was in on the action, as we can see by an ordinance passed on June 15, 1840, setting up regulations for routine funding of the roads leading to the City of Montreal.[2] This structure predates Governor General Thomson's Board of Works, but the intent was the same. Lessons had been learned all across the colonies in the previous decades, and the 1840s would see a burst of road building, based on those lessons. The result would be many miles of much better roads.

In fact, the Upper Lachine Road (as opposed to the Lower Lachine Road along the river), would be macadamized soon after William Weller and the governor general rushed into the city. An experimental approach was used initially. Several small pieces of road in the area were macadamized in order to work out the best construction methods, and in particular, to determine how to moderate the normally high cost of this type of road. On this day, however, Mr. Weller was quite happy to run on a familiar dirt road for the last stage of the trip into Montreal.

Much development had occurred to the west of Montreal over the previous decades, as commercial activity increased and populations grew. The doubling of the population of Upper Canada in the 1830s had impacted all of the various routes of immigrants up the St. Lawrence. Inns, taverns, and blacksmith shops, carriage works, tanneries, and general stores all popped up along the turnpike at points where villages drew people, or at creeks where water power determined the location of mills.

Old maps of Montreal Island show how the landscape approaching the west side of Montreal has changed over time. A map from 1744[3] shows a sizable lake, named Lac St. Pierre, halfway between the old city of Ville Marie and Lachine. A small canal runs from Lachine to the west end of Lac St. Pierre, and the St. Pierre River flows from the east end of the lake, down to the shoreline, and across from Ile St. Paul. Settlement is shown along the south shore of Lac St. Pierre and along the north shore of the St. Lawrence River.

Then, in a map from 1834,[4] there is no Lac St. Pierre, but a river is shown running between the Coteau St. Pierre (Upper Lachine Road) and the Lachine Canal, with a road labelled Cote St. Paul, running on the south side of the canal. Nearer Montreal, the roads, the canal, and the river converge at Saint Henri, where the river heads south and the road continues into the western approach to Montreal.

Saint Henri was a strategic location on the main road from Montreal to Lachine. Its location had been determined by the presence of excellent water power to operate the tanneries established there in the 1680s. The fur trade made tanneries a necessity, and several were established outside the population centres in order to have them close to the market, but not close enough for the stench and effluent to bother the well-heeled residents of Montreal.

By the time William Weller drove down the turnpike in 1840, there was a cluster of buildings along the road at the village of Saint Henri, several of them housing busy tanneries. This legacy was brought to light in 2015, when an archeological dig preceding construction of the Turcot interchange unearthed remains of Village des Tanneries, which was often the name used for Saint Henri. Unfortunately, the site could not withstand the onslaught of progress, but the artifacts were recovered and represent an important part of the local history of this area.[5]

The driver urged the team up the long, steep hill by the tanneries, through Saint Henri and on to Montreal. The closer they came to the city, the more activity there was on the road, and the more potential there was for delay. Clusters of buildings lined the roadway at intersections, and the road was busy with wagons and people on foot and horseback. There was little snow left on the road due to the thaw, so there were fewer sleighs and more carriages, even though it was clear that the snow would be back soon and probably with a vengeance. Winter was not over yet.

William Weller's approach to the city of Montreal would be very tactical yet simple in its execution. He would follow the turnpike road all the way into the city where it became St. Jacques Street and then follow this primary road all the way to McGill Street. Notre Dame Street began on the east side of McGill in those days, but instead of going east from there, the travellers would turn south on McGill, a wide and convenient street, where the surface was good and risk of delay was minimal. That would place the sleigh within a short distance of their destination.

That destination was the Exchange Coffee House, a very popular hotel and inn located near the western edge of Old Montreal, north of the business area on Rue

St. Paul. After the War of 1812-1814, the obsolete fortifications of Old Montreal were removed and modern streets installed in their place. On the west side, this resulted in the wide and convenient McGill Street, named after Peter McGill,[6] who was a member of the commission responsible for demolishing the fortifications and building the new streets.

The city had grown to the west over the years, but this area was still seen as the western side of Montreal. The main part of the city, including notable buildings such as Notre Dame Cathedral, was located farther east. For stagecoach operators, the area around McGill and College Streets had provided ideal locations for their stage offices. Horace Dickinson, along with his collaborators and competitors, had offices in this area since the 1820s, and as a result, hotels and inns in the area represented the beginning and ending points for stage runs that went in all directions. Besides the ever-present stages to and from Upper Canada, many stages went east to Quebec, and then on to the other British colonies on the east coast. Many headed down Lake Champlain, to meet lines from Boston and New York. Like the General Stage Office in Toronto, this was a critical transportation hub.

The Exchange Coffee House had been taken over in 1836 by Matthew Jesse Doolittle, who had moved from Burlington, Vermont, where for some years he had operated a hotel along with several stage lines between Burlington and Montreal.[7] Besides having a reputation as a well-run hotel and inn, it also hosted a group of businessmen who conducted their stock transactions in the second floor of the building, starting in the 1820s. This activity would continue in this location until 1874, when the Montreal Stock Exchange was chartered, after more than forty years of informal trading. Then, in 1883, the Exchange moved to the Commodities Exchange building on St. Sacrament Street.

33.1 This advertisement in the 1842 Montreal Directory shows that the Exchange Coffee House was owned and operated by M.J. Doolittle and was located on Exchange Court, off St. Paul Street.

The building that housed the Exchange Coffee House was not located on a street, but was situated beside an inner courtyard, within a maze of buildings. A topo map of Montreal from 1846[8] provides granular detail of the streets and buildings in this area, with names written in the English form used at the time. McGill Street is one block west of St. Peter Street, which forms the west side of the block. St. Paul Street is on the south side, St. Nicholas Street is on the east side, and St. Sacrament Street is on the north. The building faced south to St. Paul Street, looking down a long alley.

There were two narrow alleys that led into the courtyard in front of the Exchange Coffee House: one off St. Peter Street and one off St. Paul Street. Another building on the courtyard had, until a few months before the arrival of the governor general, hosted the stage office for the Upper Canada stage lines. The approach off either of these streets into the narrow alleys was challenging, but the stage drivers often made a deliberate show of it by racing around the tight corners at breakneck speed and clattering up to the front of the Exchange Coffee House, with dust flying and pedestrians fleeing for their lives. It was a great joke for the drivers and somewhat of a routine spectacle for patrons of the hotel.[9]

The City of Montreal had been incorporated in 1832, and by 1840, boasted a population of forty thousand, divided almost half and half between English and French-speaking residents. The tensions between these two traditional foes had broken into armed conflict during the Rebellion of 1837 and 1838, and the repression afterwards made matters worse. A couple of streets south of the Exchange Coffee House sat the building that, a decade later, housed the Canadian Parliament, when it was burned to the ground by angry Tory sympathizers. They simply could not accept the idea of compensation for anyone who rebelled against the British authority. Calmer heads would ultimately prevail, but the underlying problem persisted.

However, on this Tuesday afternoon, February 18, 1840, the gentleman reclining in the sleigh that sped down the turnpike from Lachine had very clear instructions about how to solve these problems, once and for all. Governor General Thomson would unite the two provinces of Upper and Lower Canada into one Legislature, and he would change what he saw as an archaic bureaucratic system of administration, giving it a modern form, according to what he believed to be the superior English model. He had succeeded dramatically in Upper Canada, but that was only half the job. He saw great difficulties ahead in Lower Canada, and was anxious to be on the scene so he could take charge and see it through.

The sleigh manoeuvred around wagons, sleighs, and people on St. Jacques Street as the travellers grew ever closer to their destination. Soon they approached McGill Street, where William Weller turned the team south, down the broad boulevard. He was very familiar with this area due to many meetings with other stage line operators, who had their offices along the southern end of McGill Street. The runners slid quietly over the well-tramped surface of the road, passing Recollect Street on the left and St. Maurice Street on the right.

As they passed St. Lemoine Street on the left, William Weller pulled out his horn for one last time on this trip, blowing forcefully to alert the folks at the Exchange Coffee House that the governor general was arriving any minute. This alert was not to make sure the stable boys had a fresh team ready, so it may have been unnecessary in the circumstances, but the driver was tired, his arms ached painfully, and he was about to complete the most amazing project of his life. Everyone was darn well going to hear about it!

The sound of the horn shattered the silence in the yard outside the Exchange Coffee House. Two well-dressed men standing on the front step of the hotel stopped puffing on their after-dinner cigars and glanced down the alley toward St. Paul Street. Mr. McCullough said to Mr. McGregor, "Was that a mail stage horn? Are there stages arriving at this hour?" Mr. McGregor shrugged, and both men went back to their cigars.

At St. Paul Street, there was traffic on the street, but other drivers knew to defer to the mail stage when they heard the horn, almost like modern drivers moving over to the side when they hear a siren. In this case, they gaped at the weird contraption flying down the street, having never seen such an odd vehicle. Some people may have noticed the queen's coat-of-arms on the side door and surmised that the governor general might be in attendance. According to their particular political frame of mind, they might salute or sneer.

William Weller blew the horn again, just after turning left onto St. Paul Street, longer and louder than any blast in the last day and a half. It was a noisy place, this city, and he wanted to make sure that Mr. Doolittle and his helpers would hear it over the clank of beer mugs and laughter of patrons at the bar.

The heavy front door of the hotel flung open and a skinny fourteen-year-old boy scrambled out onto the porch, as he pulled his coat over skeletal arms and balanced a large floppy hat on top of unruly blond hair. He no sooner reached the cigar smokers than another blast from the horn caused him to stop and strain toward the sound.

Jimmy Hayward had worked at the Exchange Coffee House for almost two years, and had learned that everything he could do to help a patron could mean coins jangling in his pocket. He was smart, quick, and anxious to please, although sometimes a bit too exuberant, if you asked Mr. Doolittle, the innkeeper. The young man immediately raced across the courtyard and

33.2 Exchange Coffee House. This sketch, which appeared for the first time in the Montreal Daily Witness newspaper on December 7, 1896, shows the alley and the Exchange Coffee House.

climbed up onto the heavy water trough that stood near the alley. With one arm encircling the lamp post, he focussed his eyes on the south end of the alley, where he could see vehicles on St. Paul Street. Gas lighting had been installed in primary locations around Montreal in the last few years, and one of them was located at the corner of St. Paul and the difficult little alley.

As the sleigh crossed St. Peter Street, Mr. Weller took the reins more tightly in hand and slowed the team just before turning to the left into the small alley on the north side of St. Paul Street.

At the lamp post, the boy strained forward and saw a team of two horses rounding the corner from St. Paul Street pulling a small, odd-looking sleigh. It raced down the alley toward him. "Is it the governor general?" Jimmy thought out loud to himself. He had heard men talking about a newspaper article this morning, saying that William Weller, the well-known stagecoach king, had left Toronto early Monday morning, carrying the governor general and his aide-de-camp. The intent, so the newspaper said, was to make a fast trip to Montreal. Could this conveyance coming down the alley be William Weller and the governor general?

The boy stared intently at the approaching team and sleigh. There was no scheduled mail stage at this time in the evening, and besides, this sleigh, as much as he could see of it, was like no other he had ever seen. It must be the governor general! But so soon? How could they have driven from Toronto to Montreal in what amounted to only a day and a half? Jimmy was young, but he had learned something about the stage lines, and he could hardly believe that such a thing was possible.

But as the sleigh emerged from the shadows, he recognized Mr. Weller on the bench, driving the team. The famous stage driver had been in the hotel only a few months before and had spoken to all the hands before leaving for Cornwall. Jimmy remembered his smile.

As Jimmy climbed down from his perch on the water trough, he yelled at the top of his lungs, "The governor general is here! The governor general is here!"

A few quick strides of his fourteen-year-old legs took him past Mr. McCullough and Mr. McGregor, who were still engrossed in their cigars. He reached the front door of the hotel, swung the door all the way open, and yelled, "Mr. Weller is here with the governor general. It is the governor general, for sure!"

Mr. Doolittle was behind the bar and did not even look up before yelling back at the boy, "Nonsense! Don't be silly. They only left yesterday morning. It's far too soon for them to be here."

Jimmy stood in the middle of the lobby of the hotel and yelled at the top of his lungs once more. "The governor general is here. The governor general is here. Mr. Weller is driving into the courtyard! Right now!"

The master of the Exchange Coffee House was a portly gent with a white apron stretched over his large belly. He grumbled about the irresponsibility of youth as he wiped his hands on his apron and started toward the door to see for himself. Jimmy followed him, dancing circles around the older man, as the two made their way through the door.

Mr. Weller was happy to see that there were no other vehicles in the long, narrow alley, or in the courtyard in front of the Exchange Coffee House. The driver encouraged the team up the alley in quick time and yelled at the top of his lungs, "The Exchange Coffee House, at your service, Guvner!" With that, he swung the team around and reined them in, stopping the sleigh in the courtyard across from the front door of the hotel.

Mr. Doolittle and Jimmy Hayward came out onto the front step of the hotel and were met by a very fine two-horse team, stomping and snorting in the yard, in front of a very odd-looking sleigh. The driver was pulling on the reins and talking to the horses, calming them after their intense and exciting arrival.

Jimmy Hayward pointed to the crest on the door of the sleigh and poked his boss in the arm saying, "Look! There is the queen's coat-of-arms![1] I told you it was the governor general!"

Mr. Doolittle was convinced and already turning back toward the hotel. A stream of commands came from his mouth as he stepped quickly back into the hotel. "Get the governor general's supper ready! Prepare his room! Alert the stable master to care for the team and sleigh! Hop to it now! The governor general is here!"

34
Tell Me the Time!

THE STAFF OF THE EXCHANGE COFFEE HOUSE KNEW THE DRILL. THE GOVERNOR general had taken the best rooms in the hotel in the previous October, after arriving in Lower Canada.[1] He had only stayed in Montreal for a few weeks, but his habits and desires were quickly established. The hotel staff were well aware of their duties when it came to satisfying the most powerful man in the colonies. At the commands of the proprietor, the entire hotel came alive with activity and anticipation.

Out in the yard, the two bay horses stomped their feet in excitement and shook their heads with pride, as they revelled in the calm and friendly words of the driver. Mr. Weller was praising this handsome pair for their good behaviour in the last stage from Lachine into Montreal. Steam rose from their sweating backs and haunches as they gradually calmed down. It was not a long run, at only nine miles, but he had asked them for more speed than might normally be the case. He had still been concerned about meeting the terms of the contract and would take advantage of every bit of speed he could muster, as long as it did not hurt the horses.

Mr. Weller tied the reins to the sleigh and then sat quietly there on the bench, where he had laboured mightily for the last day and half. Except for an hour at Belleville, and a couple of times to deal with obstacles in the road, he had remained on the bench, driving and driving and driving. He was stiff and tired and finally had a quiet, peaceful moment of rest.

Jimmy Hayward went back out to the yard and was able to assist Mr. Weller as he slowly climbed down from the sleigh. Mr. Weller's boots landed on the ground with a thud. For a few unsteady seconds, he struggled to gain his balance. Then, before the boy could grab him, Mr. Weller's body teetered backwards, and he fell towards the hotel. His feet scrambled to keep up but were too slow. In an instant, he found himself lying on his back, half reclining on a snow bank.

No more had Mr. Weller come to rest in his impromptu easy chair, than the door of the sleigh was flung open and the tall military form of Captain Le Marchant emerged, striding quickly across the yard to the assistance of his driver.

"Mr. Weller! Are you hurt, sir? Are you all right?" said the captain. "I am so sorry I could not get out of the sleigh fast enough to catch you. I watched as you fell and was alarmed that you might hurt yourself."

Mr. Weller was lying still with his eyes closed. It seemed like he was asleep in a warm, comfortable bed. In a moment, he opened his eyes, and a wide smile came over his face. He looked up at Captain Le Marchant with smiling eyes and said, "I'm fine, Captain, just resting a moment in this soft place. It has been a difficult trip, and I am glad it is over."

The captain responded, "Well, that it has, sir, but it would be much better to rest inside the hotel. Here, let me help you up."

Captain Le Marchant reached out to Mr. Weller, and the driver grasped his hand and began to stand up. Suddenly, however, Mr. Weller let go of the captain's hand and flopped back onto the snow.

"What is the time? I must record the time! Captain, please take my pocket-watch over to the lamp light and tell me the time."

Although Captain Le Marchant was taken aback for a moment, he understood very well what he was being asked to do. Mr. Weller pulled a pocket-watch out of an inside coat pocket and handed it over. They had practiced this procedure before they left Toronto, so the captain knew exactly how to handle Mr. Weller's time-piece.

Here was another example of the progressive nature of William Weller. At this time, pocket-watches were considered luxury items, designed more for show than for accurate time-keeping. Mr. Weller, on the other hand, incorporated this tool into his stagecoach system, in order to make sure he was delivering both mail and passengers on schedule. In this, he was a bit ahead of his time.

Captain Le Marchant took the time-piece and stepped to the front porch of the hotel, where two gas lights shed a bright light for a few yards. Mr. Weller dug into another pocket in his coat and produced a piece of paper and a short pencil.

The captain studied the pocket-watch, and glanced to see if Mr. Weller was ready to write. "It is forty minutes after six o'clock, sir."

Mr. Weller quickly wrote that down on the paper, just below the time he had written down when they left Toronto. He then engaged in some intense figuring and writing, while Captain Le Marchant looked on in anticipation.

"We've done it, Captain Le Marchant! We are within our time! We did it! We did it!" A smile as wide as the hotel front door broke out on Mr. Weller's face.

Captain Le Marchant came back to him with a hand outstretched. "Congratulations, Mr. Weller! It is a fine accomplishment! Very well deserved!"

Captain Le Marchant handed the pocket-watch back to Mr. Weller, who stowed it, along with the paper and pencil, back into the pocket of his coat. The captain extended both of his hands this time, and Mr. Weller gratefully lifted himself out of his comfortable chair in the snow.

By this time, the governor general was on the ground, and hotel staff were beginning to unstrap the baggage from the rear of the sleigh. The governor general strode over to his two travelling companions and took Mr. Weller by the hand, shaking it energetically. "Congratulations, Mr. Weller. I overheard the good news. I can't say I am surprised that you have come in under time, and I am very grateful for your efforts. Are you quite all right, sir? You fell in a most opportune location, so I trust you are not hurt?"

Governor General Thomson was genuinely concerned for Mr. Weller's health and was delighted at his success in meeting the terms of the contract. It would cost some money, but that was trivial in light of the fact that he was back in Montreal.

The three men joked and laughed as they brushed the snow from Mr. Weller's clothes. The governor general playfully lifted Mr. Weller's fur hat from his head and daintily dabbed it with his fingers, much to the delight of his companions. It was a joyful moment. The modern reader might think of it as a victory lap after a long race or high fives after scoring a goal. The men knew they had participated in something special and were proud and happy at their success. But they were also very glad it was done. Now they could bask in the moment.

Mr. McCullough and Mr. McGregor were amused at the sight. Here were three grown men, all dressed in practical winter garments – fur hats and coats and heavy boots – but they were acting like giddy school children. All three had been travelling, but the driver of the sleigh was distinguished from his passengers by the general dirty appearance of his clothes. The weather in the last couple of days had varied from snow flurries to rain, the temperature below freezing at night and slightly above during the day. The driver had been open to the flying mud, slush, and snow from the horses' hooves, and it showed. But it didn't seem to matter at all in the flush of celebration.

Soon, however, fatigue and hunger began to calm the merriment. Governor General Thomson stepped toward the hotel and suggested that they retire to a warm and comfortable room, where they might enjoy a well-deserved meal and some celebratory libations. The three stepped toward the front porch of the hotel and were met by Mr. Doolittle, who bowed deferentially to the governor general and praised the three gentlemen profusely, directing them to the governor general's spacious rooms.

The men were just inside the hotel when suddenly Mr. Weller turned around and stepped quickly back out into the yard, striding to the team and sleigh. The stable master was preparing to move the conveyance into the stable area, but Mr. Weller stopped him and asked for a moment. He walked to the front of the team and took a few seconds to speak quietly with each of the horses, then he stepped back and addressed the team as a whole.

When he had thanked the team properly, he climbed onto the sleigh and reached under the bench, pulling out his grip. He sat it on the end of the bench and opened the top. First, the small piece of fur, which had been his cushion on the bench, was laid carefully inside. Then he reached over and removed the horn from its holder, held it up, wiped some mud from its brass surface, and placed it carefully into the grip. Next, he pulled the whip out of its holder and folded it up to fit inside the grip.

These items, along with his pocket-watch, were important tools in the busy life of a stagecoach driver, especially those engaged in the more demanding role of running Royal Mail coaches. William Weller was always aware of having the right tool for the right job, and he had learned very early in life to take good care of his own tools. On a more immediate level, these particular tools had contributed to his success, and he was grateful.

Now he was ready for a good meal and a soft chair!

35

In Montreal

AT NOON ON WEDNESDAY, NINETEEN GUNS ON THE BATTERY ON SAINT HELEN'S Island boomed a salute to welcome the governor general to Montreal.[1] This was a ritual that took place any time the governor general entered the city, and it was specifically performed to welcome him to the seat of government. However, this time was different. It was less than twenty-four hours since Mr. Weller had delivered the governor general to his quarters in the Exchange Coffee House, so the celebration signified something more.

Word spread very quickly of William Weller's amazing accomplishment in setting what we would call a land-speed record. Nobody had ever travelled the route between Toronto and Montreal in so short a time. It was a spectacular achievement and only served to bolster the already solid reputation of the Stagecoach King of Cobourg.

Political junkies, on the other hand, responded by ramping up the already-charged discussions about what the governor general was up to. Almost immediately, stories took flight to link his quick arrival in Montreal with the fate of Quebec. Pundits in Toronto had already likened his departure from Toronto to rats leaving a sinking ship, and the people of Quebec could not help but see something ominous in his early arrival in the province. What was to come next?

The *Montreal Courier* was rather tongue-in-cheek about Mr. Thomson's arrival. "The Governor-General arrived, from Toronto on Tuesday evening, in 36 hours, which is quite as rapid a movement, as that he made in the minds of the Upper

Canada Legislators, in regard to the Union and the Clergy Reserves questions. Both are unprecedented."[2] Unprecedented, indeed!

The article also included details about the trip. The governor general had arrived at the Exchange Coffee House at twenty minutes before seven on Tuesday evening after travelling three hundred and seventy-six miles and stopping to change horses twenty-four times. The trip was completed in thirty-five hours and forty minutes which was more than two hours under the time limit of thirty-eight hours set out in the contract. Mr. Weller had met the terms of his contract with time to spare.

The same article mentioned that a second sleigh was bringing other members of the governor general's retinue. One report suggested that William Weller's eldest son, Lorenzo Reed Weller, was the driver of this second sleigh, which had left Toronto later in the day on Monday with some of the governor general's baggage and "other members of his suite." Lorenzo Weller had turned eighteen only a few weeks before, and folks may have questioned whether William Weller should put his teenage son in charge of such an important job.

Lorenzo Reed Weller was born in 1822 when the family still lived in Canton, Saint Lawrence County, New York. He was twelve when his father moved the family to Cobourg in 1834, and one can expect that his father enjoyed the company of his son on the bench as he drove stagecoaches and travelled around the countryside, building up his business. The young fellow was a fast learner and a capable hand.

Lorenzo Weller would marry Corintha Bettes of Brighton in October 1843, and in 1845, we see advertisements in the *Cobourg Star* describing him as captain of the *Forester*, his father's steamboat on Rice Lake.

We have a testimonial regarding the work of the young steamboat captain in an article in the *Cobourg Star* in June 1845: "Mr. Weller starts a six-horse coach every morning for the Rice Lake, with an excellent most careful driver, where it meets the Forester steamboat; this boat is under the command of Mr. Weller, Jr., and his attention to his passengers and punctuality in the delivery of freight are earning him not only favour from the public in the shape of praise, but also, we are glad to hear, in a more substantial form."[3]

Lorenzo R. Weller appears to have demonstrated the same attention to detail and concern for the comfort of patrons as his father, and at the young age of twenty-four, would gain a reputation as a very capable steamboat captain. Soon after his father died in 1863, Lorenzo Weller would move to Cedar Rapids, Iowa and enjoy a solid reputation as a respected book keeper until his death in 1901. In light of these facts, it might not be unreasonable to suggest that William Weller asked his most trusted associate, his son, to make sure that the baggage and the remaining members of the governor general's suite made it safely to Montreal.

It seems that the trip was a tough experience for the teenaged driver. The sleigh carried a good deal of baggage strapped to the top and rear along with three or four people on board. An account of the trip that appears in the *Montreal Daily Herald* in 1895 says: "…Mr. Weller's eldest son followed to Montreal with some of the Governor's aides, and did not arrive until twenty-four hours later, all pretty well used up."[4] No doubt, this was the most challenging experience of Lorenzo Weller's young life.

The *Montreal Gazette*, after reporting on the firing of the guns, continued on February 20, "We are informed that His Excellency is in good health, and that he enjoyed his rapid journey in the true spirit of a Canadian winter traveller. Mr. Murdoch, Chief Secretary, Captain Campbell, and Mr. Baring, A.D.C., have also arrived in town – the first named last night."[5] It might be inferred from this that Mr. Murdoch, chief secretary to the governor general, was the primary individual driven to Montreal in the second sleigh piloted by Lorenzo Weller.

On the same day, the *Montreal Herald* had a slightly different description of the arrival of the governor general, focussing more on his state of health, which had been a major topic of discussion in both provinces. "His Excellency walked out yesterday, and appeared to enjoy a better state of health than what we were led to anticipate from the accounts previously received."[6]

It was well known that Mr. Thomson had serious ongoing health issues, and it was felt such a strenuous trip might further undermine a fragile constitution. This proved not to be the case, but the competing political pundits would naturally use anything like this to cast doubt on the governor general in his aggressive pursuit of reform. It was all grist for the mill.

However, in the midst of all the euphoria, a tragic accident spoiled the moment. On Wednesday evening, the day after Mr. Weller and the governor general had arrived in Montreal, a sleigh was travelling east of Gananoque, carrying some of the governor general's domestic servants as well as numerous pieces of baggage. While the sleigh was proceeding, one of the servants loaded a pistol and placed it on his lap. Then, when he turned to secure a piece of baggage, the pistol fell onto the floor and discharged. The ball went through the seat in front, fatally injuring a French Canadian passenger.[7]

The newspaper reports of this incident do not say that this was the sleigh driven by Lorenzo Weller, although it is exactly the same route and around the same time that he was said to have brought the chief secretary to Montreal, arriving the evening of the nineteenth. There may have been more than one sleigh carrying the governor general's servants and baggage to Montreal, but it is a tantalizing possibility that the eighteen-year-old son of Mr. Weller may have been forced to cope with this extremely distressing event.

In any case, both William Weller and Governor General Thomson would have seen this incident as a sour note at the end of their trip. It had all gone so well, all the way from Toronto to Montreal without so much as a scratch for man or beast. How could it end with such a senseless and tragic accident as this?

William Weller and his son Lorenzo stayed in Montreal for a couple of weeks after the trip to rest up, taking in the sights and having discussions with stage operators and stagecoach manufacturers. Before they left, however, the governor general requested their attendance at Government House. In a heart-felt ceremony, the governor general presented his driver with a beautiful gold watch. He had been extremely impressed with the efforts of Mr. Weller in planning the trip so meticulously and in exerting himself so persistently and skillfully on the bench for the entire trip. In light of this, he felt some token of his appreciation was in order.

The Wellers would be home in Cobourg by March 11, when the *Cobourg Star* included a suitably respectful piece: "Mr. Weller, we are glad to say has returned from Montreal none the worse in health and pocket for his late arduous undertaking. He has with him a very neat gold watch, with suitable inscription, very appropriately presented to him by His Excellency the Governor in Chief, in acknowledgement of the distinguished public service he succeeded in performing."[8]

The *Toronto Examiner* contained a small item in its March 23 issue, which said: "Previous to Mr. Weller's departure for Upper Canada he received a valuable gold watch, enclosed in a very neat Mahogany case, with the following inscription: "Presented to Mr. Weller by the Right Hon. C.P. Thomson, Governor-General of British North America, in remembrance of having conveyed His Excellency from Toronto to Montreal, in 35 hours and 40 minutes. – February, 1840."[9]

Mr. Weller cherished the gold watch for the rest of his life. Amazingly, it has been protected by the Weller family to this day. The author has seen the gold watch, which is in the possession of a family member who prefers to remain anonymous.

36

After the Trip: The Governor General

THE GOVERNOR GENERAL SET TO WORK IMMEDIATELY ON RETURNING TO MONTREAL. One of the first things he did was to remove Mr. Chatterton from his position as a magistrate in Cobourg. One can imagine the joyful flourish of the pen as Governor General Thomson set his signature to the order. This generated a good deal of indignant copy in the *Cobourg Star*, particularly from the injured party.

Mr. Chatterton responded to an associate, "While we thank our excellent contemporary of the *Niagara Chronicle* for the handsome and gentlemanly manner in which he has considered the subject of our late dismissal, we assure him that we are quite as unable as himself to discover the motives that actuated the infliction upon us of so signal a mark of Vice-regal displeasure."[1] As always, there were folks on both sides of this issue. Mr. Chatterton would continue to be editor of the *Cobourg Star* newspaper until 1847.

For the governor general, it was back to the political wars. In a letter sent to London from Montreal on March 13, he wrote, "I have been back three weeks, and have set to work in earnest in this province."[2] He felt very strongly that the greatest difference in Lower Canada compared to Upper Canada was the abject hatred between the English and French. At least the men in Upper Canada argued over positions and financial prospects, which seemed natural to him. However, fighting strictly over race regardless of the practical issues, thought Mr. Thomson, was the worst situation he had ever seen.

He pulled no punches regarding conditions in Lower Canada. "There is positively no machinery of government. Everything is to be done by the governor or his secretary. There are no heads of departments at all, or none whom one can depend on..."[3] As a long-time member of the Board of Trade in London, he was derisive of the lack of organization. "The wise system hitherto adopted has been to stick two men into some office whenever a vacancy occurred; one Frenchman and one Britisher! Thus we have joint Crown surveyors, joint sheriffs, &c., each opposing the other in everything he attempts."[4] As far as Mr. Thomson was concerned, all of this would be swept away with the union of the provinces, which would result in a new government structure based on departments, with department-head hires based on merit. Well, at least it would be a start.

His masters in London were impressed. Lord John Russell sent a dispatch to the governor general, dated from Downing Street, March 20, 1840, in which he said, "The promptitude with which you have acted in ascertaining the sentiments of the Special Council, – the decision which you made to resort in person to the Upper Province, – the conciliatory spirit in which you met the Legislature of that Province, – and the zeal for Her Majesty's service and the good of Her people, which you have on all occasions evinced, have been observed by the Queen with the greatest satisfaction, and have inspired Her Majesty with a confident hope, that you may successfully complete the work you have so ably commenced."[5]

Wow! That was the ultimate in terms of career possibilities, which was never far from Thomson's thoughts. Maybe his work in Canada would, after all, result in the peerage he so much desired. He had been promised as much when he left England, and it was beginning to look like his dream might come true. For the son of a merchant, elevation to a peerage would be the greatest revenge for all the condescension and slights from the most noble men of the land.

Governor General Thomson set to work on several major issues. He wanted to see the cities of Quebec and Montreal incorporated in order to provide a legal framework for enforcement of laws and regulations. Closely tied to this was the touchy question of the seminary of St. Sulpice, which he also wanted to incorporate so that a satisfactory settlement could be negotiated regarding the "gradual extinction of seigneurial dues."[6] Talk about jumping in with both feet! Here was a way to make lots of folks very angry right away. But he forged ahead.

Over the next few months the governor general worked hard to pass numerous bills in the Legislature of Lower Canada in order to prepare for the union and the new form of government. As a break, he took several trips up the Richelieu and St. John rivers, much refreshed by the air and exercise. His health stabilized for a time, and he was in good spirits regarding the prospects of success.

In July 1840, there was a trip to Nova Scotia, where he addressed a serious conflict in the government there. The underlying problems were similar in all the colonies, and he recommended to his masters in London a restructuring of the executive council to include only members of the government; in other words, what we might call cabinet government. This was another highly contentious situation, and the trip was not good for Mr. Thomson's health, which would deteriorate over the next year.

The government in London was ready to approve Thomson's bills and in particular to allow for the union of the provinces. However, before proceeding with that step, they needed to adjust the role of the governor general in anticipation of the new united Province of Canada. This seemed like a good time to reward Mr. Thomson for his efforts in Canada. As a result, on August 19, 1840, Charles Poulett Thomson was elevated to a peerage with the full title of "Baron Sydenham of Sydenham in Kent and Toronto in Canada."[7] From that point forward he would be referred to as Lord Sydenham.

A quick trip to Upper Canada included Kingston and Hamilton but deliberately avoided the Tory strongholds of Toronto and Cobourg, disappointing many and resulting in a flood of nasty words in the newspapers. William Weller worked with the Board of Police in Cobourg to compose a properly respectful address, which could not be delivered in person but was sent along to the governor general by courier.

On February 5, 1841, Lord Sydenham issued a proclamation that February 10 would be the date on which the union of Upper and Lower Canada would take place, resulting in the Province of Canada.[8] Then, on February 15, he summoned the Parliament of Canada to meet at Kingston, which he had selected for the seat of government. This gave a huge boost to the movers-and-shakers of Kingston but was bitterly opposed by many in Montreal and Toronto, for their own obvious reasons.

Sydenham had selected Kingston because it was the most central location in the new united Province of Canada and provided excellent accommodations and services. Truth be told, he preferred Kingston because it provided distance from the strong French influence in Montreal, which was, in effect, the target of the union in the first place. In Kingston, he hoped the French would have less effect and the English would eventually dominate.

There was a fine line to walk regarding the conflict between French and English in Quebec. The governor general had worked hard to co-operate with the more moderate elements of the French groupings in Quebec, always trying to minimize the power of the more extreme forces. He wanted to maintain a strong degree of self-government for the French component of the new Province of Canada, but he insisted that this component not be powerful enough to limit the development of Upper Canada, which was expected to grow dramatically in the next decades. The solution to this dilemma was to create a Legislature with equal representation from Canada East (today's Quebec) and Canada West (today's Ontario). Theoretically, the English would then have a majority position with Canada West and the English minority in Canada East working together.

In hind-sight, it is easy for us to offer a snide remark such as, "Sure, how's **that** workin' for ya?" Over the next two decades, even with responsible government after 1848, the Province of Canada experienced legislative gridlock as one side could always muster enough support to block major developments that might benefit the other side. By the early 1860s, it was this seemingly intractable problem that would motivate George Brown and John A. Macdonald to bury their battle-worn political and personal hatchets and work together toward a federal union of all the British North American colonies.

Confederation would occur on July 1, 1867 and was a celebrated event, but nation building is less an event than a process. The platform for this big change had been constructed during the preceding decades when structures for local government and then true responsible government were put in place in the individual provinces. If he had been there in 1867, Lord Sydenham might have blanched to see Britain give away so much authority to the colonies, but he might also take satisfaction from the fact that he had contributed to the development of Canada, in his own particular way.

Elections were set in Canada East for April 8, 1841 and campaigning began in earnest. History shows that Thomson participated directly to shape the result of this election in Canada East. He directed the moving of polling places and provided funding for goons who intimidated voters. This was one of the most violent elections in an era of common election violence but when questioned about his involvement, Sydenham responded lamely that the local magistrates controlled elections and could do as they wished.[9] Besides, if you asked anyone on the reform side, they might smirk and suggest that it served them right. Everybody knew that the Family Compact had used the same tactics for years in Upper and Lower Canada. In any case, the result was a victory for the governor general's reform efforts and eventually most of his bills were passed.

On June 14, 1841, the first Parliament of the new Province of Canada met in Kingston. The building where they met would later be part of Kingston Hospital, and there were also government offices in a row of low stone buildings on Ontario Street. Lord Sydenham had delayed his return to Kingston due to very poor health but eventually took up residence in Alwington House, a stone mansion south of King Street, on the western side of Kingston. An historical plaque has been installed on Alwington Place, south of King Street and just east of Sir John A. Macdonald

Boulevard. The plaque is planted in a traffic island across from a lovely red brick house that occupies the ground where the original Alwington House stood.[10]

Unfortunately, Lord Sydenham would not live to enjoy his peerage for very long. In July of 1841, he experienced serious health problems that forced him to resign as governor general. He was planning to return to England soon, when on September 4, while riding back from one of his routine excursions into the countryside, his horse stumbled and threw off the rider. Thomson's foot stuck in the stirrup and his leg was broken. Over the next few days, the wound became infected, and Lord Sydenham passed away in great agony on September 19, only six days after his forty-second birthday.[11]

The death of a governor general was a big event in the colonies, but this one was particularly newsworthy because of the young age of the man and the work he had been engaged in before he died. Some degree of civility was maintained in the newspapers, at least initially, although the Tory forces were not at all displeased that the man who had worked so hard to destroy their power base was now out of the picture. They only hoped that his campaign of reform could be halted and reversed before it caused too much damage to their interests.

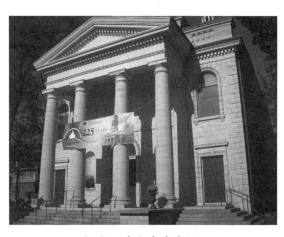

36.1 St. George's Cathedral, Kingston

The *Kingston Chronicle & Gazette* reported that between six and seven thousand people lined the roads to witness Lord Sydenham's interment in the crypt beneath St. George's Cathedral on September 24. Egerton Ryerson extolled the governor general's "...noble mind which conceived those improvements and originated the institutions which will form a golden era in the annals of Canadian history."[12] On the other hand, in private, the governor general's one-time landlord in Toronto, Sir John Beverly Robinson, referred to "...that despicable Poulett Thomson."[13]

37

After the Trip: William Weller

WILLIAM WELLER AND HIS SON LORENZO HAD RETURNED TO COBOURG AFTER COL-lecting the gold watch and the sum of one thousand pounds as a result of a wager placed on the trip. There was hardly time to take a breath. The *Cobourg Star* included an announcement in its March 25 issue stating that navigation was open early this year due to the persistent warm weather.[1] The opening of navigation was a seasonal tipping point for those in the transportation business because it meant that steamboats would ply Lake Ontario, carrying the Royal Mail and lots of passengers on the main routes between Montreal and Toronto.

Mr. Weller had to make sure all the stages, horses, and men were ready and that connecting arrangements had been made. Steamboats would seem to draw passengers away from the bumpy land stage lines, but in effect, more passengers in general meant more demand for the shorter runs and some folks welcomed good alternatives to the still risky and unreliable steamboats. Mr. Weller recognized that it was not a zero-sum game. The pie was growing, so his business would succeed by having the right product, managed effectively, along with lots of marketing to get the word out.

There was a persistent advertising campaign for the new Telegraph Line from Toronto to Hamilton with Mr. Weller's new, colourful six-horse stages.[2] The Toronto and Kingston Mail Stage was also advertised in all the papers at this time, claiming that high-quality stagecoaches driven by skillful drivers would complete this run in forty-six hours, with connections to steamboats and other stage lines in all directions. There were arrangements with stages going west to Queenston, London, and Detroit as well as eastward connections for Montreal, Quebec; Utica, Watertown, and Albany, New York.[3]

The operation of these complex stage lines was done in conjunction with the growth and development of the carriage works, which, besides turning out the much vaunted new six-horse stagecoach, was becoming known as the source for quality carriages of all types with satisfied customers across the province. The more mundane carrying trade also required wagons and sleighs of all kinds to meet the needs of teamsters and contractors who were busy moving the goods of this burgeoning land.

William Weller would benefit in many ways from his spectacular accomplishment in 1840. It boosted his brand as the Stagecoach King, which meant increased paying customers for all his stage lines. His reputation was also enhanced in his home community of Cobourg where his participation in local affairs would grow over the following years. He would continue his involvement in the Board of Police, and when District Councils were created as a result of Mr. Thomson's reforms, he would become a member of Newcastle District Council, re-elected for many years as the councillor for the East Ward of Cobourg. In 1842, he would be granted leave from his duties for the rest of the session, as reported in the *Cobourg Star*,[4] probably to attend to business interests that caused him to travel.

On the other hand, William Weller's only attempt at elected office at the provincial level was not successful in 1848. He came into the race late in the campaign, encouraged by his friends to run. His campaign speech, which was printed in the newspapers, as was the practice at the time, insisted that he was not for any party or faction but was for: "Wheat at a dollar a bushel, and good roads to your own doors."[5]

A good measure of the high regard felt for Mr. Weller in Cobourg and area is that very little invective was thrown his way during this nasty and hard-fought election. Mr. Chatterton at the *Cobourg Star* deliberately avoided printing anything derogatory about the town's worthy citizen (and a major client for advertising in the *Star*), even to the point of contradicting others who suggested the *Star* had printed something controversial. The only negative comment about William Weller to come out of this election campaign was the rather weak pronouncement by his Tory neighbour, D'Arcy Edward Boulton, that everybody always knew he was a reformer anyway.[6] In spite of this, Mr. Weller was selected as the first mayor of the town of Cobourg in 1850, a position he would hold three times, including the last two years of his life.[7]

Oh yes, and there was the matter of the £1,000 that he had won in a wager after meeting the terms of his contract. What would he do with such a large sum of money? We don't know for sure, of course, but it may be that this additional infusion of funds allowed William Weller to go ahead and purchase property to the east of Cobourg, possibly as a retirement home for his father.

The Land Registry Records for Hamilton Township show us that William Weller purchased 41 acres of land to the east of Cobourg, Concession B, Lot 9, in December 1840.[8] During the 1840s, we see David Weller living on this land, until his death in 1851. Here is one more piece of evidence regarding the character of William Weller, who demonstrated by his actions that he was an effective businessman, faithful family man, and dedicated public servant.

William Weller passed away on September 19, 1863, while he held the office of mayor.[9] He was truly mourned as a very accomplished businessman and a strong and fair advocate for the people of Cobourg.

William Weller was successful when he piloted the governor general to Montreal in record time in 1840. His reputation was embellished in the eyes of the public and his pocket book was enhanced accordingly. But he was only forty years old and many more accomplishments lay ahead.

One thing was clear to everyone: you needed to keep an eye on the Stagecoach King!

NOTES

Chapter 1. Beverly House

1. "Here it may be mentioned that while he was in England engaged upon 'Canada and the Canada Bill' his house in Toronto (Beverly House) was let to the Governor-General of Canada, Mr. Poulett Thompson (afterwards Lord Sydenham)." Major-General Charles Walker Robinson, C.B., *Life of Sir John Beverly Robinson,* Bart., C.B., D.C.L., Chief Justice of Upper Canada, pg. 295, Ontario Archives, ABD-4504

2. "If you could pop in upon us suddenly how much surprised you would be, on walking up to your house, to find it in the full glare of lights, and with two sentries posted in front," Ibid.

3. "Mr. Weller signalled to give the horses their head, and the four-in-hand started from Government House on the road to Montreal." *Montreal Daily Herald,* February 16, 1895, "By Post to Montreal, Lord Sydenham's Famous Drive by Stages in 1840 From Toronto to Montreal Over Bad Roads in 36 Hours", a clipping found in a scrapbook in the Madelein Muntz Collection, St. Catharines Museum, ALC.IV.4, 2006.73.873. (The team was only two horses, not a four-in-hand as would be commonly expected, but the reference to Government House is important because it confirms that they left from Beverly House and not from the General Stage Office in Toronto.)

4. Robert E. Saunders, "Sir John Beverly Robinson," *Dictionary of Canadian Biography*, Vol. 9, University of Toronto/Université Laval, 2003–, accessed November 16, 2016, http://www.biographi.ca/en/bio/robinson_john_beverley_9E.html.

5. John Lownsbrough, "D'Arcy Boulton," *Dictionary of Canadian Biography*, Vol. 6, University of Toronto/Université Laval, 2003–, accessed November 17, 2016, http://www.biographi.ca/en/bio/boulton_d_arcy_1759_1834_6E.html.

6. Phillip Buckner, "Charles Poulett Thomson, 1st Baron SYDENHAM," *Dictionary of Canadian Biography*, Vol. 7, University of Toronto/Université Laval, 2003–, accessed August 19, 2017, http://www.biographi.ca/en/bio/thomson_charles_edward_poulett_7E.html.

7. *Upper Canada Gazette,* Toronto, Thursday, February 13, 1840, Metropolitan Toronto Reference Library, Toronto, Newspaper Collections, *Upper Canada Gazette,* Microfilm ES HPL CESH, Vol. @, June 22 1820 – March 9, 1848.

8. "This was, it was said, the indirect cause of getting the union measure through the Upper Canada Parliament." Major-General Charles Walker Robinson, C.B., *Life of Sir John Beverly Robinson*, Bart., C.B., D.C.L., Chief Justice of Upper Canada, pg. 296, Ontario Archives, ABD-4504

9. *Charles Poulett Thomson, Memoir of the Life of The Right Honourable Charles Lord Sydenham*, G.C.B., with a Narrative of His Administration in Canada, edited by his brother, G. Poulett Scrope, Esq. M.P., page 148, downloaded from University of Toronto, Thomas Fisher Rare Book Library, https://archive.org/details/memoiroflifeofr00scro

10. "A Military Guard and Band were in attendance at the residence of the Governor General, when his Excellency took his departure." *British Colonist,* February 18, 1840, Metropolitan Toronto Reference Library, Toronto, Newspaper Collections, NL OTAR.

11. Family tree information for William Weller's family can be seen at http://www.treesbydan.com/, a source that also includes items regarding the Toronto to Montreal trip and later events in William Weller's life. Treesbydan was created by the author as a resource for family history researchers.

12. J. Ross Robertson, *Landmarks of Toronto*, 1894, Vol. 1, page 221. The Coffin Block is mentioned on page 221 followed by two sketches of The Fish Market area showing the building positioned at the point of Front and Market Street. William Weller is mentioned on page 223 as operator of the Telegraph Line of stages between Toronto and Hamilton, one of several he operated.

13. The *British Colonist,* February 18, 1840, Digital Kingston Newspaper Archives – http://vitacollections.ca/digital-kingston/

14. "At this time Weller did not usually act in the capacity of coachman, but, considering it a great honour to drive the Governor, he decided to mount the box himself." Edwin C. Guillet, *Early Life in Upper Canada,* page 566

Chapter 2. Departure

1. Edgar Andrew Collard, *Montreal Gazette*, "The Hasty Journey of William Weller," in the column "All Our Yesterdays," found in the Madelein Muntz Collection, St. Catharines Museum. Collard wrote the column called "All Our Yesterdays" in the Montreal *Gazette* from 1944 until just before his death in 2000.
2. Edwin C. Guillet, *Early Life in Upper Canada*, page 561
3. *The Varsity*, The University of Toronto's Student Newspaper, October 28, 2012, http://thevarsity.ca/2012/10/28/a-brief-history-of-toronto-street-lamps/.
4. Edwin C. Guillet, *Early Life in Upper Canada*, page 566

Chapter 3. John Street to King Street

1. J. Ross Robertson, *Landmarks of Toronto*, 1894, Volume 1, page 470.
2. Ibid., 511.
3. Ibid., 207.
4. Ibid., 470.
5. Ibid., 523.

Chapter 4. King Street West

1. J. Ross Robertson, *Landmarks of Toronto*, 1894, Volume 1, page 360.
2. Ibid., 304.
3. Phillip Buckner, "Sir George Arthur," in *Dictionary of Canadian Biography*, Vol. 8, University of Toronto/Université Laval, 2003–, accessed August 12, 2017, http://www.biographi.ca/en/bio/arthur_george_8E.html.
4. Alan Wilson, "John Colborne, Baron Seaton," *Dictionary of Canadian Biography*, Vol. 9, University of Toronto/Université Laval, 2003–, accessed August 21, 2017, http://www.biographi.ca/en/bio/colborne_john_9E.html.
5. The Historicist: "The Warmest Welcome, At An Inn" by Kevin Plummer, http://torontoist.com/2011/12/historicist-the-warmest-welcome-at-an-inn/
6. Edith G. Firth, *Dictionary of Canadian Biography*, John George Howard, http://www.biographi.ca/en/bio/howard_john_george_11E.html
7. J. Ross Robertson, *Landmarks of Toronto*, 1894, Volume 1, page 362.
8. Ibid., 239.

9. Henry Scadding, *Toronto of Old*, Chapter XXX, The Harbour – Its Marine, 1800-1814, original page 535 (on right in square brackets), page 241 of 306 in PDF version, Gutenberg ebook, ISO-8859-1.

10. J. Ross Robertson, *Landmarks of Toronto*, 1894, Volume 1, page 36.

11. Robert L. Fraser, "William Warren Baldwin," *Dictionary of Canadian Biography*, Vol. 7, University of Toronto/Université Laval, 2003–, accessed August 21, 2017, http://www.biographi.ca/en/bio/baldwin_william_warren_7E.html.

12. Michael S. Cross and Robert Lochiel Fraser, "Robert Baldwin," *Dictionary of Canadian Biography*, Vol. 8, University of Toronto/Université Laval, 2003–, accessed August 21, 2017, http://www.biographi.ca/en/bio/baldwin_robert_8E.html.

13. John Ralston Saul, *Louis-Hippolyte LaFontaine & Robert Baldwin*, page 119.

Chapter 5. King Street East to St. James Cathedral

1. Edwin C. Guillet, *Early Life in Upper Canada*, University of Toronto Press, 1933, page 93.

2. J. Ross Robertson, *Landmarks of Toronto*, 1894, Volume 1, page 6.

3. Robert J. Burns, "Thomas Ridout," *Dictionary of Canadian Biography*, Vol. 6, University of Toronto/Université Laval, 2003–, accessed August 21, 2017, http://www.biographi.ca/en/bio/ridout_thomas_6E.html.

4. J. Ross Robertson, *Landmarks of Toronto*, 1894, Volume 1, page 81.

5. William R. Wilson, "Samuel Lount and Peter Matthews," "Historical Narratives" http://www.uppercanadahistory.ca/tt/tt10.html

6. Frederick H. Armstrong and Ronald J. Stagg, "William Lyon Mackenzie," *Dictionary of Canadian Biography*, Vol. 9, University of Toronto/Université Laval, 2003–, accessed August 21, 2017, http://www.biographi.ca/en/bio/mackenzie_william_lyon_9E.html.

7. On This Site, Historical Plaque, 1 Toronto Street, re hanging of Samuel Lount and Peter Matthews, http://torontoplaques.com/Pages/Samuel_Lount_and_Peter_Matthews.html

8. "1842 Cane Topographical Plan of the City and Liberties of Toronto," Historical Maps of Toronto, http://oldtorontomaps.blogspot.ca/2013/01/1842-cane-topographical-map-of-city-and.html

9. J. Ross Robertson, *Landmarks of Toronto*, 1894, Volume 1, page 508.

10. J. Ross Robertson, *Landmarks of Toronto*, 1894, Volume 1, page 505.

11. G. M. Craig, "John Strachan," *Dictionary of Canadian Biography*, Vol. 9, University of Toronto/Université Laval, 2003–, accessed August 12, 2017, http://www.biographi.ca/en/bio/strachan_john_9E.html.

12. J. Ross Robertson, *Landmarks of Toronto*, 1894, Volume 1, page 506.

Chapter 6. King Street East to Market Square and East

1. Alexander M. Ross, "William Henry Bartlett," *Dictionary of Canadian Biography*, Vol. 8, University of Toronto/Université Laval, 2003–, accessed June 20, 2016, http://www.biographi.ca/en/bio/bartlett_william_henry_8E.html.

2. *Cobourg Star*, January 1, 1840, Cobourg Public Library, microfilm collection.

3. J. Ross Robertson, *Landmarks of Toronto*, 1894, Volume 1, page 62.

4. Ibid., 235.

5. Robert J. Burns, "William Jarvis," *Dictionary of Canadian Biography*, Vol. 5, University of Toronto/Université Laval, 2003–, accessed December 22, 2016, http://www.biographi.ca/en/bio/jarvis_william_5E.html.

6. J. Ross Robertson, *Landmarks of Toronto*, 1894, Volume 1, page 129.

7. Douglas Leighton and Robert J. Burns, "Samuel Peters Jarvis," *Dictionary of Canadian Biography*, Vol. 8, University of Toronto/Université Laval, 2003–, accessed December 22, 2016, http://www.biographi.ca/en/bio/jarvis_samuel_peters_8E.html.

8. Christopher Armstrong, "James Austin," *Dictionary of Canadian Biography*, Vol. 12, University of Toronto/Université Laval, 2003–, accessed August 31, 2017, http://www.biographi.ca/en/bio/austin_james_12E.html.

9. J. Ross Robertson, *Landmarks of Toronto*, 1894, Volume 1, page 15.

10. Ibid., 132.

11. Henry Scadding, *Toronto of Old*, Chapter XV, King Street, From Caroline Street to Berkeley Street, original page 196, page 91 of 306 in PDF version, Gutenberg ebook, ISO-8859-1.

Chapter 7. Across the Don

1. Alan Wilson, "John Colborne, Baron Seaton," *Dictionary of Canadian Biography*, Vol. 9, University of Toronto/Université Laval, 2003–, accessed August 13, 2017, http://www.biographi.ca/en/bio/colborne_john_9E.html.

2. *Upper Canada Gazette*, September 22, 1827, Toronto Metropolitan Reference Library, microfilm, ES SC C, Oct 1824 –1845.

3. Ibid.

4. J. Ross Robertson, *Landmarks of Toronto*, 1894, Volume 1, page 134.

5. York Pioneer and Historical Society, http://www.yorkpioneers.org/aboutus.html

6. Jeanine Avigdor, "Scadding Cabin 1794, Toronto's Oldest House," page 6 (Booklet available from York Pioneers.)

Chapter 8. East of the Don

1. Joanne Doucette, *Leslieville: Pigs, Flowers and Bricks*, 2016, ISBN #978-0-9952645-0-2, available online at https://archive.org/details/PigsFlowersAndBricksFeb32017

2. Ontario Heritage Trust, The Ashbridges Estate, Historical Plaque at Ashbridges Estate, 1444 Queen Street, East, Toronto, Ontario.

3. Toronto Historical Board, Norway Post Office, Historical Plaque located at 32 Kingston Road, north side, just east of Woodbine.

4. Lillian F. Gates, "Asa Danforth," *Dictionary of Canadian Biography,* Vol. 6, University of Toronto/Université Laval, 2003–, accessed August 13, 2017, http://www.biographi.ca/en/bio/danforth_asa_6E.html.

5. Robert R. Bonis, *A History of Scarborough*, published by Scarborough Public Library, 1968, pg. 77

6. *Kingston Chronicle*, December 12, 1829, page 2, Digital Kingston Newspaper Archives – http://vitacollections.ca/digital-kingston/

Chapter 9. Highland Creek and the Rouge River

1. Clancy Delbarre, *Highland Creek Village*, Centennial Community & Recreation Association (CCRA), http://www.ccranews.com/history.html

2. Robert R. Bonis, *A History of Scarborough*, published by Scarborough Public Library, 1968, pg. 77

3. *Cobourg Star*, April 20, 1836, Cobourg Public Library, microfilm collection.

4. "Civil Secretary's Correspondence," Upper Canada Sundries, September 1836, (R.G. 5, A 1, Volume 170). A copy of this document was sent to me by Linda Smith, a fellow researcher interesting in William Weller.

5. William Robertson Wood, *Past Years in Pickering*, Chapter XIX, The Road, the River and the Bay, page 161.

Chapter 10. Pickering Township

1. *Pickering News*, April 3, 1896, from the Pickering-Ajax Digital Archives.
2. Phillip Buckner, "Charles Poulett Thomson, 1st Baron Sydenham," *Dictionary of Canadian Biography*, Vol. 7, University of Toronto/Université Laval, 2003–, accessed August 13, 2017, http://www.biographi.ca/en/bio/thomson_charles_edward_poulett_7E.html.
3. Ibid.
4. Ibid.
5. *Memoir of the Life of The Right Honourable Charles Lord Sydenham, G.C.B., with a Narrative of His Administration in Canada*, edited by his brother, G. Poulett Scrope, Esq. M.P., page 15 & 16.
6. Ibid., 97.
7. Louise K. Rorke, "Pickering's First Settler," an article copied from the Pickering Women's Institute scrapbook, available in the Pickering-Ajax Digital Archives. (The given name Mike used here cannot be verified.)
8. "Old Post Inn is Ajax's oldest building," *News Advertiser*, Sunday, March 29, 1992, page 5, available on Pickering-Ajax Digital Archive.
9. Old Post Inn, 365 Kingston Road East, Ajax, Designated Heritage Property, No. 127, https://www.ajax.ca/en/livinginajax/historicalajaxlandmarks.asp

Chapter 11. Perry's Corners (Whitby)

1. H. E. Turner, "Peter Perry," *Dictionary of Canadian Biography*, Vol. 8, University of Toronto/Université Laval, 2003–, accessed February 10, 2017, http://www.biographi.ca/en/bio/perry_peter_8E.html.
2. Ibid.
3. Ibid.
4. T. E. Kaiser, M.D, *Historic Sketches of Oshawa*, Benjamin Wilson, page 5, downloaded from Oshawa Public Library - http://localhistory.oshawalibrary.ca/pdfportal/pdfskins/kaiser/kaiser.pdf
5. Ibid., 11, 12.
6. "Loss of the *Speedy*," The Oracle, *Upper Canada Gazette*, York, Saturday, November 3, 1804, (FLM UPCG) Legislative Library of Ontario, available on microfilm through inter-library loan to the Brighton Public Library.

Chapter 12. Darlington Township

1. Thomas Courtice, "Courtice Family History, Sketch of the History and Times of the Lake Christopher Courtice of Darlington, Ontario," June 1900, for the Courtice Picnic in 1921, available at http://www.ontariogenealogy.com/Durham/courticefamilyhistory.html
2. Charles Taws, "Who Was Charles Bowman Anyway?" Clarington Museums and Archives, http://www.claringtonpromoter.ca/downloads/feature/feature-2011-10.pdf

Chapter 13. Clarke Township (Newcastle)

1. A. B. McCullough, "Samuel Wilmot," *Dictionary of Canadian Biography*, Vol. 12, University of Toronto/Université Laval, 2003–, accessed February 14, 2017, http://www.biographi.ca/en/bio/wilmot_samuel_12E.html.
2. *Illustrated Historical Atlas of the Counties of Northumberland and Durham, Ont., Completed, Drawn, Published from Personal Examinations and Surveys by H. Beldon & Co., Toronto, 1878,* reprinted by Mika Silk Screening Limited, Belleville, Ontario, 1972, pages 11 & 12.
3. "Newcastle History," Newcastle Settlement, Newcastle BIA, http://villageof-newcastle.ca/community/history/
4. David Weller, www.treesbydan.com, the author's genealogy web site.
5. *Upper Canada Gazette*, January 7, 1830, copied from microfilm (Reel 6 – May 29, 1828 – Dec 31, 1831) at The Metro Reference Library, Toronto, June 11, 2016.
6. *Upper Canada Gazette*, January 7, 1830, copied from microfilm at The Metro Reference Library, Toronto.
7. *Kingston Chronicle*, January 2, 1830, page 2, copied from Digital Kingston.

Chapter 14. Hope Township

1. *Cobourg Star*, December 14, 1839, Cobourg Public Library microfilm collection.
2. *Cobourg Star*, January 1, 1840, Cobourg Public Library microfilm newspaper collection.
3. A. Arnot Craick, "Port Hope Historical Sketches," Port Hope, Sept. 1901, http://www.porthopehistory.com/phhistsketchescraick/phhistsketches_index.htm.

4. William Weller, www.treesbydan.com. Look up William Weller (1799-1863) (#91527) and trace back to John Weller (1694-1755)(#91515); see Eliakem Weller (1737-1781)(#33692) and his son Asa Weller (1761-1825)(#8942).

5. *Illustrated Historical Atlas of the Counties of Northumberland and Durham, Ont., Completed, Drawn Published from Personal Examinations and Surveys by H. Beldon & Co., Toronto, 1878*, reprinted by Mika Silk Screening Limited, Belleville, Ontario, 1972, pages 5 & 6.

6. "Walton Street Heritage Conservation District, Downtown Port Hope, recognized": 1997/10/06, Listed: 2007/07/24, Canada's Historic Places, http://www.historicplaces.ca/en/rep-reg/place-lieu.aspx?id=7792

7. William Furby (presumed), "O. T. Letters, Old Timer Letter One," from *The Port Hope Guide*, August 30, 1877, http://www.porthopehistory.com/rememberph/otletter1.html.

8. Ibid.

9. O'Brien, Brendan, *Speedy Justice, The Tragic Last Voyage of His Majesty's Vessel Speedy*, Speedy Sails, Page 83, Published for the Osgoode Society by University of Toronto Press.

10. William Furby (presumed), "O. T. Letters, Old Timer Letter Five," from the *Guide,* October 4, 1877, http://www.porthopehistory.com/rememberph/otletter5.html. (J. D. Smith is John David Smith (1786-1849), son of Elias Smith and Catharine Molenaer.)

11. Ibid.

12. William Furby (presumed), "O. T. Letters, Old Timer Letter Eleven," from the *Guide,* November 22, 1877, http://www.porthopehistory.com/rememberph/otletter11.html.

Chapter 15. Cobourg

1. William Weller, www.treesbydan.com, The first census or assessment records for Hamilton Township that mention William Weller are in 1834, related to ¼ acre in Concession A, Lot 16, which is the location of his stagecoach business in downtown Cobourg, north of King and east of Division. Hamilton Township Census and Assessment records are found online at http://www.eagle.ca/westhistory/genealogy.htm.

2. *Cobourg Star*, December 18, 1830, Cobourg Public Library, microfilm collection.

3. *Illustrated Historical Atlas of the Counties of Northumberland and Durham, Ont., Completed, Drawn, Published from Personal Examinations and Surveys*

by H. Beldon & Co., Toronto, 1878, reprinted by Mika Silk Screening Limited, Belleville, Ontario, 1972, pages 5 (Hope Twp.) & 31 (Hamilton Twp.).

4. Hereward Senior, "George Strange Boulton," *Dictionary of Canadian Biography*, Vol. 9, University of Toronto/Université Laval, 2003–, accessed March 1, 2017, http://www.biographi.ca/en/bio/boulton_george_strange_9E.html.

5. *Upper Canada Gazette*, "An Act to Alter certain parts of an Act, passed March 2, 1805", York, Legislative Library of Ontario, available on microfilm (FLM UPCG) through inter-library loan to the Brighton Public Library.

6. Dan Buchanan, *Murder in the Family: The Dr. King Story*, Launched Into Eternity, page 153, Dundurn Press, July 2015.

7. Carla Jones, *Forgotten Cemetery: The Facts Exhumed*, Cobourg and District Historical Society, January 27, 2015, document is located at http://cdhs.ca/histories.

8. "Sacred to the Memory of Mercy Wilcox, wife of Wm. Weller of Cobourg, who departed this life 20 Aug 1843m Aged 39 Years. In life Amiable, in suffering Patient, in death Blessed." Madelein Muntz, Transcription of inscription on the Memorial of Mercy Wilcox, William Weller's first wife. Photo taken by Madelein Muntz some time in the 1960s. The photo is very blurry; text is included under the photo. A further note says the location of the stone was in the southeast corner of the Old Kirk Burying Ground, Cobourg. This is from the scrapbook section of the Madelein Muntz Collection, St. Catharines Museum, ALC.IV.4, 2006.73.873.

9. Peter Ennals, "Zacheus Burnham," *Dictionary of Canadian Biography*, Vol. 8, University of Toronto/Université Laval, 2003–, accessed February 27, 2017, http://www.biographi.ca/en/bio/burnham_zacheus_8E.html.

10. *Cobourg Star*, January 18, 1831, Cobourg Public Library, microfilm collection. This is the first edition of the Cobourg Star.

11. Peter Ennals, "James Gray Bethune," *Dictionary of Canadian Biography*, Vol. 7, University of Toronto/Université Laval, 2003–, accessed February 26, 2017, http://www.biographi.ca/en/bio/bethune_james_gray_7E.html.

Chapter 16. Five Hours From Toronto

1. *Cobourg Star*, February 19, 1840, Cobourg Public Library, microfilm collection.

2. C. B. Sissons, *A History of Victoria University*, page 18, University of Toronto Press, Toronto, 1952.

3. Edwin C. Guillet, *Cobourg – 1798-1948*, page 129.

4. *Cobourg Star*, May 4, 1836, Cobourg Public Library, microfilm collection.

5. *Cobourg Star*, March 11, 1840, Cobourg Public Library, microfilm collection.

6. Alfred Elisha Munson (1824-1904) (#91720), www.treesbydan.com.

7. John Witham, "Frederick Preston Rubidge," *Dictionary of Canadian Biography*, Vol. 12, University of Toronto/Université Laval, 2003–, accessed August 14, 2017, http://www.biographi.ca/en/bio/rubidge_frederick_preston_12E.html.

8. Peter Ennals, "Robert Henry," *Dictionary of Canadian Biography*, Vol. 8, University of Toronto/Université Laval, 2003–, accessed February 26, 2017, http://www.biographi.ca/en/bio/henry_robert_8E.html.

9. Edwin C. Guillet, *Victorian Cobourg*, Mika Publishing Company, Belleville, Ontario, 1976, page 108-123. (Reprinted from the *Canadian Review*, 1937, by permission of the publisher and author.)

10. Peter Ennals, "Robert Henry," *Dictionary of Canadian Biography*, Vol. 8, University of Toronto/Université Laval, 2003–, accessed February 26, 2017, http://www.biographi.ca/en/bio/henry_robert_8E.html.

11. *Brief Biography of D'Arcy Edward Boulton*, Cobourg Public Library, Image Database, Boulton Family 03-03, http://images.ourontario.ca/Cobourg/48391/data

Chapter 17. Grafton

1. Barnum House, Grafton, Ontario, Canada's Historic Places, Formally Recognized: 1982/07/23, Listed on the Canadian Register: 2014/02.19, http://www.historicplaces.ca/en/rep-reg/place-lieu.aspx?id=19799.

2. Thomas Major Spalding (1780-1852) (#45298), www.treesbydan.com.

3. Margaret McBurney & Mary Byers, *Homesteads: Early buildings and families from Kingston to Toronto*, University of Toronto Press, 1979, page 165.

4. John Grover (1771-1847) (#39921), www.treesbydan.com,

5. The Grafton Inn, Grafton, Ontario, https://www.thegraftoninn.ca/

6. Denis F. Lawless, *Lawless Family of Haldimand Township*, http://www.ontario-genealogy.com/Northumberland/lawlessfamilyhaldimand.html

7. Benjamin Ewing (1776-1852) (#65050), www.treesbydan.com,.

8. *Cobourg Star*, February 6, 1833, Cobourg Public Library, microfilm collection.

Chapter 18. Wicklow and Colborne

1. Edwin C. Guillet, M.A., *Early Life in Upper Canada*, page 568, University of Toronto Press, 1933.

2. Susan Burnham Greeley, "Sketches in the Past," *The Colborne Chronicle*, Friday, June 21, 1974, Cramahe Digital Archives, Cramahe Township Public Library, http://vitacollections.ca/cramahelibrary/3084231/page/4?n=3

3. Nathaniel Herriman (1816-1881) (#94615), www.treesbydan.com.

4. Susan Burnham Greeley (1806-1904) (#33781), www.treesbydan.com.

5. "Colborne-Cramahe," *Illustrated Historical Atlas of the Counties of Northumberland and Durham, Ont., Completed, Drawn, Published from Personal Examinations and Surveys by H. Beldon & Co., Toronto, 1878*, reprinted by Mika Silk Screening Limited, Belleville, Ontario, 1972, page ix (Colborne & Cramahe).

6. Charles Beale, "Distinguished Colborne homes share connections," *Northumberland Today*, November 19, 2014, http://www.northumberlandtoday.com/2014/11/19/distinguished-colborne-homes-share-connections

7. Didier Prioul, "James Pattison Cockburn," *Dictionary of Canadian Biography*, Vol. 7, University of Toronto/Université Laval, 2003–, accessed March 4, 2017, http://www.biographi.ca/en/bio/cockburn_james_pattison_7E.html.

Chapter 19. Brighton

1. Municipality of Brighton, *That's Just The Way We Were, Brighton Memories*, page 2, published by the Brighton History Book Committee, 2006.

2. *Cobourg Star*, January 27, 1836, Cobourg Public Library, microfilm collection.

3. Schedule D, New Townships, from "An Act to make certain alterations in the Territorial Divisions of Upper Canada." [2d August, 1851], CAP. V., Statutes, 1851 Vol. III 1792 1851, PDF copy provided by staff at Osgoode Hall Law School Library, Toronto.

4. Proctor House Museum, http://www.proctorhousemuseum.ca/.

5. The Brighton Barn Theatre, http://www.brightonbarntheatre.ca/.

6. Simpson Cairn, near entrance to Presqu'ile Park, transcribed by the author.

7. Buchanan, Dan, *The Old Percy Road*, PDF can be downloaded from www.treesbydan.com, History section.

8. William Hawley Sanford (1814-1870) (#17907), www.treesbydan.com,

9. John Drummond Smith (1761-1842) (#45126), www.treesbydan.com,

Chapter 20. Trent Port and Belleville

1. John Bleecker, c1762-1807, Murray Township, Ancestry.com, Freepages, http://freepages.genealogy.rootsweb.ancestry.com/~saylormowbray/bleecker.html

2. John Witham, "Nicol Hugh Baird," *Dictionary of Canadian Biography*, Vol. 7, University of Toronto/Université Laval, 2003–, accessed August 15, 2017, http://www.biographi.ca/en/bio/baird_nicol_hugh_7E.html.

3. Randy Saylor, "Trent River Ferry and Bridges – 1794-1834," Section 10. 1831-1834 – Petitions of John V. Murphy, http://freepages.genealogy.rootsweb.ancestry.com/~saylormowbray/rivertrent.html

4. Cyrus Weaver (1800-1856) (#12722), www.treesbydan.com.

5. Robert J. M. Shipley, "John Walden Meyers," *Dictionary of Canadian Biography*, Vol. 6, University of Toronto/Université Laval, 2003–, accessed August 15, 2017, http://www.biographi.ca/en/bio/meyers_john_walden_6E.html.

6. Gerald Boyce, *Belleville: A Popular History*, page 88, Belleville Public Library.

7. *Upper Canada Herald*, January 10, 1837, copied from Digital Kingston.

8. George Singleton (c. 1750-1789) (#38169), www.treesbydan.com.

9. Mary G. Plumpton, *The Rambling River, History of Thurlow Township*, published by Thurlow Township Council, Ontario Intelligencer Limited, 1967, page 5.

10. Alexander Chisholm (1748-1808)(#38171), www.treesbydan.com.

11. Larry Turner, "Billa Flint," *Dictionary of Canadian Biography*, Vol. 12, University of Toronto/Université Laval, 2003–, accessed August 15, 2017, http://www.biographi.ca/en/bio/flint_billa_12E.html.

12. Armand P. La Barge, *Billa Flint, King of Hastings County*, Kirby Books, Page 60.

Chapter 21. Shannonville, Deseronto, and Napanee

1. C. M. Johnston, "John Deserontyon," *Dictionary of Canadian Biography*, Vol. 5, University of Toronto/Université Laval, 2003–, accessed August 22, 2017, http://www.biographi.ca/en/bio/deserontyon_john_5E.html.

2. "Township of Tyendinaga," Hastings County, The Canadian County Atlas Digital Project, http://digital.library.mcgill.ca/countyatlas/Images/Maps/TownshipMaps/has-m-tyendinaga.jpg

3. William Canniff, *History of the Settlement of Upper Canada (Ontario) With Special Reference to the Bay of Quinte*, Chapter XIX, Page 207

4. George Rawlyk and Janice Potter, "Richard Cartwright," *Dictionary of Canadian Biography,* Vol. 5, University of Toronto/Université Laval, 2003–, accessed August 15, 2017, http://www.biographi.ca/en/bio/cartwright_richard_5E.html.

5. Walter S. Herrington, *History of the County of Lennox and Addington,* The Macmillan Company of Canada, Limited, 1913, Toronto, The Beginning of Napanee, Page 211

Chapter 22. Morven and Odessa

1. J. Douglas Stewart and Mary Stewart, "John Solomon Cartwright," *Dictionary of Canadian Biography,* Vol. 7, University of Toronto/Université Laval, 2003–, accessed March 10, 2017, http://www.biographi.ca/en/bio/cartwright_john_solomon_7E.html.

2. Walter S. Herrington, K.C., *History of the County of Lennox and Addington,* The Macmillan Company of Canada, Limited, Toronto, 1913, Page 157.

3. "John Loudon McAdam," Wikipedia, https://en.wikipedia.org/wiki/John_Loudon_McAdam

4. Walter S. Herrington, K.C., *History of the County of Lennox and Addington,* The Macmillan Company of Canada, Limited, Toronto, 1913, Page 172.

5. John Matthias Fralick (1767-c.1852) (#24573), www.treesbydan.com.

6. *British Whig,* April 15, 1834, Digital Kingston.

7. Ibid.

8. *Kingston Herald,* Tuesday, February 18, 1840, Digital Kingston.

9. Parker Smith Timmerman (1813-1897) (#44969), www.treesbydan.com.

10. Margaret McBurney and Mary Byers, *Homesteads, Early Buildings and Families from Kingston to Toronto,* University of Toronto Press, 1979, pages 83 and 84.

Chapter 23. Kingston

1. J. K. Johnson and P. B. Waite, "Sir John A. Macdonald," *Dictionary of Canadian Biography*, Vol. 12, University of Toronto/Université Laval, 2003–, accessed August 15, 2017, http://www.biographi.ca/en/bio/macdonald_john_alexander_12E.html.

2. *Kingston Chronicle,* February 19, 1840, Digital Kingston.

3. Orville Luther Holley, *The Picturesque Tourist: Being a Guide Through the Northern and Eastern States and Canada*, Tour Through Canada, page 224, available on Google Books.

4. Fernand Ouellet, "John George Lambton, 1st Earl of Durham," *Dictionary of Canadian Biography,* Vol. 7, University of Toronto/Université Laval, 2003–, accessed March 16, 2017, http://www.biographi.ca/en/bio/lambton_john_george_7E.html.

5. "Durham Report," *The Canadian Encyclopedia,* http://www.thecanadianency-clopedia.ca/en/article/durham-report/

6. "Historic Walking Tours, City of Kingston," https://www.cityofkingston.ca/explore/culture-history/history/walking-tours

7. *Memoir of the Life of The Right Honourable Charles Lord Sydenham, G.C.B., with a Narrative of His Administration in Canada*, edited by his brother, G. Poulett Scrope, Esq. M.P., page 323.

8. Fort Frontenac National Historic Site of Canada, Canada's Historic Places, Formally Recognized: 1923/05/25, Listed on the Canadian Register: 2009/04/29, http://www.historicplaces.ca/en/rep-reg/place-lieu.aspx?id=12130

9. *Kingston Chronicle*, June 4, 1829, Digital Kingston. (Description is available but not the image. Images are available for items re the passing of the bill and tenders for collecting tolls.)

10. *British Whig*, February 21, 1834, page 3, Digital Kingston.

11. "Pittsburgh Township," The Canadian County Atlas Digital Project, http://digital.library.mcgill.ca/countyatlas/Images/Maps/TownshipMaps/fro-m-pittsburgh.jpg

12. "Barriefield Heritage Conservation District, City of Kingston," https://www.cityofkingston.ca/residents/heritage-conservation/districts/barriefield

Chapter 24. Gananoque

1. "Howe Island: Frontenac County, Early Settlers," http://freepages.genealogy.rootsweb.ancestry.com/~theislands/howeisland.html

2. Historical Plaque in Willowbank Cemetery, erected by descendants of the Lloyd family.

3. Elizabeth M. Morgan, "Joel Stone," *Dictionary of Canadian Biography*, Vol. 6, University of Toronto/Université Laval, 2003–, accessed March 22, 2017, http://www.biographi.ca/en/bio/stone_joel_6E.html.

4. Bray Heritage with Economic Planning Group FoTenn Consultants, *Gananoque Cultural Plan*, Prepared for the Town of Gananoque, December 31, 2010, Page 9, https://www.gananoque.ca/sites/gananoque.ca/files/00-146_GananoqueCulturalPlan_Final%20(2)_0.pdf.

5. C. J. Shepard, "John McDonald," *Dictionary of Canadian Biography*, Vol. 8, University of Toronto/Université Laval, 2003–, accessed March 24, 2017, http://www.biographi.ca/en/bio/mcdonald_john_1787_1860_8E.html.

6. Leeds & 1000 Islands Historical Society, "Walking tour of Lansdowne," http://www.ltihistoricalsociety.org/walkingtour.html

7. Nathaniel Mallory (1742-1808) (#94682), www.treesbydan.com.

8. Mallorytown Glass Works, Historical Plaque, erected July 1998 by the Macoy Masonic Lodge No. 242.

Chapter 25. Brockville and Maitland

1. Doug Grant, Brockville History Album, "The Albion Hotel – no longer a Brockville Landmark," 10-21 King St. E., The Long History of the Hotel, https://brockvillehistoryalbum.wordpress.com/2008/02/16/the-albion-hotel-no-longer-a-brockville-landmark/

2. Ian MacPherson, "William Buell, Jr.," *Dictionary of Canadian Biography*, Vol. 9, University of Toronto/Université Laval, 2003–, accessed April 5, 2017, http://www.biographi.ca/en/bio/buell_william_1792_1862_9E.html.

3. Ephraim Jones (1750-1812) (#93548), www.treesbydan.com.

4. Ian MacPherson, "William Buell, Sr.," *Dictionary of Canadian Biography*, Vol. 6, University of Toronto/Université Laval, 2003–, accessed April 5, 2017, http://www.biographi.ca/en/bio/buell_william_1751_1832_6E.html.

5. Ian Pemberton, "Levius Peters Sherwood," *Dictionary of Canadian Biography*, Vol. 7, University of Toronto/Université Laval, 2003–, accessed April 5, 2017, http://www.biographi.ca/en/bio/sherwood_levius_peters_7E.html.

6. Armand P. La Barge, *Billa Flint, King of Hastings County*, Kirby Books, Page 15.

7. "Leeds and Grenville County Court House National Historic Site," Canada's Historic Places, http://www.historicplaces.ca/en/rep-reg/place-lieu.aspx?id=7635

8. Wayne Lowrie, "New owner plans restoration of storied Maitland tower," *Post Media Network*, Friday, June 23, 2017, http://www.recorder.ca/2017/06/23/new-owner-plans-restoration-of-storied-maitland-tower

9. "Homewood Museum, Canada's Historic Place," Ontario Heritage Trust, http://www.historicplaces.ca/en/rep-reg/place-lieu.aspx?id=8870

10. The Blue Church, Historical Plaque, erected by the Archaeological and Historical Sites Board, Department of Public Records and Archives of Ontario.

Chapter 26. Prescott, Johnstown, Edwardsburgh

1. Frank Mackey, *Steamboat Connections: Montreal to Upper Canada, 1816-1843*, A Clearing of the Decks, page 157, accessed at McGill-Queen's University Press, http://www.mqup.ca/steamboat-connections-products-9780773520554. php

2. Mrs. John Graves Simcoe, *The Diary of Mrs. John Graves Simcoe, Wife of the First Lieutenant-Governor of the Province of Upper Canada, 1792-6*, Through the Rapids in Bateaux, page 99, Prospero, Canadian Collection, Toronto, 2001.

3. Susannah Moodie, *Roughing It In The Bush*, Chapter Three, Our Journey Up The Country, Coles Publishing Company Limited, Toronto, 1980, Pages 59-75

4. D. E. Fitzpatrick, "William Gilkison," *Dictionary of Canadian Biography*, Vol. 6, University of Toronto/Université Laval, 2003–, accessed April 7, 2017, http://www.biographi.ca/en/bio/gilkison_william_6E.html.

5. "Prescott Heritage, The Fort Town, Founding of the Town," http://www.prescott.ca/en/live-here/Live-Here-History-and-Heritage.asp

6. "Fort Wellington National Historic Site," Parks Canada, http://pc.gc.ca/en/lhn-nhs/on/wellington

7. "Battle of the Windmill National Historic Site," Parks Canada, https://www.pc.gc.ca/en/lhn-nhs/on/windmill

8. Julian Gwyn, "Sir William Johnson," *Dictionary of Canadian Biography*, Vol. 4, University of Toronto/Université Laval, 2003–, accessed April 9, 2017, http://www.biographi.ca/en/bio/johnson_william_4E.html.

9. Earle Thomas, "Sir John Johnson," *Dictionary of Canadian Biography*, Vol. 6, University of Toronto/Université Laval, 2003–, accessed April 9, 2017, http://www.biographi.ca/en/bio/johnson_john_6E.html.

10. "Hugh Munro Jr.," Clan Munro USA, Genealogy Pages, http://www.clanmunrousa.org/gen/getperson.php?personID=I50028&tree=1

11. "Edwardsburgh Cardinal," Township History, http://www.twpec.ca/and-more/about-the-township/

Chapter 27. Iroquois and Williamsburg

1. "Galop Canal," St. Lawrencepiks – Seaway History, http://stlawrencepiks.com/seawayhistory/beforeseaway/galop/

2. J. K. Johnson, "John Munro," *Dictionary of Canadian Biography*, Vol. 4, University of Toronto/Université Laval, 2003–, accessed April 10, 2017, http://www.biographi.ca/en/bio/munro_john_4E.html.

3. 3."Allen Paterson," Roy F. Fleming, Clan Munro USA, Genealogy Pages, http://www.clanmunrousa.org/gen/getperson.php?personID=I22049&tree=1

4. P. G. Cornell, "James Morris," *Dictionary of Canadian Biography*, Vol. 9, University of Toronto/Université Laval, 2003–, accessed April 5, 2017, http://www.biographi.ca/en/bio/morris_james_9E.html.

5. "John William Loucks," Ancestry, http://wc.rootsweb.ancestry.com/cgi-bin/igm.cgi?op=GET&db=kareoleson&id=I317

6. John K, Mahon, *The Ward of 1812*, James Wilkinson, page 213, Da Capo Press, Inc., New York, 1972.

7. "Williamsburg Township," The Canadian County Atlas Digital Project, http://digital.library.mcgill.ca/countyatlas/Images/Maps/TownshipMaps/sto-m-williamsburg.jpg

8. "Cook's Tavern and Livery, Upper Canada Village," http://www.uppercanada-village.com/things-to-do/tour-the-village/cook-s-tavern-and-livery/

Chapter 28. Ten Lost Villages

1. "The Lost Villages," http://www.ghosttownpix.com/lostvillages/

2. "Great Lakes St. Lawrence Seaway System," Seaway History, http://www.great-lakes-seaway.com/en/seaway/history/

3. Frank Mackey, *Steamboat Connections: Montreal to Upper Canada, 1816-1843*, A Clearing of the Decks, page 56, accessed at McGill-Queen's University Press, http://www.mqup.ca/steamboat-connections-products-9780773520554.php

4. *Kingston Chronicle*, December 25, 1830, page 3, Digital Kingston.

5. "Cornwall Township," The Canadian County Atlas Digital Project, Stormont County, http://digital.library.mcgill.ca/countyatlas/Images/Maps/TownshipMaps/sto-m-cornwall.jpg.

6. Edwin C. Guillet, *Pioneer Travel In Upper Canada*, Chapter VII – Roads and Road-Builders, page 134, University of Toronto Press, 1933, Reprinted 1963.

7. "Cornwall Canal," St. Lawrencepiks – Seaway History, http://stlawrencepiks.com/seawayhistory/beforeseaway/cornwall/

8. "Moses-Saunders Power Dam," Cornwall, Wikipedia, https://en.wikipedia.org/wiki/Moses-Saunders_Power_Dam

Chapter 29. Cornwall

1. "Auberge Chesley's Inn," 40 First Street West, Cornwall, http://www.chesleysinn.ca/en/

2. J. F. Pringle, "Lunenburg or The Old Eastern District," (1890, 2009), image reprint CD. (Milton, Ontario: Global Heritage Press, 2011), page 291. (This refers to a violent storm in 1846 in Cornwall. It demonstrates that the Chesley's Inn building exterior was clapboard in its earlier life and was bricked later, as we see it today.)

3. *Cobourg Star*, February 26, 1840, Cobourg Public Library, microfilm collection.

4. J. F. Pringle, "Lunenburg or The Old Eastern District," (1890, 2009), image reprint CD. (Milton, Ontario: Global Heritage Press, 2011), page 160, 161.

5. Ibid., 162, 163

6. "Cornwall Community Museum," Cornwall, https://cornwallcommunitymuseum.wordpress.com/page/37/?app-download=nokia

7. C. M. Livermore and N. Anick, "John McDonald," *Dictionary of Canadian Biography,* Vol. 9, University of Toronto/Université Laval, 2003–, accessed April 17, 2017, http://www.biographi.ca/en/bio/mcdonald_john_1866_9E.html.

8. Inverarden House, Montreal Road, Cornwall, Canada's Historic Places, Recognized: 1995/09/21, Listed on the Canadian Register: 2008/06/10, http://www.historicplaces.ca/en/rep-reg/place-lieu.aspx?id=9488

Chapter 30. Glengarry

1. Robert J. Burns, "Robert Isaac Dey Gray," *Dictionary of Canadian Biography,* Vol. 5, University of Toronto/Université Laval, 2003–, accessed April 20, 2017, http://www.biographi.ca/en/bio/gray_robert_isaac_dey_5E.html.

2. "Gray's Creek Conservation Authority," Raisin Region Conservation Authority, Glengarry County, https://www.rrca.on.ca/view.php?id=53

3. "Sir John Johnson House National Historic Site," Parks Canada, http://www.pc.gc.ca/en/lhn-nhs/on/johnjohnson

4. E.A. McDougall, "John Bethune," *Dictionary of Canadian Biography*, Vol. 5, University of Toronto/Université Laval, 2003–, accessed February 26, 2017, http://www.biographi.ca/en/bio/bethune_john_1751_1815_5E.html.

5. "Bethune-Thomson House," 19730 John Street, Williamstown, Glengarry County, http://www.heritagetrust.on.ca/en/index.php/properties/bethune-thompson-house

6. John Nicks, "David Thompson," *Dictionary of Canadian Biography*, Vol. 8, University of Toronto/Université Laval, 2003–, accessed August 17, 2017, http://www.biographi.ca/en/bio/thompson_david_1770_1857_8E.html.

7. "Glengarry House," Cornwall, Ontario, Canada's Historic Places, Recognized: 1921/05/21, Listed on the Canadian Register: 2009/08/11, http://www.historic-places.ca/en/rep-reg/place-lieu.aspx?id=13373

8. "Cooper Marsh," Raisin Region Conservation Authority, Glengarry County, http://www.rrca.on.ca/view.php?id=52

9. "Raisin Region Conservation Authority, Glengarry County," https://www.rrca.on.ca/

10. "Glengarry Cairn National Historic Site," Cairn Island, South Lancaster, in the St. Lawrence River, now part of Akwesasne, http://www.ontarioplaques.com/Plaques/Plaque_Stormont49.html

11. "Lancaster Township," Glengarry County, The Canadian County Atlas Digital Project, http://digital.library.mcgill.ca/countyatlas/Images/Maps/TownshipMaps/sto-m-lancaster.jpg

Chapter 31. Lower Canada

1. "Soulanges Canal," St. Lawrencepiks – Seaway History, http://stlawrencepiks.com/seawayhistory/beforeseaway/soulanges/

2. *Cobourg Star*, January 27, 1836, taken from the Kingston Chronicle, Cobourg Public Library, microfilm collection.

3. *Coteau-du-lac National Historic Site*, The locks canal of Coteau-du-Lac, Parks Canada, https://www.pc.gc.ca/en/lhn-nhs/qc/coteaudulac/activ/sentiers-trails/fort-coteau-du-lac/07-canal-ecluses-locks

4. John Beswarick Thompson, "John Simpson," *Dictionary of Canadian Biography*, Vol. 10, University of Toronto/Université Laval, 2003–, accessed February 4, 2017, http://www.biographi.ca/en/bio/simpson_john_1788_1873_10E.html.

5. John Ralston Saul, *Louis-Hippolyte LaFontaine & Robert Baldwin*, Extraordinary Canadians, Penguin Canada, pg. 112.

6. "Coteau-du-Lac National Historic Site," Parks Canada, Coeau-du-Lac, Quebec, http://www.pc.gc.ca/en/lhn-nhs/qc/coteaudulac

7. Frank Mackey, *Steamboat Connections: Montreal to Upper Canada, 1816-1843*, A Clearing of the Decks page 162, accessed at McGill-Queen's University Press, http://www.mqup.ca/steamboat-connections-products-9780773520554.php

Chapter 32. On the Ice to Lachine

1. "Taschereau Bridge, Quebec," https://en.wikipedia.org/wiki/Taschereau_Bridge
2. "Galipeault Bridge, Quebec," https://en.wikipedia.org/wiki/Galipeault_Bridge
3. Daniel Houle, Jean-David Moore and Jean Provencher, Direction de la Recherche Forestière, Ministère des Ressources Naturelles et de la Faune, Québec, Canada, "Ice Bridges on the St. Lawrence river as an Index of Winter Severity from 1620 to 1910," Published Online Feb 15 2007, available from *American Meteorological Society, Journals* Online, http://journals.ametsoc.org/doi/full/10.1175/JCLI4025.1
4. "The French Dream," Lachine Canal National Historic Site, Parks Canada, http://www.pc.gc.ca/en/lhn-nhs/qc/canallachine/decouvrir-discover/natcul1
5. Gerald J. J. Tulchinsky, "The Construction of the First Lachine Canal, 1815-1826," A thesis, Department of History, McGill University, Montreal, June 1960, page 18, available for download from McGill Library and Collections, PID 112940, http://digitool.library.mcgill.ca/R/?func=dbin-jump-full&object_id=112940&local_base=GEN01-MCG02
6. Ibid., 96.
7. "Pavillon de L'Entrepol," Musée de Lachine, Montreal's Museums, http://museesmontreal.org/en/museums/musee-de-lachine-pavillon-de-l-entrepot
8. "The Fur Trade At Lachine" National Historic Site, Parks Canada, https://www.pc.gc.ca/en/lhn-nhs/qc/lachine
9. John S. Galbraith, "Sir George Simpson," *Dictionary of Canadian Biography*, Vol. 8, University of Toronto/Université Laval, 2003–, accessed July 20, 2017, http://www.biographi.ca/en/bio/simpson_george_8E.html.

Chapter 33. The Governor General Is Here!

1. "Previous to the introduction of macadam in 1841 and for years later many of the streets in Quebec were known as planked roads." George Gale, *Historic Tales of Old Quebec*, Quebec, The Telegraph Printing Company, 1920, Presented to the Library of the University of Toronto by David Hayne, downloaded from University of Toronto – Robarts Library, https://archive.org/details/historictalesofo00galeuoft.
2. "3 VICTORIA, CAP XXXI. An Ordinance to provide for the improvement of the Roads in the neighborhood of, and leading to the City of Montreal, and to raise a fund for that purpose. Assented to 15th June, 1840." *Ordinances And*

Acts of the Montreal Turnpike Trust, Montreal, Printed by the Gazette Printing company, 1897, downloaded from University of Alberta Libraries – The CIHM Monograph Collection, https://archive.org/details/cihm_53455

3. "Carte De Lisle De Montreal Et De Ses Environs," Ville de Montreal Gestion de documents et archives, http://www2.ville.montreal.qc.ca/archives/democratie/ democratie_fr/media/images/contenu/expo/pieces/inspection/BM5-C-26-050.jpg

4. "Carte de Lisle de Montréal," 1834, par Jobin, Atlas Du Paysage du Mont Royal, http://ville.montreal.qc.ca/siteofficieldumontroyal//sites/default/ files/8_1834_carte_de_lile_de_montre_al_par_jobin.pdf

5. Marian Scott, "Progress versus the past in St.-Henri – This is 300 years of history," *Montreal Gazette,* September 13, 2015, http://montrealgazette.com/news/ local-news/progress-versus-the-past-in-st-henri-this-is-300-years-of-history

6. Robert Sweeny, "Peter McGill," *Dictionary of Canadian Biography,* Vol. 8, University of Toronto/Université Laval, 2003–, accessed August 18, 2017, http:// www.biographi.ca/en/bio/mcgill_peter_8E.html.

7. *The Doolittle Family in America, Part IV,* compiled by William Frederick Doolittle, 1904, The Sayers and Waite Printing Co., Digitized by Google, pages 388 & 389.

8. Topographical and Pictorial Map of the City of Montreal, Surveyed and Drawn by James Cane, Civil Engineer, downloaded from McGill Library, http://public-content.library.mcgill.ca/gis/data/historic/cane/data/Cane_1846_150dpi.jpg

9. Edgar Andrew Collard, "The Hasty Journey of William Weller," "All Our Yesterdays," *Montreal Gazette,* Madelein Muntz Collection, St. Catharines Museum. (E.A. Collard wrote the column called "All Our Yesterdays" in the *Montreal Gazette* from 1944 until just before his death in 2000. This clipping shows no date.)

Chapter 34. Tell Me The Time

1. Phillip Buckner, "Charles Edward Poulett Thomson, 1st Baron Sydenham," *Dictionary of Canadian Biography,* Vol. 7, University of Toronto/Université Laval, 2003–, accessed August 19, 2017, http://www.biographi.ca/en/bio/ thomson_charles_edward_poulett_7E.html.

Chapter 35. In Montreal

1. *Montreal Gazette*, February 20, 1840, Toronto Metropolitan Reference Library, microfilm, ES SC C, Oct 1824 –1845.
2. *Cobourg Star*, February 26, 1840, Colonial, Lower Canada, from the *Montreal Courier*, Cobourg Public Library, microfilm collection.
3. *Cobourg Star*, June 18, 1845, Cobourg Public Library, microfilm collection.
4. *Montreal Daily Herald*, February 16, 1895, "By Post to Montreal, Lord Sydenham's Famous Drive by Stages in 1840 From Toronto to Montreal Over Bad Roads in 36 Hours," a clipping found in a scrapbook in the Madelein Muntz Collection, St. Catharines Museum, ALC.IV.4, 2006.73.873.
5. *Montreal Gazette*, February 20, 1840, Toronto Metropolitan Reference Library, microfilm, ES SC C, Oct 1824 –1845.5
6. *Montreal Herald*, February 20, collection of items re the trip in the *British Colonist*, 1840 02 26, Toronto Metropolitan Reference Library, microfilm.
7. *Upper Canada Herald*, Kingston, February 25, 1840, Toronto Metropolitan Reference Library, microfilm
8. *Cobourg Star*, March 11, 1840, Cobourg Public Library, microfilm collection.
9. *Toronto Examiner*, March 23, 1840, [From the *Montreal Courier*], Toronto Metropolitan Reference Library, microfilm

Chapter 36. After The Trip: The Governor General

1. *Cobourg Star*, March 11, 1840, Cobourg Public Library, microfilm collection. (Chatterton)
2. Governor General Charles Poulett Thomson, *Memoir of the Life of The Right Honourable Charles Lord Sydenham, G.C.B., with a Narrative of His Administration in Canada*, edited by his brother, G. Poulett Scrope, Esq. M.P., page 175.
3. Ibid., 175, 176.
4. Ibid., 176.
5. Lord John Russell, "Copy of a Dispatch from Lord John Russell to Right Honourable C. Poulett Thomson," 20 March 1840, No. 18, Correspondence: - Affairs of Canada, page 50, from "Copies or Extracts of Correspondence Relative to the Reunion of the Provinces of Upper and Lower Canada, Early Canadiana" Online, http://eco.canadiana.ca/view/oocihm.9_01442/51?r=0&s=1

6. Governor General Charles Poulett Thomson, *Memoir of the Life of The Right Honourable Charles Lord Sydenham, G.C.B., with a Narrative of His Administration in Canada*, edited by his brother, G. Poulett Scrope, Esq. M.P., page 177.

7. Ibid., 197.

8. Ibid., 210.

9. Phillip Buckner, "Charles Edward Poulett Thomson, 1st Baron Sydenham," *Dictionary of Canadian Biography*, Vol. 7, University of Toronto/Université Laval, 2003–, accessed August 19, 2017, http://www.biographi.ca/en/bio/thomson_charles_edward_poulett_7E.html.

10. Government House 1832, Historical Plaque at side of Alwington House, Kingston, erected by Archaeological and Historic Sites Board of Ontario.

11. *Cobourg Star*, September 22, 1841, Cobourg Public Library, microfilm collection.

12. Phillip Buckner, "Thomson, Charles Edward Poulett, 1st Baron SYDENHAM," in *Dictionary of Canadian Biography*, Vol. 7, University of Toronto/Université Laval, 2003–, accessed August 19, 2017, http://www.biographi.ca/en/bio/thomson_charles_edward_poulett_7E.html.

13. Ibid.

Chapter 37. After the Trip: William Weller

1. *Cobourg Star*, March 25, 1840, Cobourg Public Library, microfilm collection.

2. *Cobourg Star*, December 18, 1839, Cobourg Public Library, microfilm collection.

3. *Cobourg Star*, January 1, 1840, Cobourg Public Library, microfilm collection.

4. *Cobourg Star*, November 30, 1842, Cobourg Public Library, microfilm collection.

5. *Cobourg Star*, December 15, 1847, Cobourg Public Library, microfilm collection.

6. *Cobourg Star*, December 29, 1847, Cobourg Public Library, microfilm collection.

7. *Cobourg Star*, January 23, 1850, Cobourg Public Library, microfilm collection.

8. *Land Registry Records of Hamilton Township*, Abstract Index Book for Concession A, B&S 6211, Concession B, Lot 9, 41 acres, Instrument Date Dec 8, 1840, Registration Date Feb 24, 1841, Northumberland County Archives, Town of Cobourg, Cobourg Public Library.

9. *Cobourg Sentinal*, September 26, 1863, Cobourg Public Library, microfilm collection.

SOURCES

1842 Cane Topographical Plan of the City and Liberties of Toronto, Historical Maps of Toronto, http://oldtorontomaps.blogspot.ca

A History of Victoria University, C. B. Sissons

Ancestry.com

Auberge Chesley's Inn

Belleville: A Popular History, Gerald Boyce

Billa Flint, King of Hastings County, Armand P. La Barge

"Brief Biography of D'Arcy Edward Boulton," Cobourg Public Library, http://images. ourontario.ca/Cobourg

British Colonist, Metropolitan Toronto Reference Library

"Brockville History Album," Doug Grant, https://brockvillehistoryalbum.word-press.com

Canada's Historic Places, http://www.historicplaces.ca/en

Cobourg – 1798-1948, Edwin C. Guillet

Cobourg and District Historical Society

Cobourg Public Library, microfilm collection

Cobourg Sentinal

Cobourg Star

Centennial Community & Recreation Association (CCRA), http://www.ccranews.com/

"Civil Secretary's Correspondence," Upper Canada Sundries, Ontario Archives

Clarington Museums and Archives, http://www.claringtonpromoter.ca/

Cornwall Community Museum

"Courtice Family History, Sketch of the History and Times of the Lake Christopher Courtice of Darlington, Ontario," Thomas Courtice

Cramahe Digital Archives, Cramahe Township Public Library

Dictionary of Canadian Biography, http://www.biographi.ca/en/bio

Digital *Kingston Newspaper* Archives – http://vitacollections.ca/digital-kingston/

Early Canadiana Online, http://eco.canadiana.ca

Early Life in Upper Canada, Edwin C. Guillet

Gananoque Cultural Plan, Bray Heritage with Economic Planning Group FoTenn Consultants

Grafton Inn, Grafton, Ontario, https://www.thegraftoninn.ca/

Great Lakes St. Lawrence Seaway System

Hamilton Township Census and Assessment, http://www.eagle.ca/westhistory/genealogy.htm.

Historic Sketches of Oshawa, T.E. Kaiser, M.D.

Historic Tales of Old Quebec, George Gale,

Historic Walking Tours, City of Kingston

Historical Narratives by William R. Wilson, http://www.uppercanadahistory.ca

History of the County of Lennox and Addington, Walter S. Herrington,

History of the Settlement of Upper Canada (Ontario,) With Special Reference to the Bay of Quinte, William Canniff

Homesteads: Early Buildings and Families from Kingston to Toronto, Margaret McBurney & Mary Byers

Ice Bridges on the St. Lawrence River as an Index of Winter Severity from 1620 to 1910, Daniel Houle, Jean-David Moore and Jean Provencher, Direction de la Recherche Forestière, Ministère des Ressources Naturelles et de la Faune, Québec

Illustrated Historical Atlas of the Counties of Northumberland and Durham, Ont., H. Beldon & Co., Toronto

Land Registry Records, Cobourg Public Library

Landmarks of Toronto, J. Ross Robertson

Lawless Family of Haldimand Township, Denis F. Lawless

Leslieville: Pigs, Flowers and Bricks, Joanne Doucette

Life of Sir John Beverly Robinson, Bart., C.B., D.C.L., Chief Justice of Upper Canada, Ontario Archives, ABD-4504

Louis-Hippolyte LaFontaine & Robert Baldwin, John Ralston Saul

Lunenburg or The Old Eastern District, J.F. Pringle

Madelein Muntz Collection, St. Catharines Museum

McGill Library

Memoir of the Life of The Right Honourable Charles Lord Sydenham, G.C.B., with a Narrative of His Administration in Canada, edited by his brother, G. Poulett Scrope, Esq. M.P.,

Montreal Gazette

Murder in the Family: The Dr. King Story, Dan Buchanan

"Newcastle History, Newcastle BIA," http://villageofnewcastle.ca/community/history/

Northumberland Today

Ontario Heritage Trust

Osgoode Hall Law School Library

Parks Canada

Past Years in Pickering, William Robertson Wood

Pickering-Ajax Digital Archives

Pioneer Travel in Upper Canada, Edwin C. Guillet, University of Toronto Press, 1933.

Port Hope Guide, http://www.porthopehistory.com/rememberph

Port Hope Historical Sketches, A. Arnot Craick

Post Media Network

Prescott Heritage

Raisin Region Conservation Authority

Reminiscences of Mr. J.H. Dorwin, Montreal in 1816, Mr. J.H. Dorwin

Roughing It In The Bush, Susannah Moodie

Scarborough Public Library

Speedy Justice, The Tragic Last Voyage of His Majesty's Vessel Speedy, O'Brien, Brendan, St. Lawrencepiks – Seaway History

Steamboat Connections: Montreal to Upper Canada, 1816-1843, Frank Mackey

That's Just The Way We Were, Brighton Memories, Municipality of Brighton

The Canadian County Atlas Digital Project, http://digital.library.mcgill.ca/countyatlas/Images/Maps/TownshipMaps

The Canadian Encyclopedia, http://www.thecanadianencyclopedia.ca

"The Construction of the First Lachine Canal, 1815-1826," A thesis, Gerald J.J. Tulchinsky

The Diary of Mrs. John Graves Simcoe, Wife of the First Lieutenant-Governor of the Province of Upper Canada, Mrs. John Graves Simcoe,

"The Historicist," Kevin Plummer, http://torontoist.com

"The Lost Villages," http://www.ghosttownpix.com/lostvillages/

The Picturesque Tourist: Being a Guide Through the Northern and Eastern States and Canada, Edited by Orville Luther Holley

The Rambling River, History of Thurlow Township, Mary G. Plumpton

The Varsity, The University of Toronto's Student Newspaper

The Ward of 1812, John K, Mahon

Toronto Historical Board

Toronto of Old, Henry Scadding

Treesbydan, www.treesbydan.com

University of Alberta Libraries

Upper Canada Gazette, Toronto Metropolitan Reference Library

Upper Canada Gazette, York, Legislative Library of Ontario

Upper Canada Herald

"Upper Canada Village," http://www.uppercanadavillage.com

Victorian Cobourg, Edwin C. Guillet

Ville de MontrealGestion de documents et archives

"Walking tour of Lansdowne," Leeds & 1000 Islands Historical Society

Wikipedia, https://en.wikipedia.org/wiki

York Pioneer and Historical Society, http://www.yorkpioneers.org/aboutus.html

ILLUSTRATIONS

16.2 Albion Hotel, Cobourg, Cobourg and District Images, http://images.ourontario.ca/Cobourg/19016/data?n=3

18.1 Carrying a Rail, C. W. Jefferys, Library and Archives of Canada, Image #1972-26-536

18.2 The Keeler Tavern, East Colborne, Cramahe Township Public Library, Digital Archives, Image #1776666

19.1 Proctor Inn, Highway #2, west of Brighton, photo by author

19.2 Hodges Tavern, 156 Main Street, Brighton, photo by author

20.1 Covered Bridge at Trent Port, Quinte West Public Library, http://images.ourontario.ca/QuinteWest/2686051/data

20.2 Belleville Looking East by Thomas Burrowes, 1830, Archives of Ontario, Image #I0002229

22.1 Four Mile Marker, 7318 County Road 2, west of Morven, photo by author

22.2 Fralick Tavern, 7222 County Road 2, west of Morven, photo by author

22.3 Timmerman Store, 155 Man Street, Odessa, photo by author

23.1 Coffee House, 75-77 Princess St., Kingston, photo by author

23.2 Cataraqui Bridge, Kingston, Toronto Reference Library, Baldwin Collection, Image #JRR 1373 Cab II

24.1 McDonald House, 30 King Street East, Gananoque, photo by author

25.1 Brockville Court House, Brockville, Brockville History Album, Doug Grant, https://brockvillehistoryalbum.wordpress.com/

26.1 Forwarding Museum, 201 Water St., Prescott, photo by author

27.1 Battle of Crysler's Farm Monument, Upper Canada Village, 13470 County Road 2, Morrisburg, photo by author

29.1 Chesley's Inn, 40 First Street West, Cornwall, photo by author

32.1 Ice Road, Montreal to Laprairie c. 1840 by Phillip Bainbrigge, Library and Archives of Canada, Image #ICON191683

32.2 Lachine Canal, Boulevard Saint-Joseph, Lachine, Quebec, photo by author

33.1 Exchange Coffee House Advertisement, Montreal Directory 1842, page 214, http://www.collectionscanada.gc.ca/obj/001075/f2/nlc003599.pdf

33.2 Exchange Coffee House, Courtyard off Rue Saint-Paul, Montreal, first appeared in the Daily Witness, Montreal, 7 December 1896

36.1 St. George's Cathedral, 270 King St. East, photo by author

INDEX

C

M

N ———

O

P

Richardson, Rebecca (ne Dennis), 25
Richmond Street, Toronto, 4
Richmond Township, Lennox County, 122, 123
Rideau Canal, Kingston, 139, 140, 146, 147, 162, 195
Ridout Street, Port Hope, 77
Ridout, John, 38
Ridout, Joseph, 28
Ridout, Percival, 28
Ridout, Thomas, 38, 41
Rivière Rouge, Quebec, 196
Rivière-Beaudette, Quebec, 192
Robinson, John Beverly, 3, 4, 8, 18, 32, 83, 126, 226
Robinson, Peter, 83
Robinson, Sarah, 4
Roblin Hill, Napanee, 125, 128
Roblin, David, 125
Rose Ellery Park, Brighton, 110
Roseberry Hill, Hope Township, 75, 76
Royal Exchange Hotel, Kingston, 141
Royal Mail, 11, 45, 55, 81, 117, 175, 178, 196, 227
Royal Mail Line, 45, 56, 65, 68, 75, 79, 92, 93, 104, 112, 217
Rouge Hill, 55, 58
Rouge River, 27, 55, 56, 58, 61
Rouge River Valley, 18, 55, 56
Roughing It In the Bush, Susanna Moodie, 163
Rubidge, Frederick Preston, 93
Rue Recollect, Montreal, 210
Rue Saint-Jacques, Quebec, 206, 208, 210
Rue Saint-Lemoine, Montreal, 210
Rue Saint-Maurice, Montreal, 210

Rue Saint-Paul, Montreal, 209, 210-212
Rue Saint-Peter, Montreal, 209, 210, 212
Russell, Lord John, 223
Russell, New York, 175
Ryerson, Egerton, 90, 226

S

Saint-Anne-de-Bellevue, Quebec, 198, 199
Saint Helen's Island, Montreal, 218
Saint-Henry, Quebec, 206, 208
Saint-Zotique, Quebec, 177, 192
Salem, Cramahe Township, 107
Santa Cruz, Stormont County, 174
Scadding Cabin, Toronto, 47
Scadding, Henry, 42, 47
Scadding, John, 47
Scarborough Township, York County, 50, 51, 53, 58
Scarborough Village, 52
Second Street West, Cornwall, 180
Seminary of St. Sulpice, Montreal, 223
Shakespeare Hotel, Toronto, 24
Sharp, John, 66
Sheik's Island, Cornwall Township, 176-179
Shelter Valley Creek, Grafton, 100
Sidney Township, Hastings County, 76, 115
Simcoe County, 30
Simcoe Street, Oshawa, 65
Simcoe Street, Toronto, 4
Simcoe, Lady John Graves, 162
Simcoe, Lieutenant Governor John Graves, 25, 27, 38, 41, 47, 65, 83, 112, 144, 177, 186

Y

Printed in Canada